Blazing Trails

HBJ BOOKMARK READING PROGRAM, EAGLE EDITION

Margaret Early

G. Robert Canfield

Robert Karlin

Thomas A. Schottman

Sara Krentzman Srygley

Evelyn L. Wenzel

Level 11

Blazing Trails

HARCOURT BRACE JOVANOVICH, PUBLISHERS

New York   Chicago   San Francisco   Atlanta   Dallas   and   *London*

ACKNOWLEDGMENTS: For permission to reprint copyrighted material, grateful acknowledgment is made to the following sources:

ADDISON-WESLEY PUBLISHING COMPANY: Adapted from *501 Balloons Sail East* (titled "The Wind Watchers") by Edith Battles. © 1971 by Edith Battles, a Young Scott Book.

ISAAC ASIMOV: Adapted from "Benjamin Franklin Changes the World" by Isaac Asimov from *Cricket* Magazine, 1976.

ATHENEUM PUBLISHERS: "The Whales Off Wales" from *One Winter Night in August and Other Nonsense Jingles* by X. J. Kennedy (a Margaret K. McElderry Book). Copyright © 1975 by X. J. Kennedy. "The Dream Woman" from *The Apple Vendor's Fair* by Patricia Hubbell. Copyright © 1963 by Patricia Hubbell.

BRANDT & BRANDT LITERARY AGENTS, INC.: "Nancy Hanks" from *A Book of Americans* by Rosemary & Stephen Vincent Benét. Copyright 1933 by Rosemary & Stephen Vincent Benét. Copyright renewed © 1961 by Rosemary Carr Benét.

COWARD, MCCANN & GEOGHEGAN, INC.: Adapted from *Mary's Monster* (titled "Curiosities from the Cliffs") by Ruth Van Ness Blair. Copyright © 1975 by Ruth Van Ness Blair. Illustrations by Richard Cuffari, reprinted by permission from *Mary's Monster.* Illustration copyright © 1975 by Richard Cuffari. "The Temper of Tempe Wick" from *This Time, Tempe Wick?* by Patricia Lee Gauch. Copyright © 1974 by Patricia Lee Gauch. Adapted from *The Little Riders* by Margaretha Shemin. Copyright © 1963 by Margaretha Shemin. Adapted from *The Cabin Faced West* (titled "Hamilton Hill: September 18, 1784") by Jean Fritz. Copyright © 1958 by Jean Fritz.

THOMAS Y. CROWELL, PUBLISHERS: An adaptation of the text from pages 10 to 20 of *Maria Tallchief* (titled "Truly a Ballerina") by Tobi Tobias. Copyright © 1970 by Tobi Tobias. Based on text excerpts from *Ghost Towns of the American West* (titled "Golden Ghosts") by Robert Silverberg. Copyright © 1968 by Robert Silverberg. Text adaptation of "The Seeing Stick" by Jane Yolen. Text copyright © 1977 by Jane Yolen.

CURTIS BROWN, LTD.: Adapted from "The Peddler's Pack" by Charlotte MacLeod. Copyright © 1976 by Charlotte MacLeod.

DOUBLEDAY & COMPANY, INC.: "He Reached for the Stars" and "The Secret of the Sea" adapted from *Pioneers and Patriots* by Lavinia Dobler and Edgar A. Toppin. Copyright © 1965 by Doubleday & Company, Inc. Adapted from *The Camels — Ships of the Desert* (titled "The Ship of the Desert") by George Laycock. Copyright © 1975 by George Laycock. "I Go Forth to Move About the Earth" by Alonzo Lopez from *The Whispering Wind,* edited by Terry Allen. Copyright © 1972 by the Institute of American Indian Arts.

E. P. DUTTON: Adapted from *Little Rascal* (titled "A Boy and a Raccoon") by Sterling North. Copyright © 1965 by Sterling North.

AILEEN FISHER: "Comma in the Sky" from *In the Woods, In the Meadow, In the Sky* by Aileen Fisher. Scribners, New York, 1965.

BARTHOLD FLES LITERARY AGENCY: Adapted from "Light My Fire" (titled "Feliciano!") from *Challenged by Handicap: Adventures in Courage* by Richard B. Lyttle. Copyright © by Richard B. Lyttle.

FOLLETT PUBLISHING COMPANY: "A Modern Dragon" from *Songs from Around a Toadstool Table* by Rowena Bennett. Copyright © 1967 by Rowena Bastin Bennett.

FOUR WINDS PRESS, A DIVISION OF SCHOLASTIC MAGAZINES, INC.: *Petronella* by Jay Williams. Text copyright © 1973 by Jay Williams.

GOLDEN GATE JUNIOR BOOK DIVISION OF CHILDRENS PRESS, CHICAGO: Adapted from *A Tree Is Something Wonderful* (titled "Giants in the Earth") by Elizabeth K. Cooper and Padraic Cooper. © 1972. Adapted from *Living Lights — The Mystery of Bioluminescence* (titled "Living Lights in Our World") by Alvin and Virginia Silverstein. © 1970.

GREENWILLOW BOOKS (A DIVISION OF WILLIAM MORROW & CO.): "The Snopp on the Sidewalk" from *The Snopp on the Sidewalk and Other Poems* by Jack Prelutsky. Copyright © 1976, 1977 by Jack Prelutsky.

GROSSET & DUNLAP, INC.: "Glory, Glory . . ." from *Twenty-Six Ways of Looking at a Black Man* by Raymond R. Patterson. Copyright 1969 by Raymond R. Patterson.

HARCOURT BRACE JOVANOVICH, INC.: Excerpts on pp. 90 and 91; 201–03; 368 and 369 (text and art); 450 and 451; and diagrams on pp. 325 and 326; from *Concepts in Science* (Purple) Newton Edition by Paul F. Brandwein et al. Copyright © 1975 by Harcourt Brace Jovanovich, Inc. Excerpts on pp. 248 and 249; 298 and 299; from *Language for Daily Use,* Explorer Edition (Purple) by Mildred A. Dawson et al. Copyright © 1978 by Harcourt Brace Jovanovich, Inc. Excerpts on pp. 47 and 48; 344 and 345 (text and art); 452 and 453; 497–99; from *Balance in Your Life* (Purple) by Sam F. Seeley et al. Copyright © 1977 by Harcourt Brace Jovanovich, Inc. Excerpts on pp. 370 and 371 (text and art) from *Growth in Mathematics* (Purple) by David W. Wells et al. Copyright © 1978 by Harcourt Brace Jovanovich, Inc. Entries on pp. 51–54; 66; 67; taken from (or adapted from) *The HBJ School Dictionary.* Copyright © 1977, 1972, 1968 by Harcourt Brace Jovanovich, Inc.

HARCOURT BRACE JOVANOVICH, INC., AND THE BODLEY HEAD: Adapted from "The Oba Asks for a Mountain" in *Olode the Hunter and Other Tales from Nigeria* (British title: *Ijapa the Tortoise and Other Nigerian Tales*) by Harold Courlander with Ezekiel Aderogba Eshugbayi. Copyright © 1968 by Harold Courlander.

HOLT, RINEHART AND WINSTON, PUBLISHERS: Adapted from *Poor Richard in France* by F. N. Monjo. Copyright © 1973 by Ferdinand Monjo and Louise L. Monjo.

HOUGHTON MIFFLIN COMPANY: Excerpts on pp. 45 and 46; 198–200; 249–51; 319; 424 and 425; from *Windows on Our World: The United States* by Anderson and King. Copyright © 1976 by Houghton Mifflin Company. *The Toothpaste Millionaire,* by Jean Merrill. Copyright © 1972 by Houghton Mifflin Company.

HOUGHTON MIFFLIN COMPANY AND GEORGE ALLEN & UNWIN LTD.: From "Oliphaunt" from *The Adventures of Tom Bombadil* by J. R. R. Tolkien. Copyright © 1962 by George Allen & Unwin Ltd.

iv

Contents

APPRECIATING LITERATURE

Part **2** You Can't Help Laughing

READING TO LEARN
Part 3 Expressions 159

APPRECIATING LITERATURE

Part **4 The Poet's Way**   253

READING TO LEARN

Part 5 Learning About America's Past   279

APPRECIATING LITERATURE

Part **6** How They Told It 373

READING TO LEARN

Part **7** Discoveries, Ideas, and Inventions 407

To the Reader

Blazing Trails—that is what you will be doing as you explore this book. Like a pioneer, you will be traveling new roads, discovering new ideas, and learning skills. You will learn about some of nature's mysteries. You will enjoy stories that will make you laugh. You will read about people and the different ways they express themselves through music, the arts, science, poems, and folktales. You will read articles and stories about America's past. You will learn about discoveries and ideas that have made our lives today richer and better. You may even learn about your own hometown.

Your book, *Blazing Trails,* is divided into eight parts. In Parts 1, 3, 5, and 7, you will learn to improve your reading skills through Skills Lessons, Vocabulary Studies, and Textbook Studies. The reading selections are yours to enjoy as you explore new information. In Parts 2, 4, 6, and 8, you will discover ways to understand and appreciate literature. The selections and poems are yours to enjoy as you laugh and dream with the characters and writers.

When you read, you often follow new roads in new directions. You are a pioneer discovering new territory and learning new skills. So lead the way—discover *Blazing Trails.*

Part **1**

Learning About Living Things

Using Context Clues to Find Word Meaning

What would you think if you saw the sign above on the left? You probably wouldn't know what to think. But suppose you saw the sign on the right? Now you would know that an ibex is an animal you can find at the zoo. In fact, an ibex is a wild goat that looks like the animal below.

You were able to tell that an ibex is an animal when you saw it on the sign with other animal names. The word *ibex* was used in a context that gave you a clue to its meaning.

Context means "the words or sentences around a certain word." Writers often tell you what a new word means by defining it in context. Here is an example:

Snakes and turtles are reptiles — cold-blooded animals that have no legs or very short legs.

In the sentence above, the word *reptiles* is defined in context. The context often helps to explain a word even if a definition is not given. Read this sentence:

Tigers usually hunt their prey at night.

Perhaps you know what *prey* is. If you don't, you can tell from the context that prey is something that is hunted. If you wanted to know the word's exact meaning, you could check a dictionary. You would find that *prey* means "any animal taken by another for food."

3

Synonyms

The clue to a word you don't know may be a **synonym** — a word that has the same or nearly the same meaning as another word. Thinking about what you are reading helps you to see such clues. Read this sentence:

I called my dog "Rascal" because he was such a mischief.

If you know the meaning of the word *mischief*, you may be able to figure out the meaning of the name "Rascal." If you know what *rascal* means, you may be able to figure out that a mischief is a person or animal that teases or is naughty.

Antonyms

Sometimes when you come to a word you don't know, there will be an **antonym** — a word with an opposite meaning — in the same context. Read the sentence below. Think about the meaning of the word *immense*.

We had expected all the tigers to be little, but one of them was immense.

If you do not know what *immense* means, what clue will help you? The word *but* signals an opposite idea. You might, therefore, reason that *immense* must have an opposite meaning from *little*.

Try This

Read the sentences below. Using clues in the context to help you, figure out the meaning of each word in italics. Then make up a sentence using each word.

1. Bees are able to *transmit* their knowledge of the location of honey to other bees by a "dance" that is full of messages.
2. Although people may not be able to *interpret* the bees' messages, other bees can easily tell what the dance means.
3. It appears that bees don't have to learn the "steps" of the dance. They know what the "steps" mean by *instinct*.

The Larger Context

Clues to the meaning of a word are often right in the sentence that contains the word. But sometimes you need to look further. Read the two sentences below.

All kinds of stones come out of a volcano. Pumice is one kind.

You know from the two sentences above that *pumice* is one kind of volcanic stone. The larger context of the paragraph tells you even more about *pumice*:

Pumice looks like a sponge. It is the lightest stone in the world. It's so light that if you put it in water, it will float. That's because it's filled with gas bubbles. The lava was thrown out with such force that the gas in it couldn't escape.

Now you know quite a bit about *pumice*. The full paragraph explained it. Remember to look for *all* the information you can find about a new word.

Try This

Read the following paragraph. Then, in one sentence, explain what *diatoms* are.

Algae are simple plants that grow in water or damp places. They lack true roots, stems, or leaves. One kind, the *diatom*, is a major food source for animals that live in the sea. They also produce much of the earth's oxygen. Diatoms make up the slippery coatings on the stems of large water plants and on rocks.

VOCABULARY STUDY

Multiple Meanings

"I have here a very unusual item, ladies and gentlemen. What am I bid for this *dribbling perch* that comes with its own *litter*?"

"Excuse me, please. What do you mean by **perch**? Is that thing a *freshwater fish,* or is it a *high resting place,* such as for a bird?"

"The answer to your questions, madam, is yes. Now, who will start the bidding for the *dribbling perch*?"

"Hold it! What do you mean by **dribbling**? Is that perch thing *drooling,* or is it *bouncing or kicking a ball very quickly*?"

"The answer to your questions, sir, is yes. Now, come on folks. Let's get this auction under way. First, we have the *dribbling perch* and its *litter. . . .* Do I hear fifty dollars?"

"No. Not until you tell us what the **litter** is. Is it a *group of puppies or other young that were born at one time,* or is it *rubbish*?"

"The answer to that question is also yes! YES! YES! YES! Now please, ladies and gentlemen, I beg you. Give me a bid."

"I wouldn't give you two cents for that thing!"

"*I* wouldn't give you a quarter!"

"A quarter! The lady in blue says a quarter. Do I hear fifty cents?"

"Yes! Fifty cents!"

"One dollar!"

"Twenty dollars!"

"Do I hear twenty-five dollars? No? Going once . . . going twice . . . SOLD to the gentleman for twenty dollars! An excellent buy, sir. Will you pay for it with cash or a check?"

"You know, I like the idea of words having more than one meaning. I think I'll write you a check!"

8

Word Play

1. What do *perch, dribbling,* and *litter* mean in the sentences below?

   a. The first time I went fishing, I caught a **perch**.
   b. I looked up and saw the bird on its **perch**.
   c. Basketball players do a lot of **dribbling** during a game.
   d. The monster was **dribbling** water from its mouth.
   e. We cleaned up the **litter** on the sidewalk.
   f. That kitten is the cutest in the **litter**.

2. Look up *check* in a dictionary. Make up a sentence for each different meaning of the word.

Summertime can be wonderful for . . .

A Boy and a Raccoon

by Sterling North

How do you feed a baby raccoon that weighs less than one pound?

Some people feed them with a medicine dropper or a doll's bottle. But I fed my tiny raccoon through a clean wheat straw. I took warm milk in my mouth. Then I tilted the hollow straw downward to his mouth and watched him suck eagerly.

I called my raccoon "Rascal" because he was such a mischief. He had shining black eyes, a mask like a little bandit, and five black rings around his fluffy tail. His whispered trills were full of wonder and curiosity. High up in the wide-spreading oak tree behind our house, there was a hole. The hole made a good home for Rascal. Here he dreamed away his first two months, sleeping happily between feedings.

10

At the foot of this great tree lay my big Saint Bernard, Wowser. He was a dependable watchdog who protected all my pets.

Wowser was a handsome animal weighing 170 pounds. Only a brave dog or a foolish person would have tried to disturb Wowser's new friend, my little raccoon, Rascal.

One day in June, Wowser and I heard a trill at the hole in the tree. A moment later, we saw two bright eyes shining from a small, black mask. Rascal was peeking out at the world below from the door of his home. Soon he began backing down the tree like a little bear, tail first.

Wowser was worried. He yelped a question or
two and looked up to see what I thought about this
new problem. I told my dog not to worry, but to
watch what happened.

I had a shallow minnow pool not far from the
tree. Rascal hurried to the little pond and started
fishing. His hands searched the shallows, while his
eyes gazed far away, as though he were thinking
of something else entirely. Soon his clever little
hands caught a minnow. He began washing it
back and forth, as raccoons do with almost
everything they eat. Rascal carried his minnow to
the edge of the pool, very pleased with himself. He
began eating the small fish in polite, little bites.
Then he started exploring the back yard around
the oak tree.

Having explored his little world, my raccoon
climbed the tree and disappeared into his safe
home in the hollow of the oak. Wowser sighed with
relief. Rascal was again safely in his nest. He had
not hurt himself in any way.

The Mystery of the Disappearing Sugar

My father and I lived together in a little town in Wisconsin. He let me keep any number of pets and let me wander as free as the wind over meadows and hills. I knew that he would not mind having Rascal eat with us. From the attic I carried down the family high chair, last used when I was a baby.

At breakfast the next morning I put a shallow bowl of warm milk on the tray of the high chair. Rascal stood in the chair, placing his hands on the edge of the tray. He could reach the milk easily. He drank the milk, hardly dribbling a drop. In fact, his table manners were better than those of many children. My father smiled at our new breakfast companion. I was delighted at Rascal's good behavior.

All went well until I offered Rascal a lump of sugar. He took it between his two hands and began washing it back and forth in his milk, just as he had washed the fish. In a moment or two, of course, it melted entirely away. You could not imagine a more surprised little raccoon!

First he felt all over the bottom of the bowl to see if he had dropped it. Then he looked in his right hand. No sugar lump! Next he looked in his left hand. No sugar lump there either!

Finally he turned to me and shrilled a sharp question: Who had stolen his lump of sugar?

When I stopped laughing, I gave him a second lump. He thought about washing it, but then a look came into his shining eyes. He took the sugar directly into his mouth and chewed it happily.

Rascal was a very bright raccoon. When he learned a lesson, he learned it for life. Never again did he try to wash a lump of sugar.

Rascal, the Speed Demon

A boy, a bicycle, a little raccoon! Imagine the adventures we had! Rascal had become a speed demon. He liked nothing better than whizzing down a steep hill. This lovable little animal had the heart of a lion. He liked to stand in the basket of my bicycle with his feet wide apart and his hands holding the front rim of the basket. His natural goggles made him look like a racing driver. His small button of a nose pointed straight into the wind, and his whiskers blew back nearly to his ears as his long tail streamed out behind.

Sometimes he shared the bicycle basket with bunches of radishes that I raised in my garden and sold to the grocery stores. Other times, when we went to the river to fish, Rascal shared the basket with my box of fishing tackle.

Summer Fun

Summer passes all too quickly for an active boy of eleven. Rascal and I often went fishing below the dam in the river. I fished for big, fighting silver catfish in my favorite hole, below a pleasant sand-bar. Rascal, meanwhile, fished in the shallows along the edge of the bar. He often grabbed a crayfish—those little monsters that look so much like small, freshwater lobsters. These he washed and ate, tail first, with great delight.

Even with mowing lawns and working in my
garden, I always found time to read. I would lie in
the hammock and listen to all the sounds of
summer.

Sometimes my father would hang a sign on the
office door: GONE FOR THE DAY.

Then, I'd fill a picnic basket with sandwiches
and a few bottles of soda. My father and Rascal
and I would climb happily into the front seat of
our car, with the top back and the windshield
down. All three of us wore goggles—Rascal's being
natural, of course. He liked to perch between us on
the back of the seat. He looked joyfully ahead as
we headed up the road toward Lake Koshkonong.

Here we hunted for arrowheads, searched a nearby cave, or swam in the cold water. Rascal was a fine swimmer, dog-paddling along beside us until he grew tired. He thought of me as his protector when we were in deep water. He would climb on my shoulder or my head for a rest. Often I would float on my back and raise my chest above the water. This gave him a better resting place. As soon as he had caught his breath, he would dive in again. Then he would paddle along bravely through the little waves as we explored the coves and grassy points along the sandy shore.

Sterling North is a well-known author of books for young people. This selection comes from his book **Little Rascal.** Even as a boy in 1918, Mr. North believed that wild animals should not be kept as pets. Though he enjoyed Rascal's visits, he knew that the raccoon belonged in its natural home—the forest. He showed how much he truly loved Rascal when he encouraged the raccoon to return to the wild at the end of the summer.

18

Understanding What You've Read

1. How old was Rascal when the boy first found him?
2. How did the boy know that his father would not mind having Rascal in the house?
3. What things showed that Rascal was bright?
4. Why did the boy let the raccoon sleep in a tree, fish for minnows, and swim in the lake?
5. What might have happened if the boy had not encouraged the raccoon to return to the wild?

Applying the Skills Lesson

What is the meaning of each of the words in italics below? Choose one of the meanings given below the sentences. What words in the context give you clues to the meanings of the words?

1. Rascal carried his *minnow* to the edge of the pool. . . . He began eating the small fish in polite, little bites.

   a. a small, freshwater fish   b. a kind of rock

2. All three of us wore *goggles* — Rascal's being natural, of course.

   a. tall hats   b. large eyeglasses, with side guards

3. His whispered *trills* were full of wonder and curiosity.

   a. warbling sounds   b. movements

Using Context Clues

Whenever you read a textbook, use all your skills to understand the meanings of new words. Look for context clues that may help you. Notice any words printed in boldface or italic type. They may be defined in context, or they may be found in the glossary of your textbook.

As you read the following textbook selections, use the side-notes to help you find clues to the meanings of new words.

Using Context Clues in Science

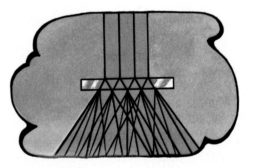

Words in headings like this will usually be explained. What is *scattering*?

SCATTERING. When light passes through things, it does not always travel in the same way. For example, when light passes through some things, such as frosted glass, it scatters. That is, the light separates and goes in many directions. If you were to look at this kind of glass, you could see light shining through it. However, you could not see objects very well through the glass.

Things which you cannot see through very well, such as frosted glass, are *translucent.* Thin cloth and thin paper are such things. When do you think it is important to have something that scatters light?

A word in italics is often explained or defined in context. What does this word mean?

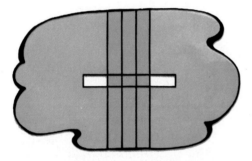

PASSING STRAIGHT THROUGH. Light can pass through some things in another way. It can pass straight through these things. Such things are *transparent.* Some transparent things are clear glass, air, and water. Because light can pass straight through transparent things, you can see through them clearly. What other transparent things can you think of? When might you want to be able to see through something?

Very often, examples are given to help you understand a new word. What examples are given to help you understand the word *transparent*?

— *Exploring Science:* Green Book
Laidlaw Brothers

Building Skills

1. The following words are defined or explained in context. What does each word mean?

    a. translucent   b. transparent   c. scattering

2. Which of the following clues to new words appear in the selection?

    a. a word in boldface
    b. a word in italics
    c. examples
    d. a picture or diagram

Using Context Clues in Social Studies

The first four sentences tell about *iron ore*. What is the difference between *iron* and *iron ore*?

Iron is never found in its pure form in nature. It is always mixed with soil and rock. The mixture is called iron ore. The iron is locked into the ore. The only way to get it out is to heat the ore to a very high temperature. Iron melts before rock does. When the iron melts, it runs out from the rest of the ore, which remains solid. Separating iron from ore in this way is called smelting. People have made iron this way for thousands of years. It is the way we still make iron today.

What word is defined in context in this sentence?

THE RECIPE. The recipe for ironmaking also has not changed over the years. It calls for three things. One, of course, is iron ore. Another is a fuel that can make a fire hot enough to melt iron. The third is a mineral called lime-stone. When iron is melted out of the ore, it is not really pure. There are still bits of rock, dirt, and other things mixed with it. Limestone helps get them out. It melts along with the iron and mixes with these other things. Together, they float to the top. That floating stuff is called slag. The slag is then skimmed off. What remains is pure iron.

—People in the Americas
Silver Burdett

> **Limestone may be a new word to you. The context tells you what it is (a mineral), and what it does. What does *limestone* do in ironmaking?**

> ***Slag* is defined in context. What is *slag*?**

Building Skills

Not every new word in the selection is defined in context. See if you know what each word below means. Match each word in column 1 with its meaning in column 2.

1	2
1. skimmed	a. any natural substance, such as coal, that is not a plant or animal
2. mineral	b. removed floating matter from the surface of a liquid
3. recipe	c. a type of mineral, such as marble, that contains calcium
4. fuel	d. a set of directions or a way to get a desired result
5. limestone	e. something that produces energy

SKILLS LESSON

Clues to Word Meaning

You find new words everywhere. You find them in your textbooks and in the books you read for fun. You find them when you talk with people or when you watch TV. What are some other places in which you find new words?

Suppose you meet a new word in your reading. What are some of the things you can do to learn what it means?

Look at the following list of things you can do to learn new words.

- You can use what you know about sound–letter relationships. You can try to divide the word into syllables. When you can say the word, you often find that you have heard it before. It may not really be a "new" word after all.
- You can look for clues to meaning within the word. Is it a compound word? Is there a prefix or suffix? Does the word have a root within it?
- You can look for clues in the context. Other words in the same sentence or in other sentences may give you help.
- You can look up the word in a glossary or dictionary.

Do you need to do all these things with every new word? Of course not. Often, however, you will use two or three clues to help you find the meaning of a new word.

Using Sound–Letter Relationships

You know what sounds letters stand for. So you can **decode** most words that you've never seen in print before. When you do so, you often find that they're words you know "by ear." Perhaps the word *squid* is one that you have not seen before. You can pronounce it because you know what sounds its letters stand for. Once you have said the word, you may know that a squid is a sea animal with many arms.

Syllables Help in Pronouncing Words

Knowing about sound–letter relationships can help you pronounce a word like *squid*. But how do you tackle a long, unfamiliar word? Dividing a word into syllables can help you say it. Look at this sentence:

The scientist studying the *bacteria* had a *fabulous* idea.

If you don't know how to pronounce the two words in italics, you should try to divide them into syllables:

bac·te·ri·a   fab·u·lous

A syllable is a word part that has one vowel sound. *Bacteria* has four vowel letters. Each vowel letter stands for a separate vowel sound. So *bacteria* has four syllables.

Fabulous also has four vowel letters. But the *ou* together stand for one sound. So *fabulous* has three vowel sounds. This means it has three syllables.

After you have divided the word into syllables, put the sounds together and say the whole word. Your first try may not be exactly right, but it is probably close enough for you to recognize each word. Say the words *bacteria* and *fabulous*. Now do you know that bacteria are tiny living things? Did you recognize that *fabulous* means "wonderful"?

Try This

Read the sentences below. If the words in italics are new to you, try to decode them. Break them into syllables and try to say them. Once you say them, you may find you know what they mean. Match each word with one of the meanings listed below the sentence. Then look up the words in a dictionary.

1. The tiny animal could be seen only under a *microscope*.

   a. a mountain filled with caves
   b. a large animal that does not cast a shadow
   c. an instrument used to magnify very small things

2. Mopsy is just an *ordinary* dog.

   a. brown   b. common   c. fat

Word Parts Help with Meaning

Words are made up of units of meaning. The word *glowworm* has two units of meaning: *glow* and *worm*. Notice that each of these units of meaning is a whole word. These two words, when put together, form a **compound** word.

In some compound words (like *glowworm*), it is easy to see how the meaning of each word helps you understand the meaning of the compound word. In other compound words, however, the meaning of the whole word cannot be found by simply combining the meanings of the separate words. You may have to use your imagination to figure out what the compound word means. Look at the compound words below. In which ones can you find the meaning simply by combining the meanings of the separate words?

buttonhole   skyscraper   headache

You can find the meaning of *buttonhole* and *headache* by combining the meanings of the separate words. But a skyscraper is not something that scrapes the sky. It is a very tall building.

Prefixes, Suffixes, and Root Words

Prefixes are units of meaning added to the beginnings of words. **Suffixes** are units of meaning added to the ends of words. Prefixes and suffixes are not whole words. They must be added to whole words. The unit of meaning to which a prefix or suffix is added is called the **root word.**

How many units of meaning are there in *unhelpful*? If you said three, you're right. You recognized the root word *help*, the prefix *un-*, and the suffix *-ful*. *Un-* means "not," and *-ful* means "full of." So you know that the whole word means "not full of help." Find the units of meaning in each of these three words.

unhappy   helpless   successful

Try This

1. Read the sentences below. Try to pronounce each of the words in italics. Notice the units of meaning. Separate the root word from its suffix or prefix. What does each whole word mean?

   a. A mineral is a *nonliving*, natural thing.
   b. John helped the baby until she could walk *unaided*.
   c. The *courageous* girl defended her sister.
   d. The tank held a *hammerhead* shark.
   e. Daisy is *unusually* late today.

2. Combine each root word in Column A with a prefix or suffix in Column B to make a new word. Then combine the words in Column A with other words to make as many compound words as you can.

A	B
cycle	-ing
set	bi-
soft	-y
sun	re-
motor	-en
total	-ly
dress	un-

VOCABULARY STUDY

Compound Words

Here are some pictures from Martin and Ruth's snow-covered vacation. Although they enjoyed it, they're not quite sure that they would do it again.

Everything on the mountain was so white, we could hardly see where we were going. I have good eyesight, but it didn't help me this time.

Our biggest job each day was cleaning the car's windshield so we could see the road.

We were out in the terrible storm for only a minute, but our eyelashes were coated with snow. That made it hard to open our eyes!

The deer we saw seemed to enjoy the cold and the snow. It was breathtaking to see the deer leaping all around us.

Word Play

You can use the shorter words in a compound word to understand the meaning of the compound word. Match each compound word on the left with its correct meaning on the right. Make up a sentence using each compound word.

eyesight	hairs growing on the edges of the eyelids
windshield	very beautiful, taking one's breath away
eyelashes	the power of seeing; vision
breathtaking	the front window of a car

To pronounce any words that are new to you, use what you know about sound–letter relationships. Breaking new words into syllables may help you say them. Look for units of meaning in any word that is new to you.

Travelers to the southernmost part of the world enjoy watching the strange birds in . . .

PENGUIN PARADISE

by Edna M. Andreas

When people first sailed far south to Antarctica, they met a bird that walked like a human, swam like a fish, and acted like a busybody. It didn't seem to be a bird at all until it became sleepy. Then, like every other bird in the world, it tucked its bill under its wing and went to sleep.

This strange bird was a penguin. It is found only in the southern part of the world. It shows no fear of people and sometimes is quite friendly.

Rear Admiral Richard E. Byrd made his first trip to Antarctica in 1928. Day by day, he kept a record of all that happened. On December 17, he wrote the story of his first meeting with live penguins.

33

Meeting an Emperor

The Admiral's ship was sailing through the ice pack. This is a ring of floating ice which circles Antarctica. Suddenly, on some ice near the ship, Admiral Byrd spied an emperor penguin. He knew that Antarctica couldn't be very far away.

The emperor is the largest of all penguins. The one Byrd saw was nearly four feet tall. It was a handsome bird. Its back was gleaming black. Its chest feathers were the color of rich cream. On each side of its neck was a patch of golden yellow feathers. On its beak were bright orange lines. The beak was so long and the body so large that the emperor's head looked very small indeed.

The bird stood on its two feet. It looked quietly at the men as if to say, "I own this great land of ice and snow!" And this is almost true, for the emperor spends more of its life on Antarctica's shores than any other living thing. In fact, before the humans came to Antarctica, these birds had 6 million square miles of land all to themselves every winter. Other animals leave when winter and darkness come. But that is the very time the emperors raise their young!

Admiral Byrd was surprised to see how much this huge penguin looked like a person. In its fancy "coat" and "shirt," it seemed to be dressed for a grand party. Because the emperor looked so proud, the Admiral thought he should speak to it respectfully. But the penguin didn't want to speak to Byrd. It just bowed a little. Then the penguin turned and walked away.

Admiral Byrd and friends.

The Adélies

Later, Byrd met another kind of penguin, the Adélie [ə·dā′lē]. These birds are smaller than the emperors. They are also more friendly. Whatever they do, they seem to have fun.

Many of the birds came near the Admiral's ship. Some came sliding down small hills of ice on their fat, round stomachs. Some of the sailors jumped onto the ice and played with the penguins. No one knew who had more fun—the sailors or the birds.

The Adélies swam like fish behind the ship. Now and then, a bird would race across the ice on its stomach. By pushing with its flippers, the Admiral said, the Adélie could travel as fast as a person could walk.

A penguin's wings are not like other birds'. They are not built to lift the penguin's plump body off the ground. And they

Adélie feeding two chicks. The chicks will soon be old enough to leave for the sea.

are not usually called wings. They're called flippers.

A penguin's strong flippers are useful in many ways. They help to balance the bird when it walks. They serve as clubs during a fight. They help the bird glide over the snow. And, used as paddles, flippers make the penguin one of the world's best swimmers.

Who's Afraid? Not an Adélie!

As the sailors unloaded the ships, they were never alone. The Adélies followed them everywhere. The birds came close and stared with their funny round eyes. The white rings around their eyes made them look wide-awake and very wise.

Admiral Byrd soon learned that the Adélies were too curious and too fearless for their own good. Adélies are afraid of only three things in the world. They fear the leopard seals and killer whales that gobble penguins in the sea. They are also afraid of the skua [skyoo′ə] gulls that steal eggs and eat baby penguins. Nothing else can frighten an Adélie.

The birds showed that they had no fear of the great ships

nearby, or of the noisy people at work. They were not even afraid of the barking dogs that pulled the sleds.

In his book *Little America,* Admiral Byrd told about one brave Adélie. It came heading straight toward a team of nine sled dogs. The Admiral knew that it would take only one husky to kill an Adélie.

There was no stopping the noisy penguin. On and on it came. When it reached the team, it started to fight with all nine dogs at once. The nine dogs barked. The penguin squawked. The dogs tried to bite with their sharp, strong teeth. The Adélie's squawks became louder, but it didn't run away.

Admiral Byrd went after the Adélie quickly. He snatched it away from the dogs just in time. Then he carried the bird far away and put it down safely on the snow.

The dogs became quiet once more. But was the penguin quiet? No! Was it thankful to Admiral Byrd for saving its life? No, indeed! It was angry because Admiral Byrd had not let it finish the fight.

The little Adélie was still squawking as it walked away. Admiral Byrd thought the penguin seemed to be saying, "Well, I showed those dogs a thing or two!"

Understanding What You've Read

1. What is this selection chiefly about?

   a. funny things Admiral Byrd saw a penguin do
   b. life in Antarctica
   c. penguins in general, and a few individual ones

2. Why can't penguins fly?
3. What are the only things Adélie penguins are afraid of? Why are they afraid?
4. Why did Admiral Byrd rescue a penguin? How did the penguin seem to feel about being rescued?
5. Before people went to Antarctica, the penguins had the land to themselves. What effects do people have on an animal when they move into the animal's environment?

Applying the Skills Lesson

How many syllables are there in each of the words below? Pronounce each word. What does each one mean?

1. Antarctica
2. plump
3. gleaming
4. admiral
5. fearless
6. Adélie
7. emperor
8. penguin
9. squawking

In this selection, you will find many compound words. The separate units of meaning in a new word may give you a clue to the meaning of the whole word. Try to pronounce any word you find that is new to you.

On a summer evening, in a boat or on land, you may be able to see some of the lovely . . .

LIVING LIGHTS IN OUR WORLD

by Alvin *and* Virginia Silverstein

Tiny flashes of light are sprinkled through the summer evenings. These winking lights are made by living creatures called fireflies.

The firefly is not a fly. It is a dark-colored little beetle, about half an inch long. The male has four large wings and can fly swiftly through the air. But in many species, the female cannot fly.

Both male and female fireflies have something which most other beetles do not have. At the very end of its body, each firefly carries a light that it can turn on and off whenever it wants. This is no ordinary light. It is a living light.

How Living Lights Work

How does the firefly's light go on and off? Threadlike nerves reach deep into the firefly's body. Messages are carried along these nerves from the firefly's brain. This sets off a chemical reaction that makes a light flash on.

People love to watch the winking lights of the fireflies in the summer, nighttime sky. But did you know that the fireflies really use their lights as signals? They flash them on and off to signal other fireflies.

The firefly is a living light.

How often a firefly lights up depends on a number of things. First of all, it depends on the kind of firefly it is. One kind lights up every two seconds. Other kinds of fireflies light up at different rates.

You might want to signal to a firefly with a flashlight. You will have to signal at just the right time and at just the right speed—just as though you were a firefly. Some people have been able to fool fireflies with small lights. As long as the rate is right, the firefly will come toward the light.

There are more than sixty kinds of fireflies in the United States. Many other kinds of fireflies are found in different parts of the world. Some of them have very strange ways.

In Burma and in Thailand, hundreds or even thousands of fireflies may gather on a certain kind of tree growing near the water. Perched so thickly on branches that they may nearly cover the tree itself, they all light up together. No one has figured out why the Asian fireflies act in this strange way. Whatever the reason, these living lights are a breathtaking sight.

Glowworms

Some glowworms live in caves in New Zealand. They hang from the ceilings of the caves and spin sticky "fishing nets." These "nets" are similar to spider webs. Small insects that live in the caves see the bright lights and fly up to them. On the way, they are caught in the glowworms' "fishing lines." The successful glowworms pull in their sticky threads, gobble up their prey, and then lower their fishing lines again.

The tiny glowworms, grouped together in thousands on the ceilings of the caves, are a beautiful sight. About 50,000 tourists a year now visit the great Glowworm Grotto in New Zealand. There they are treated to a wonderful show.

Visitors enter the Glowworm Grotto in boats. They are carried along by an underground river. The tunnel entrance opens up into a huge cave, lighted by twinkling lights of tiny glowworms hanging from the ceiling. There are so many glowworms that their light is bright enough to read a book by. But if anyone should suddenly make a loud noise, every single light in the cave goes out. For a moment, there is darkness. Then,

slowly, one by one, the tiny lights wink on again.

Most glowworms glow only one color. But one large beetle, which lives in South America, has two different sets of colored lights. This is the railroad worm. When it is resting, a pair of bright red lights glows from its head. But when this strange creature begins to crawl, a row of bright green lights on each side of its body winks on. It looks like a little railroad train, with red headlights and green lights shining out the windows of the cars.

Living Lights in the Sea

Sometimes a ship plowing through the sea on a warm summer night may seem to set the water on fire. The wake of the ship sparkles and flashes. Floating and swimming along in the ocean currents are countless numbers of tiny creatures. Each is so small that you wouldn't be able to see it without a microscope. But together they make a dazzling show. When they are disturbed by a passing ship or a large fish, they begin to sparkle. Then, when the water is quiet again, their lights wink out, and all around them it is dark once more.

Above, glowworm with lights on.

Below, thousands of glowworms drop their "fishing lines" (sticky threads) to catch insects.

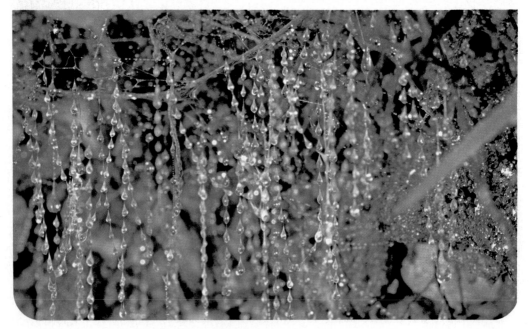

There are also many larger sea animals that glow with living lights. Some jellyfish that float on the surface of the water may start to glow when the sea is disturbed at night by a passing ship. From the ship, the jellyfish look like round dinner plates, shining in the water.

An even more exciting show of living lights on the ocean surface can be seen only a few times a year. In the waters of the West Indies, strange glowing worms live in burrows at the bottom of the sea. They are fireworms. During the summer, just two nights after each full moon, these fireworms suddenly leave their burrows and swim to the top of the sea. It is quite an unusual sight.

Many other creatures of the deep sea carry their own lights. There are shrimps and clams that glow in the dark, deep waters of the ocean. Some squids that live deep in the sea use their lights to blind their enemies.

Scientists are very much interested in living lights. Unlike sunlight, starlight, or electric light, living lights are cold lights. All the energy of the reaction is turned into light, and none is lost as heat. It is hoped that the discovery of how living lights work may someday teach people how to make cold lights to light homes, and perhaps even cities.

Understanding What You've Read

1. Why do fireflies light up?
2. What is meant by "living lights"?
3. Where does the railroad worm get its name?

Applying the Skills Lesson

1. Look for units of meaning in the words below. What is the meaning of each word?

    flashlight   railroad   glowworm

2. What is the root word of each word below? What is the meaning of each whole word?

    suddenly   successful   darkness

Understanding New Words

When you come to a new word in your textbooks, use what you know about sounds and letters to help you pronounce it. Use what you know about word parts for more help in figuring out its meaning.

The sidenotes for the first selection will help you to understand some of the words you may not know. Refer to them as you read. Try to answer the questions in them.

Understanding New Words in Social Studies

For years, people looked at wet-lands and thought only of the ways in which such land might be put to work. So they drained them and built

Two words make up this compound word. Why is this word a good name for land that is covered by water most of the time?

Sometimes the meaning of a compound word is different from the combined meaning that the separate words suggest. Must a highway be high?

The suffix *-tion* is added to *protect,* a word you might already know. (The *t* in *protect* is dropped before the suffix is added.) This suffix means "state of being." What is protection?

Many animals' names are compound words. What do you think a spoonbill looks like?

homes, highways, shopping centers, and factories where they had been.

However, wetlands are not just useless. For one thing, they provide large flat areas over which flood waters can spread out. For another, many ocean fish use wetlands along the coasts for breeding and protection. Also, the most varied animal life in the country is found in wetlands. In the swamps of southern Florida, for example, are alligators, deer, panthers, bears, snakes, and hundreds of water birds such as herons, ibis, spoonbills, storks, and gulls. Finally, wetlands are increasingly attractive as places for recreation. People who live in urban areas like to get away and visit the kinds of natural settings that wetlands offer.

— The United States
Houghton Mifflin

Building Skills

What is the root word to which a suffix has been added in each of the following words? What does each whole word mean?

1. increasingly
2. natural
3. useless
4. breeding
5. attractive
6. varied

Understanding New Words in Health

There are no sidenotes for this selection. Read it and then answer the questions that follow.

Animals that live off other animals are called **parasites.** Some parasites, like fleas, are a bother to the animals they live on. But they are not really harmful. Others can cause much harm.

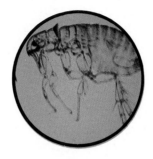

The picture at the bottom of the page also shows parasites. But these parasites do not live *on* an animal or a person. They live *inside* an animal's or a person's body. They are so small that you can't see them without a special **microscope.** They are **microorganisms.** Sometimes people call them microbes for short.

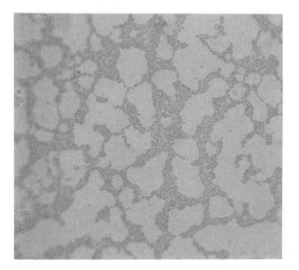

As they live inside your body, some of these microorganisms harm your body cells. Some of them give off poisons. The result is disease.

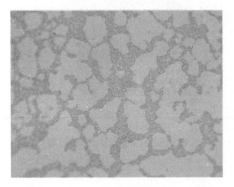

DISEASE	MICROORGANISM
Measles	virus
Poliomyelitis	virus
Mumps	virus
Smallpox	virus
Tetanus	bacteria

— Balance in Your Life: Purple
Harcourt Brace Jovanovich

Building Skills

1. The prefix *micro-* means "small." What does the word *microscope* mean?
2. What clue is given in the selection that the following words are new?

   parasites   microscope   microorganisms

3. What two words in the selection have the prefix *micro-*? What is an *organism*? (Look in the glossary if you do not know.) What is a *microorganism*?

The Dictionary

Finding the Entry Word

Have you ever looked for a word in a dictionary and not been able to find it? Perhaps it was there but was not listed among the **entry words.** Entry words are the words printed in boldface type at the left-hand side of each column in a dictionary.

Many times the word you need is related to an entry word but has a different form. Its spelling may have been changed by adding a prefix or suffix. When this is the case, you must know the root word and look for it as an entry word.

Suppose you do not understand the word in italics in the following sentence:

This weather makes the cabin seem *mustier* than ever.

You look, but you don't find *mustier* among the entry words in a dictionary. What do you do next? Look for the root word. You can guess that it is *musty*. The suffix -er has been added to the root. (Most words ending in *y* change the *y* to *i* before adding a suffix.) When you find the word *musty* in a dictionary, you will see that *mustier* is part of the entry:

> * **must·y** [mus′tē] *adj.* **must·i·er, must·i·est**
> **1** Having a moldy odor or taste. **2** Stale or old:
> *musty* humor. — **must′i·ness** *n.*

You can see that it is often important to know the root of a word in order to find it in a dictionary. However, remember that many words with prefixes or suffixes added to them *are* listed as entry words in most dictionaries.

Try This

What entry word in a dictionary would help you find each word below? Find each word in a dictionary and use it in a sentence.

1. resembled
2. mysteriously
3. silliest
4. successful
5. unavailable
6. disloyal

Using the Pronunciation Key and Accent Marks

How do you pronounce the word *amphibian?* If you don't know, a dictionary can help you. Here is the first part of a dictionary entry for this word:

* **am·phib·i·an** [am·fib′ē·ən]

The letters and symbols in brackets [ ] are the **phonetic respelling** of *amphibian.* A phonetic respelling shows you how to pronounce a word. To understand what the symbols in a phonetic respelling mean, use the **pronunciation key.**

* **add, āce, câre, pälm; end, ēqual; it, īce; odd, ōpen, ôrder; t $\widetilde{oo}$ k, p $\overline{oo}$ l; up, bûrn;** ə = a in *above,* e in *sicken,* i in *possible,* o in *melon,* u in *circus;* **y $\overline{oo}$ = u in *fuse;* oil; pout; check; ring; thin; this; zh in *vision.***

Pronunciation keys are not all the same. But some symbols like the schwa (ə) appear in most of them. Once you get used to the symbols in a dictionary, you will be able to say many of the phonetically respelled words without having to look at the key. Of course, the pronunciation key is always there when you need it for reference. Look for it at the bottom of the dictionary page or in the front of the dictionary.

* From the *HBJ School Dictionary,* © 1977 by Harcourt Brace Jovanovich, Inc. Reprinted and reproduced by permission of the Publisher.

When you are working out the pronunciation of words that have two or more syllables, you have to know which syllable to **accent,** or say with the greatest force. A mark like this ′ shows which syllable should be said with the most force. What syllable has the greatest force in am·fib′ē·ən?

In some long words, like *revolution*, two syllables are accented. This mark ′ shows which syllable is said with the greatest force. This mark ′ shows which syllable is said with lesser force. Which syllable is said with the greatest force in rev′ə·lo͞o′shən? Which syllable is said with lesser force?

Try This

* **add, āce, câre, pälm; end, ēqual; it, īce; odd, ōpen, ôrder; to͝ok, po͞ol; up, bûrn; ə** = a in *above,* e in *sicken,* i in *possible,* o in *melon,* u in *circus;* **yo͞o** = u in *fuse;* **oil; pout; ch**eck; ri**ng; th**in; **th**is; **zh** in *vision.*

Use the pronunciation key above to match each respelling in the column on the left with a word in the column on the right. Then say each word. Use a dictionary to check your work.

1. kāk	a. alphabetical
2. rek′lis	b. celebration
3. sel·ə·brā′shən	c. cake
4. al′fə·bet′i·kəl	d. reckless

Finding the Definition That Fits the Sentence

If a dictionary gives only one definition for a word, that definition is usually right for any sentence. But sometimes you must choose among several definitions. When you find one

* From the *HBJ School Dictionary,* © 1977 by Harcourt Brace Jovanovich, Inc. Reprinted and reproduced by permission of the Publisher.

that seems right for a sentence, try using it in place of the word in the sentence. If the sentence makes sense, you have probably chosen the right definition.

Let us find the meaning for *apt* and fit it into this sentence:

At that moment, Henry made an apt remark.

Suppose you find the following dictionary entry for *apt*. Which meaning is the right one for the sentence above?

> *** apt** [apt] *adj.* **1** Having a natural tendency; likely: Fish are *apt* to be biting then. **2** Quick to learn: an *apt* pupil. **3** To the point; fitting: an *apt* suggestion. — **apt'ly** *adv.* — **apt'ness** *n.*

Which meaning from the entry could have been used in place of *apt*? If you use the meaning from definition 1 or 2, would the sentence make sense? No. Try the meaning in definition 3: At that moment, Henry made a *fitting* remark.

When you check an entry in a dictionary, it is usually a good idea to check all the definitions given. Then choose the one that best fits the sentence you are reading.

* From the *HBJ School Dictionary,* © 1977 by Harcourt Brace Jovanovich, Inc. Reprinted and reproduced by permission of the Publisher.

Sometimes there are two or more words that have exactly the same spelling but are different words with different meanings. A dictionary puts a number next to each of these entry words. When you see a word marked ¹, remember that the following entry word or words will also have numbers. These entries are spelled the same way, but they are different words. Be sure to check all numbered entries to find the meaning that you want.

Try This

From each dictionary entry given, choose the definition that best fits the word in italics in each sentence below. Make up a sentence using each different meaning given.

1. The yard was covered with *concrete*.

> * **con·crete** [kon′krēt *or* kon·krēt′] **1** *n.* A hard substance formed of cement, sand, gravel, and water, used as a building and paving material. **2** *adj. use:* a *concrete* floor. **3** *adj.* Actually existing; real: A chair is *concrete*, but a dream is not. **4** *adj.* Specific; particular: Give me a *concrete* example. — **con·crete′ness** *n.*

2. I knew he was *sensitive*, so I didn't tease him.

> * **sen·si·tive** [sen′sə·tiv] *adj.* **1** Capable of feeling, reacting, appreciating, etc., quickly or easily: The ear is *sensitive* to sound; a *sensitive* thermometer; a film *sensitive* to light. **2** Easy to upset or make angry; touchy. **3** Extremely or abnormally susceptible: *sensitive* to changes in diet. **4** Tender or painful: a *sensitive* spot on the skin. — **sen′si·tive·ness** *n.*

* From the *HBJ School Dictionary*, © 1977 by Harcourt Brace Jovanovich, Inc. Reprinted and reproduced by permission of the Publisher.

VOCABULARY STUDY

Homophones

Van: Rabbits live in **burrows**.

Stan: Did you say rabbits live in *burros*?

Van: Not in burros, "the little donkeys." I'm talking about burrows, "holes in the ground that animals live in." *Burrow* and *burro* are *homophones*. They sound the same but aren't spelled the same. They don't mean the same thing, either. Rabbits live in burrows!

Stan: Oh, those! Why didn't you say so?

Van: I did. Anyway, many small animals hide in burrows when birds of **prey** fly overhead.

Stan: Birds *pray*?

Van: No. They fly down, catch animals, and eat them. *Prey* means "any animal taken by another for food."

Stan: Oh, prey, not pray. Why didn't you say so?

Van: I did. Anyway, birds of prey are often carried high up in the air by **currents**.

Stan: Little *currants* can do that?

Van: Listen carefully, Stanley. *You're* talking about currants, "little berries you use to make jelly." I'm talking about wind currents, "air that flows in definite directions."

Stan: Oh, those! Why didn't you say so?

Word Play

Give a definition for *burrow, burro, prey, pray, current,* and *currant*. Then use each word in a sentence.

If you have trouble figuring out the meaning of some words in this selection, the glossary or a dictionary can help you.

This selection is a diary account of a family's . . .

Dolphin Days

by Cynthia de Narvaez

March 15, Friday

Today was clear and cool. The sun sparkled off the blue-green water. It danced on the red and yellow toys that were spread out along the side of the pool. We waited excitedly. Suddenly a fin knifed up through the water. A gleaming gray body rolled over with a puff . . . and was gone. "There's one! There's one! Where did it go?"

A dolphin at last! Ninu, Cynta, Claudia, Felito, and I, their mother, had never seen live dolphins before.

The dolphin rose again! It gasped--and so did we. The animal was much larger than we had imagined. It moved as though it were oiled. We had expected to see dolphins like those in the movies or on TV--cute and small. But this animal from the deep sea was immense, strange, and beautiful.

A man in white pants and a red-and-white-striped shirt walked out onto the dock. He introduced himself as Michael, the trainer, and welcomed us. He greeted

Pete, the dolphin in the pool, and gave us
a short talk on dolphins. Michael told us
that they are mammals, not fish. They use
their mouths mostly for eating. They
breathe and speak through the blowhole at
the top of their heads. They can drown if
water enters the blowhole. Not only is the
blowhole the dolphin's "nose," but in it
are organs like our lips, vocal cords, and
tongue. The "tongue" serves to close the
blowhole when the dolphin dives.

The permanent "smiling" expression on a
dolphin's face seems to show that it is
joyful and friendly. In fact, dolphins are
well known for saving people's and other
dolphins' lives. Though they are usually
gentle, they are always ready to protect

themselves. They are expert shark-killers. But they will never hurt someone who has not hurt them.

There are about thirty kinds of dolphins. The bottlenose is one of the largest. Bottlenoses are often called porpoises. This is a mistake. Porpoises are smaller animals that are relatives of dolphins.

Michael told us that a dolphin's skin is very sensitive. Dolphins have good eyesight both in the air and under the sea. They can hear sounds ten miles away through the water. Their sense of taste makes up for their lack of a sense of smell.

When Michael finished talking, Pete squawked and shook his flippers as if to say, "That was great. Thank you. But now let's get on with it!"

Telling him to mind his manners, Michael threw him a basketball. Pete fielded it neatly on his beak. He swam through the pool toward a basket that hung nine feet above the water. Then he tossed the ball and scored a perfect goal. We glowed with pride, as if he had been a member of our own family.

March 17, Sunday

Yesterday, it rained. But at eight o'clock Sunday morning we went once again to the pool. At the end of the show,

Michael invited us to swim with Pete. We all accepted at once. Ninu ran to the dock, but when she came face to face with the huge animal lying in the water, she stopped. She turned to look at me, and took a few steps back.

"Swim to the end of the pool and wait," ordered Michael, unaware of her fear.

"Go on, Ninu," I said. "If you don't, I will!"

That was a real challenge. She jumped into the water, swam across the pool, and waited. Pete stayed near the dock and watched her. He seemed a bit worried about the intruder in his pool.

Michael said quietly, "Go get her, Pete!" Pete then vanished soundlessly underwater.

"Where is he?" Ninu called, searching the pool around her. Pete's big fin rose right in front of her face.

"Take hold of his fin and hang on tight," Michael called.

She did, and Pete, swimming through the water, pulled her straight to the dock.

Ninu climbed out, gasping and happy. Just then, Claudia pushed Cynta in. In great fear, Cynta swam across the pool. But Pete was waiting for her at the other side. He dived and slowly came up to tickle her. Then he presented his fin and returned her to the dock. He let her hug him. Then he twittered at her, nodding his head.

Pete then shot out of the way as I lost
my footing and fell into the chilly water.
I began to swim but soon saw that Pete had
gone ahead of me and was waiting to tow me
back. Holding onto his fin as he shot
through the water, I felt as if I were
riding on a torpedo.

Next we visited with Dove. She did no
tricks but was everybody's pet. As I
entered the water in her pen, she slid
under my arm to be hugged. Happy to have
company, she snaked around each one of us.
She floated on her back, turning around
and smiling. Each time one of us swam

toward the side of her pen to get out,
Dove moved between the edge and the
swimmer. She wanted all of us to stay. She
made noises as if to say, "How could you
desert me?"

Later we learned some interesting facts
about dolphins. Some trainers who work
with them think dolphins are as smart as—
or even smarter than—people. They believe
this because of the shape and size of
dolphins' brains and also because dolphins
learn so easily.

Dolphins use their hearing to "see" what
is around them in the water. In the
darkest waters, they are aware of a
shark—its distance, its size, and how
hungry it is—long before they can see it.
A mother dolphin can use her hearing to

tell if there are uncomfortable air pockets in her baby's stomach. She knows just where to give the baby a gentle poke with her beak to "bubble" it. Blindfolded, a dolphin can easily jump through hoops in the air or find a fish in the water.

March 18, Monday

When we arrived at the pool this morning, we found that Pete had been joined by Simo [sē′mo] and Beau Brummell [bō′ brum′əl], the two high jumpers. They played with a ball for a long while. Afterwards they swam to the dock and looked at us, showing us all their teeth. Sometimes one would sit up in the water and nod and talk to us. They would not let us touch them, but they came very close. Soon Ninu, Cynta, and I joined them in the water. This scared them. They tore around the pool at high speed. However, they soon decided that we were safe and came closer, circling each one of us. At long last, they let us touch them.

The dolphins seemed to prefer the children to me. Michael told me this was always true at first, but that one of them would soon adopt me. He made it clear that I had no choice which one it would be. The choice is always theirs. I felt like a puppy in a litter up for sale.

They delighted in playing tricks on us. They kept talking excitedly. Rough as they

were among themselves, they were never too
rough with us. As I was watching them play
with the children today, I felt a blow on
the top of my head. Then a great weight
settled on my shoulder. Simo had bounced
the ball on my head. With his head and
neck resting on my shoulder, he was
looking around into my face. I burst out
laughing and hugged him. Then he made a
sound so exactly like my laugh that I was
surprised. How happy I was that this one
seemed to have adopted me!

Understanding What You've Read

1. What is this selection chiefly about?

    a. the many things dolphins do
    b. how remarkable dolphins are
    c. a family's vacation

2. Why do some trainers think that dolphins may be smarter than people?
3. What does the author mean in saying that dolphins "speak" and "talk"?

Applying the Skills Lesson

1. What entry word would you look for to find the meaning of each word below? Remember—entry words are usually root words, but not always.

    a. circling   b. soundlessly   c. unaware
    d. snaked   e. intruder   f. uncomfortable

2. Which meaning of *litter* fits the sentence below?

> *__lit·ter__ [lit′ər] **1** *n.* Scraps or other things strewn about; clutter. **2** *v.* To make untidy or unsightly with litter: to *litter* the sidewalk with trash. **3** *n.* The young brought forth at one birth by a mammal normally having several offspring at a time. **4** *v.* To give birth to (young). **5** *v.* To have a litter. **6** *n.* Straw, hay, etc., spread as bedding for animals. **7** *n.* A stretcher for carrying sick or wounded persons. **8** *n.* A vehicle consisting of a couch on two poles carried by men or animals.

Litter

I felt like a puppy in a *litter* up for sale.

TEXTBOOK STUDY

Using Dictionaries and Glossaries

You have found that many new words in your textbooks are explained in context. But sometimes you find new words that are not explained and that you cannot decode. In such cases, you need to turn to a dictionary or to a glossary. Study the dictionary and glossary entries that follow. Refer to the sidenotes. They will help you understand some of the entries.

Using a Dictionary

* **Hai·ti** [hā′tē] *n.* **1** A country in the western part of the West Indian island of Hispaniola. **2** A former name of Hispaniola. — **Hai·ti·an** [hā′·tē-ən *or* hā′shən] *adj., n.*

hake [hāk] *n., pl.* **hake** or **hakes** A food fish related to the cod.

hal·berd [hal′bərd] *n.* A weapon used about 400 years ago, with a spear point and an ax blade on a long shaft.

hal·cy·on [hal′sē-ən] *adj.* Calm; peaceful. ◆ In myths, the *halcyon* was a bird supposed to build its nest in the water and make the winds become calm while it was nesting.

hale[1] [hāl] *v.* **haled, hal·ing** To compel to go: to *hale* into court.

hale[2] [hāl] *adj.* **hal·er, hal·est** Vigorous and healthy; robust: He felt *hale* and hearty.

Hale [hāl], **Nathan,** 1755–1776, American patriot, hanged as a spy by the British.

half [haf] *n., pl.* **halves** [havz] **1** *n.* Either of two equal or almost equal parts into which a thing may be divided, or a quantity equal to such a part: Give me *half*. **2** *adj.* Having half of a standard value: a *half* teaspoon. **3** *adj.* Not complete; partial. **4** *adv.* To the extent of a half; partially. **5** *adv.* Nearly: I was *half* inclined to refuse. **6** *adv. informal* To any extent at all: not *half* good enough.

Halberd

Each word and all the information listed about it is called an *entry*. Notice that this dictionary also lists places and people.

Sometimes, a dictionary tells you where a word comes from. Where did the word *halcyon* come from?

Pictures or diagrams in dictionaries help you to understand meanings.

How does the sentence help you to understand this meaning of *half*?

* From the *HBJ School Dictionary,* © 1977 by Harcourt Brace Jovanovich, Inc. Reprinted and reproduced by permission of the Publisher.

Building Skills

1. Answer the following questions about the dictionary entries on page 67.

   a. How many entries are there for *hale*?
   b. How many meanings are given for *half*?
   c. Who was Nathan Hale?

2. All the items listed below are found in dictionaries. Which items are part of an entry?

   a. the spelling of the entry word
   b. the entry word's meanings
   c. the pronunciation key
   d. the phonetic respelling of the entry word
   e. the guide words
   f. names of important people, places, and things

Using a Glossary

Here are several entries from a mathematics glossary. Notice that the entry words are in boldface type. They are listed in alphabetical order. Some entries include pictures or examples.

Glossary

Addition An operation on two numbers that tells how many in all or how much in all.

> **This example gives you two important terms in addition: *addend* and *sum*.**

$$\begin{array}{r} 5 \leftarrow \text{addend} \\ \text{plus} \longrightarrow +7 \leftarrow \text{addend} \\ \hline 12 \leftarrow \text{sum} \end{array}$$

$$\begin{array}{r} .26 \\ 3.41 \\ \hline 3.67 \end{array}$$

$$\frac{1}{9} + \frac{4}{9} = \frac{5}{9}$$

Addition Property of Zero The sum of a number and zero is the number itself. For example: $5 + 0 = 0 + 5 = 5$.

Angle A figure formed by two rays with the same endpoint. Angles are acute, right, or obtuse.

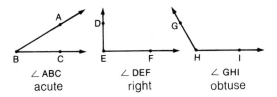

| ∠ ABC | ∠ DEF | ∠ GHI |
| acute | right | obtuse |

The measure of any right angle is 90°.

Area The number of unit squares it takes to cover the inside of a figure. The area of this figure is 10 square units.

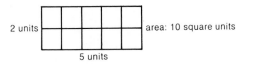

2 units   area: 10 square units
5 units

Square inch, square foot, square yard, and square centimeter and square meter are standard units for measuring area.

— Mathematics, Series M: Level 5
Macmillan

Building Skills

1. Which entries include equations to help you understand the meanings?
2. What information in the entry for *area*, in addition to the definition, helps you understand the meaning?
3. If you didn't know the meaning of a term used in a definition in the glossary, what would you do?

Recognizing Cause-and-Effect Relationships

What happened in the pictures? The snow fort melted. What caused it to melt? The hot sun *caused* it to melt. This is a cause-and-effect relationship.

Cause-and-Effect Relationships in Sentences

To understand cause and effect, you must notice how events are related. Ask yourself two questions: "What happened?" and "Why did this happen?" Look for the cause-and-effect relationship in the following sentence.

The crops were small because there was so little rain this year.

70

What happened to the crops? Your answer is an *effect:* They were small. Why did this happen? Your answer is a *cause:* There was so little rain this year.

Sometimes sentences contain word clues that show cause and effect. Look for such word clues in the two sentences below.

1. The cold winter caused the supply of heating fuel to be used up quickly.
2. As a result of the gas and oil shortages, people looked for ways to use energy from the sun.

Using the sun's energy. The heat of the sun warms the water in the bottles. The bottles hold that warmth for a long period of time and warm the air.

In sentence 1 on page 71, *caused* is a clue word. What happened? The supply of heating fuel was used up. This is the effect. Why did this happen? It happened because of the cold winter. The cold winter is the cause. In sentence 2 on page 71, *As a result* is the clue. That people looked for ways to use energy from the sun is the effect. The cause is the gas and oil shortages.

Cause-and-Effect Relationships Between Sentences

Sometimes separate sentences show cause-and-effect relationships. Again, word clues can often help you see these relationships. Look for the clues to cause and effect in each pair of sentences below.

1. In northern states, food for birds becomes scarce in the winter. Therefore, geese and ducks fly south in search of food.

2. In one area, where wolves depended on deer for food, the number of deer decreased. So, the number of wolves in that area also decreased.

In the first pair of sentences above, *Therefore* shows a cause-and-effect relationship. In the second pair of sentences, *So* is the word clue. Sometimes, however, there is a cause-and-effect relationship between sentences that do not have word clues such as *therefore* or *so*. Read the following pair of sentences. There are no word clues in them. Try to find the cause and the effect. Ask yourself "What happened?" and "Why did this happen?"

The giraffe is the tallest living four-legged animal. Giraffes are able to use the leaves of tall trees for their food supply.

You can clearly understand the relationship between these sentences if you ask yourself: What happened? (effect) Why did it happen? (cause)

(effect)→Giraffes are able to use the leaves of tall trees for their food supply.

(cause)→The giraffe is the tallest living four-legged animal.

Try This

1. In each sentence below, find the cause and the effect. Use the word clues to help you.

   a. Dad failed to shut the freezer door tightly, so the bag of ice turned to water.
   b. Because several power lines were not working in my town, we found ourselves without electricity.

2. In each pair of sentences below, find the cause and the effect. There are no word clues to help you.

   a. Camels can store enough food and water in their bodies to last them for several days. They can travel long distances in the desert.
   b. As bees gather nectar from flowers, they fertilize the flowers. Bees help both the flowers they visit and the people who enjoy honey as a food.
   c. Ants recognize the other ants that live in their nest by their odor. The ability of ants to recognize the members of their "family" helps them to protect the nest from enemies.

VOCABULARY STUDY

Synonyms

The Larsen twins were in an exploring group. They each wrote a report. They didn't want to say exactly the same thing. So, to be different, they used some *synonyms,* words that have the same or nearly the same meanings. Here are parts of their reports.

. . . I put on my **goggles** and went into the **grotto**. Once inside, most of the light disappeared. But the dark never **disturbed** me. Inside we did much climbing and walking. By the time we got outside, I was totally out of breath.

. . . I put on my special eyeglasses and went into the cave. Once inside, most of the light **vanished**. But the dark never bothered me. Inside we did much climbing and walking. By the time we got outside, I was **entirely** out of breath.

Word Play

1. What synonyms in the reports above help you to know the meaning of *goggles, grotto, disturbed, vanished,* and *entirely*?
2. Write a short report about your favorite hobby. Then rewrite your report, replacing some of the words with synonyms.

What causes city trees to die? Why was a 4,000-year-old tree called "Pine Alpha"? For the answers to these questions, look for cause-and-effect relationships in this selection.

Long before the first humans or any other animal walked on this planet, the land was filled with great, silent . . .

GIANTS IN THE EARTH

by Elizabeth K. Cooper

The moon has no trees. No trees grow on Mars. As far as we know, only one planet — Earth — has trees.

Trees are alive, just as you are. But most of them are bigger than you are, and many years older. A tree can live and keep growing as long as it gets all the things that it needs.

Every tree needs food, which it makes in its own green leaves. To make its own food, a tree needs good air, good water, and sunlight. A tree also needs the right kind of soil.

Hot lands and cold lands, high places and low ones, wet areas and dry — they all have their own kinds of trees. It is amazing how some trees manage to survive where they live.

The First Trees

Millions of years ago, strange trees and tall, treelike plants lived in the green forests. No birds sang. No bees buzzed. No rabbits, squirrels, or chipmunks ran through the leaves. Such animals had not yet begun to live on Earth. Even the dinosaurs had not yet arrived.

In time, some of the ancient trees disappeared from the Earth forever. Other kinds lived on. They changed slowly, as the Earth changed through the ages. Some of the old trees were ancestors of our pines and other cone-bearing trees.

Giant trees once grew in great forests in many parts of the world. Now most of the giants are gone, but one kind — the sequoias — live on. Most of them are in California.

Sequoia trees are named for Sequoyah, a Cherokee who invented a written language for his people.

There are two kinds of sequoia trees in California—redwoods and giant sequoias. Earth's tallest tree is a giant sequoia.

The Oldest Trees

The 3,500-year-old General Sherman is a giant tree in Sequoia National Park. It is one of the best-known trees in the world. It is 310 feet tall and more than 32 feet around. But its cones are small, with seeds just a quarter of an inch long. What a miracle that a giant tree can grow from so small a seed!

Not very long ago, some much older trees were discovered. They, too, are in California.

The Pine Alpha is not tall or wide or handsome. Nevertheless, it is a very interesting tree.

It lives high on the steep, rocky side of a mountain. It leans out over miles of wide, empty valley. In the morning it catches the first rays of sunrise. In the evening it is touched by the last glow of sunset.

Pine Alpha's trunk and branches have been peeled and cut and shaped by angry winds and blasts of sand and ice. The tree looks more dead than alive, and it is. Nine-tenths of Pine Alpha is dead. Yet the tree is still growing. It still holds live seeds that can grow into new trees. This is amazing, because Pine Alpha is 4,300 years old!

Pine Alpha's age was discovered by a scientist in 1956. With a special tool, he bored into the heart of the tree and drew out a long, thin core of wood. Then he counted the tree's growth rings —one for each year of the tree's life.

Pine Alpha is the first living tree to be dated at more than 4,000 years old. Therefore, it was named *Alpha,* after the first letter in the Greek alphabet.

Pine Alpha is not just a curiosity. It is important to scientists who study our weather. As Pine Alpha grew, its growth rings made records of weather conditions for more than 4,000 years. The U. S. Weather Service's records go back little more than 100 years. Pine Alpha's records cover a period more than forty times that long.

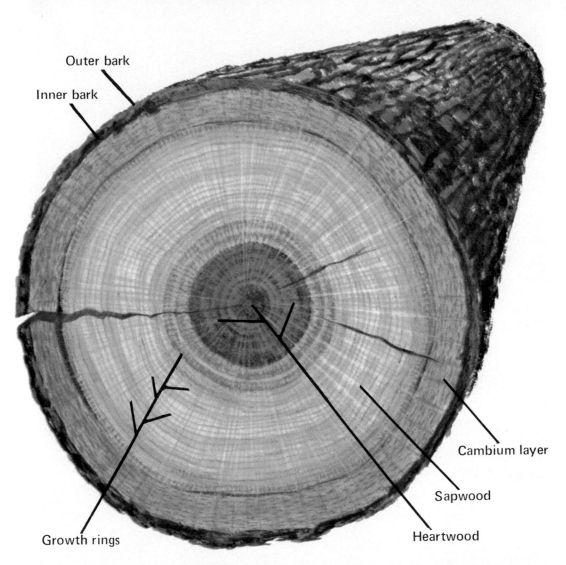

Outer bark

Inner bark

Cambium layer

Sapwood

Heartwood

Growth rings

Other trees have been studied and dated. One has been named *Methuselah,* for the oldest man in the Bible. He is said to have lived for 969 years. The Methuselah tree has been alive and growing for 4,600 years!

It is not an easy thing to visit these ancient trees. They live high above cities and towns. They are more than 10,000 feet up—on rocky slopes where few other things can grow.

City Trees

In forests and on deserts, trees grow by themselves. They spring up from seeds that fall. No one waters them when they are young. No one watches over them as they grow. Each one grows—if it gets all the things it needs. Otherwise, it dies.

City trees are different. They are brought to the city—often from tree farms—and planted by people. They are like pets. They depend on people for care and protection.

It is not always easy to keep city trees alive. Some get too hot. Many get too dry. Some are planted in poor soil. Some are bumped into by cars. And a few are hurt by people or animals. Those that live and grow are the tough ones. They are the trees that can get along in the city environment.

Plant a Tree

You can grow a real tree in a jar or even in a bottle of water. After you eat an avocado, save the seed. Put one toothpick on each side of the seed. Then put the wide end of the seed in water. The toothpicks will keep the whole seed from slipping into the jar. Watch the roots grow down. Watch the green stems grow up. Watch the green leaves grow and unfold.

When the seedling has about a dozen large leaves, it can be planted in a flowerpot filled with good soil. Of course, it can also be planted outdoors.

If you try to grow a big tree from a seed, you will almost surely be disappointed. You are better off planting a healthy, young tree that has had a head start. You can get one at a plant nursery in your own neighborhood.

The tree you plant today will grow fast or slowly, in its own way. It will grow tall and slender, or round and spreading, according to its own nature. It may live for 100 years or more.

If you plant a tree and look after it, you will feel proud, knowing you have helped a living thing to grow.

Understanding What You've Read

1. Why is "Giants in the Earth" a good title for this selection?
2. What trees mentioned in the selection have special names?
3. What have scientists learned by studying the growth rings of the giant sequoia trees?
4. Why is it not always easy to keep city trees alive?
5. What do you think people can do to help trees live longer and healthier lives?

Applying the Skills Lesson

1. In the following sentence, what is the cause? What is the effect?

    A tree can live and keep growing as long as it gets all the things that it needs.

2. Which of the two sentences below gives a cause?

    Pine Alpha is the first living tree to be dated at more than 4,000 years old. Therefore, it was named *Alpha,* after the first letter in the Greek alphabet.

3. Read the following paragraph. Which sentence gives the effect? How many causes are given for this effect?

    It is not always easy to keep city trees alive. Some get too hot. Many get too dry. Some are planted in poor soil. Some are bumped into by cars. And a few are hurt by people or animals.

In this selection, the words *as* and *when* sometimes act as word clues to cause-and-effect relationships. Look for these and other clues to cause and effect.

If you wanted to cross hot desert sands, you could ride upon . . .

The Ship of the Desert

by George Laycock

Camels, for thousands of years, have walked the hot desert sands. They have carried people and goods. Without these animals, people would not have been able to live or work in deserts.

Imagine about 1,000 camels spread out in a line and loaded with salt, silk, and tea. Once, long ago, such caravans were sent westward out of China. They crossed the mountains on trips that sometimes lasted for two months.

These strange animals, called "ships of the desert," do far more than carry people and their belongings. Camels provide milk for drinking and making cheese, and even for face cream. In some parts of the world, camels are even used as money. A person's camels are a sign of wealth. In the same way some people save money, some camel owners try to keep all the camels they can get.

Kinds of Camels

There are two different kinds of camels. You can tell the two kinds apart by the number of humps on their backs. The *Arabian* camels have only one hump. Arabian camels live in the Middle East, India, and North Africa.

The other kind of camel—
the one with two humps—is the
Bactrian. Its home country is
the Gobi Desert of northeastern
Asia. The Bactrian has shorter
legs and longer wool than the
one-humped camel. It also has
stronger, more rugged feet.
This is important because instead of having sand to walk
on, the Bactrian camels live in
rough and rocky parts of the
world.

Sometimes people talk
about another kind of camel,
the *dromedary.* The dromedary
is really a special racing model

of the one-humped camel. It is
bigger than the average Arabian one-humped camel and
can walk faster. The drome-
daries are the riding camels.

Camel History

The camel's family history
goes back millions of years.
And strangely, the camel story
leads back to North America.
The first kind of camel was
small and humpless. Another
kind of camel came later. It
stood fifteen feet high—almost
twice as high as present-day

camels. These North American animals were the ancestors of modern camels. They are believed to have spread out in two directions. One branch of the family slowly moved southward. It ended up in South America. The South American llama is a present-day cousin of the camel.

Another branch of the camel family moved northwestward, toward Alaska. Scientists believe that a belt of land once connected North America and Asia. The camels crossed over this land bridge and spread to Asia and Africa. They later died out in North America.

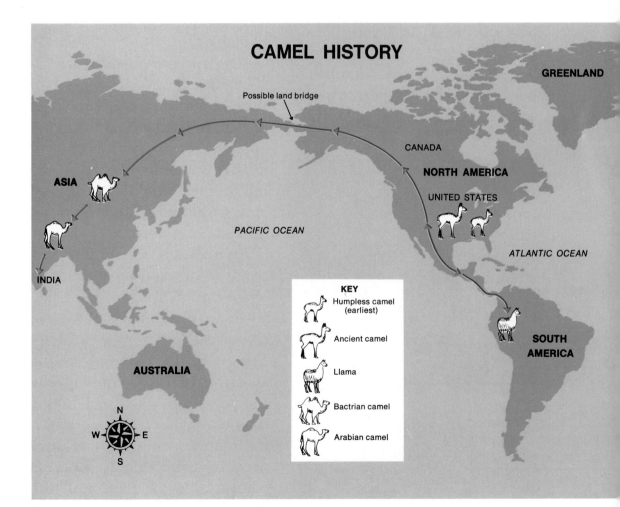

CAMEL HISTORY

Desert Life

Scientists have studied the camel carefully to find out how it can live where many other animals would die. They have found some strange answers. It is well designed for its life in the hot, dry, sandy parts of the world.

Its long legs may help it in more than walking. The hottest part of the desert is right at ground level. Up on those long legs, away from the scorching hot sands, the temperature is somewhat cooler for the camel's body.

Many people have looked at the hump on the camel's back and said, "Ah, there's the answer. The beast simply packs extra water in that hump on its back." But they are wrong about that. The camel's hump is not a big leather bag filled with water. Actually, the hump is filled with fat. There may be eighty pounds or more of fat in the hump, depending on the camel's size.

The fat provides energy to keep the camel going when there is not enough food for it to eat. If hard times last long enough, the camel's hump almost disappears. Owners can tell by the hump if the animal is in good enough condition to make a long journey.

In addition, the camel does a better job than most animals of saving water in its body. Even in the hottest places in the world, a camel gets along fine without doing much sweating at all. A camel's body temperature can also change. As the weather becomes hotter, the camel's body temperature goes up. The camel stays as comfortable as ever. And the water it would need to cool its body is saved.

You may have noticed that a camel has big, droopy eyelids and long, beautiful eyelashes. They help shade its eyes from the bright desert sun.

When the wind blows sand into a camel's face, the animal closes its nostrils. During sandstorms, the camel falls to its knees and closes its eyes. Then it stretches its long neck out, flat against the Earth, and waits for the storm to pass.

If they thought about it, camels might feel proud of themselves. Their talents are many. Their history is long. No other animal anyplace could do their work as well. Camels are the real "ships of the desert."

Understanding What You've Read

1. What is contained in a camel's hump?
2. Why do a camel's long legs prove useful in the desert?
3. Describe the two kinds of camels that lived in North America long ago.
4. Why do people call camels "ships of the desert"?

Applying the Skills Lesson

In each sentence below, there is a cause-and-effect relationship. Which words tell the cause? Which words tell the effect?

1. If hard times last long enough, the camel's hump almost disappears.
2. As the weather becomes hotter, the camel's body temperature goes up.
3. When the wind blows sand into a camel's face, the animal closes its nostrils.

TEXTBOOK STUDY

Understanding Cause-and-Effect Relationships

When you read a textbook, look for cause-and-effect relationships. Word clues like *because, so, therefore,* and *as a result* will sometimes help you see these relationships. Remember, cause-and-effect relationships are often written without these word clues. You can still see the relationships, however, if you look for them.

As you read the following selections, refer to the sidenotes. They will help you to notice the cause-and-effect relationships.

Understanding Cause-and-Effect Relationships in Science

Heating and Cooling Rock

By day, the energy of the Sun acts on the bare rock of the young mountains. How does the Sun's energy heat the rock? Heat causes rock to expand. As you might expect, the outside of the rock is heated more than the inside.

What word clue helps you see a cause and an effect in this sentence?

By night, the rock cools and contracts — but the outside of the rock cools faster than the inside. Day and night the rock expands and contracts, expands and contracts, again and

90

again. Cracks begin to show in the rock.

What causes this to happen? The cause can be found in the sentence before this one.

Water from rain and snow runs into the cracks. The water changes the rocks as they get hotter and cooler. Sometimes, when water freezes in a crack, the crack widens. If the crack widens enough, the rock may split. In time, a rock may be worn down into a handful of sand.

This sentence shows a cause and an effect. What is the effect of the water's freezing?

The breaking down of rock by weather is called weathering. Watching a mountain for a million years or so, you would see the sharp edges and pointed peaks of the young mountain being worn by weathering. You would see the edges and peaks becoming round and smooth, as the forces of weathering worked on them.

This is an effect. What causes the mountain to become round and smooth?

—*Concepts in Science:* Purple
Harcourt Brace Jovanovich

Building Skills

There is a cause-and-effect relationship in each of the sentences below. Part of each sentence is shown in italics. Is the part in italics a cause or an effect?

1. By night, the rock cools and *contracts.*
2. *If the crack widens enough,* the rock may split.
3. Watching a mountain for a million years or so, you would see the sharp edges and pointed peaks of the young mountain being worn by *weathering.*

Understanding Cause-and-Effect Relationships in Social Studies

What caused the farmers to work differently? The first sentence states the two causes.

Forests and wilderness were another important part of the American environment. They, too, forced farmers to work differently. In England, as elsewhere in Europe, farmers had hitched their plows to animals and turned over the soil. Then they raked it to break up the lumps, and planted seed. Most often their crop was wheat. In America, the settlers found few open spaces where they could start to farm. First they had to chop down the trees. Then they cleared a small spot of land where the sunshine could break through. The Eastern Woodland Indians had done the same things in the same environment for thousands of

This part of the sentence is an effect. Why was the sunshine now able to break through?

years. The settlers' plows and animals were of little use as long as there were tree stumps and roots in the ground. So they cultivated the soil by poking holes in it. When they had trouble growing wheat, they switched over to the Indian crop, corn.

—People in the Americas
Silver Burdett

These two sentences show a cause-and-effect relationship. There are actually one cause and two effects. The cause is *there were tree stumps and roots in the ground.* What are the two effects?

Building Skills

1. In the sentence below, find a cause and an effect.

   When they had trouble growing wheat, they switched over to the Indian crop, corn.

2. In the sentence below, which is told first, the cause or the effect?

   The settlers' plows and animals were of little use as long as there were stumps and roots in the ground.

Books About Living Things

Exploring City Trees and the Need for Urban Forests by Margaret J. Anderson. McGraw, 1976. This book is about the importance of city trees and the birds and animals that live in them.

Pandas Live Here by Irmengarde Eberle. Doubleday, 1973. You'll meet a family of pandas at home in the wilds of Tibet.

Cats by Nina Leen. Holt, Rinehart & Winston, 1980. The various types and behavior patterns of wild and house cats are described, with photographs, in this book.

Dolly the Dolphin by Margaret Gay Malone. Messner, 1978. This is the true story of a Florida family that adopted a dolphin.

The Emperor Penguins by Kazue Mizumura. T.Y. Crowell, 1969. The habits of these unusual birds of the Antarctic are explained in words and pictures.

Bears of the World by Dorothy Hinshaw Patent. Holiday House, 1980. This illustrated book provides information on the ways of life of seven species of bear.

A Closer Look at Deserts by Valerie Pitt and David Cook. Watts, 1976. You'll explore the world of the desert and meet many of the different kinds of plants, animals, and people who live there.

Killer Whales by Seymour Simon. Lippincott, 1978. You'll read about one of the world's largest, smartest, and most misunderstood animals.

Part 2

You Can't Help Laughing

UNDERSTANDING AND APPRECIATING LITERATURE

Humor

Humor is anything that is funny. Cartoons and stories can be humorous in many different ways.

Understanding Humor in Exaggeration and the Unexpected

Humor can come from a surprise twist that you don't expect. Read the cartoon. What is the funny surprise? You don't expect the "cat" to be a tiger. The humor comes from the **unexpected.** When you expect something normal, a cartoon or story can catch you off guard and make you laugh.

Many cartoons are funny because they show something that is hard to believe. Look at the cartoon at the right. It is funny because it exaggerates how quickly the plants are growing. **Exaggeration** makes a cartoon or story funny by showing something that is hard to believe.

Read the following story by Alvin Schwartz. Notice how the unexpected and exaggeration make the story funny.

Mule McSneed Captures a Squonk

The squonk is an animal that is so sad about the way it looks that it cries all the time. A famous hunter named Mule McSneed once caught a squonk by following its teardrops. Then he stuck the squonk in a sack and took it home. But the squonk had cried so hard that when he opened the sack, nothing was left of it but a puddle.*

What examples of exaggeration and the unexpected are humorous in the story? The first example of exaggeration is that the squonk cries *all* the time. And that Mule Mc-Sneed is able to follow and catch a squonk just by following its trail of tears is also a funny exaggeration. Then, when the author tells us that the squonk turns into a puddle by crying so hard, the author is using the unexpected to help make the story humorous.

Understanding Humor in Word Play

Some authors play on words to make a story humorous. One kind of **word play** is called a *pun*. A pun creates humor by confusing two meanings for the same word. Read the following story.

* Text adaptation of "The Squonk" from *Kickle Snifters and Other Fearsome Critters: Collected from American folklore* by Alvin Schwartz. Text copyright © 1976 by Alvin Schwartz. By permission of J. B. Lippincott, Publishers.

One day a black ant crawled up the side of a cracker box to the top. Here the ant saw a brown ant running as fast as it could around the top edge of the box.

"Why are you running around like that?" the black ant asked.

The brown ant paused and, nearly out of breath, said, "It says, 'To open this box, tear along the dotted line.'"

Why is this story funny? It is funny because of the pun on the word "tear." One meaning for "tear" is "to run hurriedly," as the ant is doing. Another meaning is "to rip or cut open." When the author includes the wrong meaning for "tear," the result is a humorous pun.

Humorous nonsense words are another type of word play. Nonsense words are not real words. "Squonk" is a nonsense word.

Nonsense words may also be mixed-up real words. Read these sentences.

"I stepped in a puddle," said Wilfred, "and my weet got fet. I mean, I stepped in a puddle and my feet got wet."

What are the funny nonsense words? "Weet" and "fet" are nonsense words. What real words did the author mix to make the nonsense words? The sounds at the beginning of the words "feet" and "wet" have been mixed.

Authors create humor in many ways. The unexpected, exaggeration, and word play are all used to create humor. Puns—words that sound the same but have different meanings—and nonsense words are two kinds of humorous word play. No matter how authors create humor, they all have the same goal—they want to make you laugh.

Try This

Read the story below. Look for word play, exaggeration, and the unexpected.

Ollepump Possum lived high in a flim-flam tree. He was always happy. If someone told him a joke, Ollepump would laugh for a week. He was a possum who saw the bright side of everything.

One day his friend Pessy warned, "Something terrible will happen someday. What will you say then? Will you *still* see the bright side?"

Just then, Ollepump's branch broke. As Ollepump tumbled past each of his friends, he smiled. "So far, everything's OK!"

Write one sentence from the story to show an example of each of the following kinds of humor:

1. word play   2. exaggeration   3. the unexpected

Writing

1. Use each of the following nonsense words in a funny sentence.

   a. bleeple (animal)   c. Streat Street (place)
   b. floober (bird)   d. fiesel-dueled engine (thing)

2. Write your own humorous paragraph about an imaginary animal called a squoodle. Use exaggeration to make your paragraph funny. You may begin with this sentence:

   The squoodle is so shy that it hides under a rock every time the wind whistles.

As you read "You Can't Help Laughing," look for the different ways humor is created in each story.

The Toothpaste Millionaire

by JEAN MERRILL

One afternoon I stopped by my friend Rufus's house to borrow his bike pump. He had about fifty bowls and pans scattered around the kitchen.

"What are you making?" I asked.

"I already made it," Rufus said.

He handed me a spoon and a bowl with some white stuff in it. I took a spoonful.

"Don't eat it," Rufus said. "Just taste it. Rub a little on your teeth. It's toothpaste."

I tried a little.

"How does it taste?" Rufus asked.

"Not bad," I said. "Better than the kind my mother buys in the pink-and-white striped tube. How'd you get it to taste so good?"

"A drop of peppermint oil," Rufus said. "But I've got other flavors, too."

He pushed three other pots across the table. The first one had a spicy taste.

"Clove-flavored," Rufus said. "You like it?"

"I don't know," I said. "It's interesting."

"Try this one."

The next sample had a sweet taste. "Vanilla," I guessed.

"Right," Rufus said.

"I like vanilla," I said. "In milkshakes. Or ice cream. But it doesn't seem quite right in toothpaste. Too sweet."

"This one won't be too sweet," Rufus said, handing me another sample.

"*Eeegh*," I said and ran to the sink to wash out my mouth. "What did you put in *that*?"

"Curry powder," Rufus said. "You don't like it? I thought it tasted like a good shrimp curry."

"Maybe it does," I said, "but I don't like curry."

Rufus looked disappointed. "I don't suppose you'd like it almond-flavored, either," he said. "I made some of that, too, but I decided not too many people would take to almond."

"What flavor is in that big plastic pan?" I asked. "You've got enough of that kind to frost twenty-seven cakes."

"That's no kind yet," Rufus said. "That's just seventy-nine cents worth of the stuff that goes in the paste. I didn't want to flavor it till I figured out the best taste."

"What does it taste like plain?" I asked.

"Well," Rufus said, "mostly you taste the bicarb."

"Bicarb!" I said. "You mean all this stuff I've been tasting has got bicarbonate of soda in it?"

Rufus grinned. "Yeah," he said. "It's probably good for your stomach as well as your teeth."

"You must have enough for ten tubes in that plastic bowl," I guessed.

"More, I bet," Rufus said.

"Why don't you squeeze the toothpaste in the tube into a measuring cup and then measure the stuff in the bowl," I suggested.

"That would be a waste of toothpaste," Rufus said. "We couldn't get it back in the tube." Rufus hates to waste anything.

"I have a better idea," he said. "I'll pack into a square pan the toothpaste I made. Then I can figure out how many cubic inches of toothpaste we have. And you can figure out how many cubic inches of toothpaste are in the tube."

"But the tube is round, Rufus," I said. "I can't measure cubic inches unless something is cube-shaped."

Rufus thought a minute. "Maybe we can squeeze the tube into a cube shape," he said.

I thought that was brilliant. But then I had another idea.

"Rufus," I said. "It says on the tube that it contains 3.25 ounces of toothpaste. Why couldn't we just weigh your paste and divide by 3.25 to see how many tubes it would make?"

"Hey—we could!" Rufus said. "You are *smart*, Kate. I'm always doing things the hard way."

That's what is really so nice about Rufus. It's not just that he gets great ideas like making toothpaste. But if *you* have a good idea, he says so.

I was pleased that I had thought of a simpler way of measuring the toothpaste, but I told Rufus, "I wish I was smart enough even to *think* of a hard way of doing something."

I *never* would have thought of measuring toothpaste in cubic inches. Partly because I never can remember exactly how to figure cubic inches. And I certainly wouldn't have thought of making a round tube cube-shaped. Would you?

Anyway it turned out Rufus had made about forty tubes of toothpaste for seventy-nine cents.

Before I finished breakfast the next morning, there was a knock on the door. It was Rufus. He was very excited.

"Kate!" he said. "Do you know what the population of the United States is?"

"No," I said. I never know things like that.

My father looked up from his paper. "According to the most recent census—over 200,000,000," he said to Rufus. My father always knows things like that.

"You're right," Rufus said. "And by now, it must be even bigger."

"Probably," my father said.

"Mr. MacKinstrey," Rufus said. "I was thinking that everybody in the United States probably uses about one tube of toothpaste a month."

"Probably," my father said.

"And if they do," Rufus said, "how many tubes of toothpaste are sold in a year?"

My father thought for a second. "Roughly two-and-a-half billion tubes."

"Right!" Rufus said.

I hate people who can multiply in their heads. Except that my father and Rufus are two of the people I like best in the world. How do you explain that?

I really don't like math at all, even when I have a paper and pencil and all the time in the world to figure something out.

And at the same time I look forward every day to Mr. Conti's math class. And how do you explain that, since that's the class where I'm always getting in trouble?

For example, the same day my father answered Rufus's population question, Mr. Conti said in math class:

"Kate MacKinstrey, would you please bring me that note."

"Well, it isn't exactly a note, Mr. Conti."

"I see," says Mr. Conti. "I suppose it's another math problem."

"It looks like a math problem, Mr. Conti."

The message from Rufus that Mr. Conti got to read that day said:

If there are 2½ billion tubes of toothpaste sold in the U.S. in one year, and 1 out of 10 people switched to a new brand, how many tubes of the new brand would they be buying?

The right answer is 250 million. It took the class a while to figure that out. Some people have trouble remembering how many zeros there are in a billion.

Then there was a second part to the note:

If the inventor of the new toothpaste made a profit of 1¢ a tube on his toothpaste, what would his profit be at the end of the year?

And it turns out that the inventor of this new toothpaste would make a two-and-a-half million dollar profit!

Well, that's how Rufus's toothpaste business started. Rufus figured out that if he sold the toothpaste for only a penny more than it cost him to make — it cost him about two cents a tube — he'd soon have millions of customers.

He had to start in a small way, of course. When he started his business, Rufus packed the toothpaste in baby food jars. A baby food jar holds about as much as a big tube, and the jars didn't cost him anything.

People with babies were glad to save jars for Rufus, as nobody had thought of a way of instantly recycling baby food jars before. When Rufus put a sign on the bulletin board at school saying that he could use the jars, kids brought us hundreds of them.

We sterilized and filled the jars. When we had about five hundred jars, Rufus and I stuffed our saddlebags with as many as they would hold and rode our bikes around the neighborhood selling the toothpaste.

We sold quite a few jars. At only three cents a jar, most people felt they could afford to give it a try, and most of the customers said it was good toothpaste.

Still, I could not see how Rufus was going to get rich on three-cent toothpaste unless millions of people knew about it. Then I had this idea about how he could get some free advertising.

Everybody in Cleveland watches a program called "The Joe Smiley Show." On the show, Joe interviews people who have interesting hobbies.

I wrote Joe Smiley a letter telling him I had this friend who had a hobby of making toothpaste and could make about two years' supply for the price of one tube. And Joe Smiley called up Rufus to ask if he would be on the show.

Rufus was very good on the show, though I was afraid that he never would get around to talking about the toothpaste. I was worried because when Joe Smiley asked Rufus how he had learned to make toothpaste, Rufus started telling about his Grandmother Mayflower.

He not only told about how she made scrapbook paste, but about how his Grandma Mayflower had made her own furnace out of two 100-gallon oil barrels. Joe Smiley was so interested in that furnace that it was hard to get him off the subject of Rufus's grandmother.

Rufus told about his grandmother taming raccoons, woodchucks, mice, chipmunks, and catbirds. And, of course, about her brushing her teeth with plain baking soda. You wouldn't think all that stuff about Rufus's grandmother would sell toothpaste. But then, as my father pointed out, you wouldn't

think Rufus's way of advertising the toothpaste would sell toothpaste, either.

Joe Smiley is the kind of guy who is always saying things are the "greatest" thing he ever heard of. Or the most "fantastic." If a girl comes on his show in a pink coat that Joe thinks is attractive, he'll say, "That's the most fantastic coat!" There's nothing that special about the coat. He just means it's nice.

What I mean is, he exaggerates. And everybody Joe has on his show is one of the greatest people he ever met or has done the most fantastic thing.

So when Joe does get to Rufus's toothpaste, he naturally gives it this big build-up. Which is what I was counting on. And what does Rufus do?

The conversation went something like this:

JOE: Now, Rufus, this fantastic toothpaste you make—I suppose it has a special, secret formula.

RUFUS: No. It's made out of stuff anybody can buy for a few cents and mix up at home in a few minutes.

JOE: Fantastic! And, of course, it's much better than the kind you buy at the store.

RUFUS: I don't know about that. But it tastes pretty good. And for about two cents you can make as much as you get in a seventy-nine cent tube.

JOE: Fantastic! And where can people get some of this great toothpaste?

RUFUS: If they live in East Cleveland, I'll deliver it to them on my bike. Three ounces cost three cents—it costs me two cents to make and I make one cent profit. If anyone outside East Cleveland wants some, I'll have to charge three cents plus postage.

JOE: Fantastic! And what do you call this marvelous new product?

RUFUS: TOOTHPASTE.

JOE: Just toothpaste? It doesn't have a name like SPARKLE or SHINE or SENSATION or

WHITE LIGHTNING or PERSONALITY PLUS?

RUFUS: No, it's just plain TOOTHPASTE. It doesn't do anything sensational such as improve your smile or your personality. It just keeps your teeth clean.

Who would have thought that telling people toothpaste wouldn't do one thing for their personality would sell toothpaste?

But three days after Rufus was on "The Joe Smiley Show," he got 689 orders for TOOTHPASTE. One came all the way from Venice, California, from a man who happened to be telephoning his daughter while she was watching the show in Cleveland. The daughter said, "There's a kid here who's selling toothpaste for three cents a jar." And her father ordered three dozen jars.

Fantastic!

Understanding What You've Read

1. How did Kate like the taste of the peppermint toothpaste? How did she feel about the curry-flavored toothpaste?
2. Find the word *curry* in a dictionary. Why might curry be an unusual flavor for a toothpaste?
3. In the TV interview between Joe Smiley and Rufus on pages 109–111, what are some of the words that Joe Smiley uses to exaggerate what Rufus says about toothpaste?
4. In the TV interview with Joe Smiley, what does Rufus say that helps you know he's a very honest person? Find sentences to support your answer.

Writing

1. Write one or more sentences describing a new toothpaste. Give your toothpaste a funny name. Tell about all the wonderful things this toothpaste will do for the people who use it. Use exaggeration to make your sentences humorous.
2. Write a few sentences or a paragraph that tells what happened to Rufus after he sold a million jars of toothpaste. Use unexpected events to make your sentences or paragraph funny.

The Book That Saved the Earth

by CLAIRE BOIKO

Characters

HISTORIAN
GREAT AND MIGHTY THINK-TANK
APPRENTICE NOODLE
CAPTAIN OMEGA
LIEUTENANT IOTA
SERGEANT OOP
OFFSTAGE VOICE

BEFORE RISE: *Spotlight shines on* HISTORIAN, *who is sitting at table down right, on which is a movie projector. A sign on an easel beside her reads:* MUSEUM OF ANCIENT HISTORY: DEPARTMENT OF THE TWENTIETH CENTURY. *She stands and bows to audience.*

HISTORIAN: Good afternoon. Welcome to our Museum of Ancient History, and to my area—things of the good old, far-off twentieth century. The twentieth century was often called the Age of the Book. In those days, there were books about everything from ants to zoology. Books taught people how to, and when to, and where to, and why to. But the strangest thing a book every did was to save the Earth. You haven't heard

113

about the Martian invasion of 1988? Really, what *do* they teach children today? Well, you know, Mars never did take over the Earth, because a single book stopped it. What was that book, you ask? A great encyclopedia? A book about rockets and missiles? A secret file from outer space? No, it was none of these. It was—but here, let me turn on the historiscope. I'll show you what happened many, many years ago, in 1988. *(She turns on projector and points it left. Spotlight on* HISTORIAN *goes out and comes up down left on* THINK-TANK, *who is seated on a raised box, arms folded. He has a huge, egg-shaped head, and he wears a long robe decorated with stars and circles.* APPRENTICE NOODLE *stands beside him at an elaborate switchboard. A sign on an easel reads:* MARS SPACE CONTROL. GREAT AND MIGHTY THINK-TANK, COMMANDER-IN-CHIEF. BOW LOW BEFORE ENTERING.*)*

NOODLE *(Bowing)*: O Great and Mighty Think-Tank, most powerful and intelligent being, what are your orders?

THINK-TANK: You left out something, Apprentice Noodle. Go over the whole thing again.

NOODLE: It shall be done, sir. *(In a singsong)* O Great and Mighty Think-Tank, Ruler of Mars and her two moons, most powerful and intelligent being—*(Out of breath)* what-are-your-orders?

THINK-TANK: That's better, Noodle. I wish to talk with our space probe to that silly little world we are going to put under our great rulership. What do they call it again?

NOODLE: Earth, your Intelligence.

THINK-TANK: Earth — of course. You see how insignificant the place is? But first, something important. My mirror. I wish to consult my mirror.

NOODLE: It shall be done, sir. *(She hands* THINK-TANK *a hand mirror.)*

THINK-TANK: Mirror, mirror, in my hand. Who is the most fantastically intellectually gifted being in the land?

OFFSTAGE VOICE *(After a pause)*: You, sir.

THINK-TANK *(Smacking mirror)*: Quicker. Answer quicker next time. I hate a slow mirror. *(He admires himself.)* Ah, there I am. Are we Martians not handsome? So much better looking than those ugly Earthlings with their tiny heads. Noodle, keep on using your mind. Someday you may have a balloon brain just like mine.

NOODLE: Oh, I hope so, Mighty Think-Tank. I hope so.

THINK-TANK: Now, call the space probe. I want to take over that ball of mud called Earth before lunch.

NOODLE: It shall be done, sir. (*She twists knobs and adjusts levers on switchboard. Electronic buzzes and beeps are heard as the curtains open.*)

*　*　*

SETTING: *The Centerville Public Library*

AT RISE: CAPTAIN OMEGA *stands at center, opening and closing card catalogue drawers in a puzzled fashion.* LIEUTENANT IOTA *is up left, counting books in a bookcase.* SERGEANT OOP *is at right, opening and closing a book, turning it upside down, shaking it, and then riffling the pages and shaking his head.*

NOODLE (*Adjusting knobs*): I can see the space crew, sir. (THINK-TANK *puts on a pair of huge goggles and turns toward the stage to watch.*) They seem to have gone into some sort of Earth building.

THINK-TANK: Very good. Make voice contact.

NOODLE (*Speaking into a microphone*): Mars Space Control calling the crew of Probe One. Mars Space Control calling the crew of Probe One. Come in, Captain Omega. Give us your location.

CAPTAIN OMEGA (*Speaking into a disc which is on a chain around his neck*): Captain Omega to Mars Space Control. Lieutenant Iota, Sergeant Oop, and I have landed on Earth without any trouble. We are now in this (*Indicates room*)—this square place. Have you any idea where we are, Lieutenant Iota?

IOTA: I can't figure it out, Captain. *(Holding up a book)* I've counted two thousand of these odd things. This place must be some sort of storage barn. What do you think, Sergeant Oop?

OOP: I haven't a clue. I've been to seven galaxies, but I've never seen anything like this. Maybe they're hats. *(He opens a book and puts it on his head.)*

OMEGA *(Bowing low)*: Perhaps the Great and Mighty Think-Tank will give us his thoughts on the matter.

THINK-TANK: Very simple, my dear Omega. Hold one of the items up so that I may view it closely. *(OMEGA holds a book on the palm of his hand.)* Yes, yes. I understand now. Since Earthlings are always eating, the place in which you find yourselves is surely a refreshment stand.

OMEGA *(To IOTA and OOP)*: He says we're in a refreshment stand.

OOP: Well, the Earthlings certainly have strange taste.

THINK-TANK: That item in your hand is called a sandwich.

IOTA *(Nodding)*: A sandwich.

OOP *(Taking book from his head)*: A sandwich?

THINK-TANK: Sandwiches are an important part of the Earth diet. Look at it closely. *(OMEGO squints at book.)* There are two slices of what is called "bread" and between them there is some sort of filling.

OMEGA: That is correct, sir.

THINK-TANK: To show that I am right, I order you to eat it.

OMEGA *(Gulping)*: Eat it?

THINK-TANK: Do you doubt the Mighty Think-Tank?

OMEGA: Oh, no, no. But poor Lieutenant Iota has not had her breakfast. Lieutenant Iota, I order you to eat this —this sandwich.

IOTA: Eat it? Oh, Captain! It's a very great honor to be the first Martian to eat a sandwich, I'm sure, but— but how can I eat before my sergeant does? *(Handing* OOP *the book; brightly)* Sergeant Oop, I order you to eat the sandwich.

OOP *(Making a face)*: Who, Lieutenant? Me, Lieutenant?

IOTA *and* OMEGA *(Slapping their chests in a salute)*: For the glory of Mars, Oop!

OOP: Yes, Captain. At once, Lieutenant. *(He opens his mouth wide.* OMEGA *and* IOTA *watch him breathlessly. He bites down on a corner of the book, and pantomimes chewing and swallowing, while making terrible faces.)*

OMEGA: Well, Oop?

IOTA: Well, Oop? *(*OOP *coughs.* OMEGA *and* IOTA *pound him on the back.)*

THINK-TANK: Was it not delicious, Sergeant Oop?

OOP *(Slapping his chest in salute)*: That is right, sir. It was *not* delicious. I don't know how the Earthlings can get those sandwiches down without water. They're as dry as Martian dust.

NOODLE: Sir, sir. Great and Mighty Think-Tank. I beg your pardon, but something just floated into my mind about those sandwiches.

THINK-TANK: It can't be worth much but go ahead. Give us your tiny bit of data.

NOODLE: Well, sir, I have seen our films of those sandwiches. I noticed that the Earthlings did not *eat* them. They used them as some sort of communication device.

THINK-TANK *(Haughtily)*: Of course. That was my next point. These are communication sandwiches. Think-Tank is never wrong. Who is never wrong?

OMEGA, IOTA, *and* OOP *(Together; saluting)*: Great and Mighty Think-Tank is never wrong.

THINK-TANK: Therefore, I order you to listen to them.

OMEGA: Listen to them?

IOTA *and* OOP *(To each other; puzzled)*: Listen to them?

THINK-TANK: Do you have rocks in your ears? I said, listen to them. *(OMEGA, IOTA, and OOP bow very low.)*

OMEGA: It shall be done, sir. *(They each take two books from the case and hold them to their ears, listening intently.)*

IOTA *(Whispering to OMEGA)*: Do you hear anything?

OMEGA *(Whispering back)*: Nothing. Do you hear anything, Oop?

OOP *(Loudly)*: Not a thing! *(OMEGA and IOTA jump in fright.)*

OMEGA *and* IOTA: Sh-h-h! *(They listen again.)*

THINK-TANK: Well? Well? Tell me. What do you hear?

OMEGA: Nothing, sir. Perhaps we are not on the correct frequency.

IOTA: Nothing, sir. Perhaps the Earthlings have sharper ears than we do.

OOP: I don't hear a thing. Maybe these sandwiches don't make sounds.

THINK-TANK: What? What? Does someone think that the Mighty Think-Tank has made a mistake?

OMEGA: Oh, no sir. No, sir. We'll keep listening.

NOODLE: Please excuse me, your Brilliance. A cloudy piece of information is rolling around in my head.

THINK-TANK: Well, roll it out, Noodle, and I will clarify it for you.

NOODLE: I seem to remember that the Earthlings did not listen to the sandwiches. They opened them and watched them.

THINK-TANK: Yes, that is quite correct. Captain Omega, those sandwiches are not for ear communication. They are for eye communication. Now, Captain Omega, take that large, bright-colored sandwich over there. It looks important. Tell me what you see. (OMEGA *picks up a very large copy of* MOTHER GOOSE, *holding it so that the audience can see the title.* IOTA *looks over his left shoulder, and* OOP *looks over his right shoulder.*)

OMEGA: It seems to contain pictures of Earthlings.

IOTA: And there seems to be some sort of code.

THINK-TANK (*Sharply interested*): Code? Code? I told you this was important. Tell me about it.

OOP: It's little lines and circles and dots. Thousands of them, next to the pictures.

THINK-TANK: Code. Perhaps the Earthlings are not as stupid as we have thought. We must break the code. We must.

NOODLE: Forgive me, your Cleverness, but did not we give our crew pills to increase their intelligence?

THINK-TANK: Stop! A thought of great brilliance has come to me. Space crew, we have given you pills to increase your intelligence. Take them and then watch the sandwich. The meaning of the code will slowly unfold before you.

OMEGA: It shall be done, sir. Remove pill. *(Crew take pills from boxes on their belts.)* Present pill. *(They hold pills out in front of them, stiffly.)* Swallow pill. *(They pop the pills into their mouths and gulp simultaneously. They open their eyes wide, and they put their hands to their foreheads.)*

THINK-TANK: Excellent. Now, break that code.

OMEGA, IOTA, *and* OOP *(Together)*: It shall be done, sir. *(They frown over the book, turning the pages.)*

OMEGA *(Brightly)*: Aha!

IOTA *(Brightly)*: Oho!

OOP *(Bursting into laughter)*: Ha, ha, ha.

THINK-TANK: What does it say? Tell me this minute. Read, Omega.

OMEGA: Yes, sir. *(He reads with great seriousness.)*

> Mistress Mary, quite contrary,
> How does your garden grow?
> With cockle shells and silver bells
> And pretty maids all in a row.

OOP: Ha, ha, ha. Think of that. Pretty maids growing in a garden.

THINK-TANK *(Alarmed)*: Stop! This is no time for laughing. Don't you see that this is serious? The Earthlings have found a way to combine farming and mining. They can actually grow crops of rare metals such as silver. And cockle shells. They can grow high explosives, too. Noodle, call our invasion ships.

NOODLE: They are ready to go down and take over Earth, sir.

THINK-TANK: Tell them to hold. Tell them new information has come to us about Earth. Iota, go on reading.

IOTA: Yes, sir. *(She reads very gravely.)*

> Hey diddle diddle! The cat and the fiddle,
> The cow jumped over the moon,
> The little dog laughed to see such sport,
> And the dish ran away with the spoon.

OOP *(Laughing)*: The dish ran away with the spoon!

THINK-TANK: Stop laughing. This is more and more alarming. The Earthlings have reached a high level of civilization. Didn't you hear? They have taught their animals music and space flight. Even their dogs have a sense of humor. Why, at this very moment, they may be starting an interplanetary attack of millions of cows! Call our ships. No invasion today. Oop, read the next code.

OOP: Yes, sir. *(Reading)*

> Humpty Dumpty sat on the wall,
> Humpty Dumpty had a great fall;
> All the king's horses and all the king's men
> Couldn't put Humpty together again.

Oh, look, sir. Here's a picture of Humpty Dumpty. Why, sir, he looks like—he looks like—*(He turns a large picture of* HUMPTY DUMPTY *toward* THINK-TANK *and the audience.)*

THINK-TANK *(Screaming and holding his head)*: It's me! It's my Great and Mighty Balloon Brain. The Earthlings have seen me. They're after me. "Had a great fall!"—That means they plan to take Mars and me! It's an invasion of Mars! Noodle, get a spaceship for me. I must escape at once. Space crew, you must leave Earth right now. But be sure to hide all trace of your visit. The Earthlings must not know that I know— *(*OMEGA, IOTA, *and* OOP *rush about, putting books back.)*

NOODLE: Where shall we go, sir?

THINK-TANK: A hundred million miles away from Mars. Order the invasion ships to leave. We are heading for Alpha Centauri, a hundred million miles away. (OMEGA, IOTA, *and* OOP *run off right as* NOODLE *helps* THINK-TANK *off left and the curtain closes. Spotlight shines on* HISTORIAN *down right.*)

HISTORIAN (*Chuckling*): And that's how one dusty old book saved the world from a Martian takeover. As you all know, in the year 2488, five hundred years after all this happened, we Earthlings resumed contact with Mars. And we even became very friendly with the Martians. By that time, Great and Mighty Think-Tank had been replaced by a very clever Martian—the Wise and Wonderful Noodle! Oh, yes, we taught the Martians the difference between sandwiches and books. We taught them how to read, too. We set up a library in the city of Marsopolis. But, as you might expect, there is still one book that the Martians can never bring themselves to read. You've guessed it—MOTHER GOOSE! (*She bows and exits right.*)

Understanding What You've Read

1. Which names of characters are humorous?
2. Why didn't the Martians know what libraries and books were?
3. What would you expect someone to do with a book? What unexpected events make the scene on pages 118–119 funny?
4. What was unexpected and funny about the Martians' understanding of the Mother Goose rhymes?

Writing

1. Write two sentences that tell what unexpected things might have happened if the Martians had landed in a playground, a zoo, or a supermarket. What might they see? What might they do?
2. Pretend that you are a Think-Tank. Write a funny paragraph to explain one of the following rhymes:

What Are Little Boys Made Of ?

What are little boys made of?
Snips and snails, and puppy dogs' tails;
And that's what little boys are made of.

A Candle

Little Nancy Etticoat
In a white petticoat
And a red nose;
The longer she stands
The shorter she grows.

Author Study:

Robert McCloskey:

An Artist with Words and Pictures

by SARA KRENTZMAN SRYGLEY

The World He Lives In

An author-artist worth knowing is Robert McCloskey. He has written eight books for young people and illustrated them with his drawings and paintings.

Telling about himself in *The Junior Book of Authors,* Mr. McCloskey said, "It is just sort of an accident that I write books. I really think up stories in pictures and just fill in between the pictures with a sentence or a paragraph or a few pages of words." Probably it isn't quite that easy. A look at his life and the books he has produced shows us that his stories and pictures are more carefully planned than Mr. McCloskey suggests.

Robert McCloskey with two of his puppets

Robert McCloskey was born in Hamilton, Ohio, in 1914. This was his home until he was a young man. He enjoyed growing up in a small Midwestern town like Hamilton. Robert played in the parks; visited the barber shop, the stores, and the public library; and went to school. He was interested in music. He learned to play the oboe, drums, and harmonica. His favorite instrument was the harmonica. He even taught his friends how to play it. He also enjoyed building model airplanes and all sorts of mechanical contraptions. He is still good at tinkering with machinery and inventing new gadgets. Recently he has been working on developing a new kind of puppet.

Very early in his life, Robert McCloskey knew that he wanted to be an artist. This ambition was encouraged when, as a high school student, he won his first national award for a calendar illustrated with woodcuts.

An art career was his dream, but it became a reality only after years of hard work. He studied art for three years in Boston and for two more years in New York. In the summers, he often went to Cape Cod and painted.

For a while he had a job drawing cartoon strips, but that work did not satisfy him. He liked to draw old Spanish ships, fierce dragons, or heroic characters from Greek and Roman myths. He knew that he wanted to illustrate books.

When he was studying in New York, Mr. McCloskey had taken some of his work to an editor of children's books, May Massee. When Miss Massee had looked carefully at his drawings, she gave him some good advice. She urged him to stop drawing things he knew little about and to concentrate on things that were familiar to him.

Mr. McCloskey took her advice. When he called again on Miss Massee, he had in his portfolio what was to become his first book. *Lentil* is about a boy growing up in a small town in Ohio. Miss Massee was enthusiastic about the book, and it was published in 1940. Robert McCloskey had begun a successful career as an author and illustrator.

Lentil was followed by other books both written and illustrated by Mr. McCloskey. In addition, he illustrated books written by other authors. Some of his books are picture books in which the pictures and the words are of equal importance in telling the story.

McCloskey was the first illustrator to win the Caldecott Medal twice. This medal is awarded every year for "the most distinguished American picture book for children." In accepting that honor for *Time of Wonder*, he said:

> With everyone clamoring for more scientists, I should like to clamor for more artists and designers. I should like to clamor for the teaching of drawing and design to every child, right along with reading and writing. I think it is most important for everyone really to see and evaluate pictures and really to see and evaluate his surroundings.[1]

The World He Imagines

As you will see, some of Robert McCloskey's own experiences are reflected in his books. The Centerburg in which Homer Price grows up is probably like Mr. McCloskey's hometown. But if he had written and drawn everything as it happened, we would not have had stories—we would have had reports of Robert McCloskey's life.

When Robert McCloskey began to think about the stories of life in the little town of Centerburg, he had to make up names for his characters. The name Homer Price recalls the ancient Greek poet Homer. He was one of the earliest storytellers we know about, and one of the greatest. His

[1] *Horn Book*, August 1958, page 245. Used by permission.

poems tell of adventures of a wandering hero, Ulysses, who left his home to fight in the Trojan War. In one of his adventures, Ulysses saved himself and his companions from evil sirens, or enchanters. He stopped up the ears of his companions so they could not hear the magic song the sirens used to get people to follow them. Robert McCloskey, at the end of "Nothing New Under the Sun (Hardly)," makes Homer Price a modern-day Ulysses.

In Mr. McCloskey's books, Homer Price and Uncle Ulysses are not great heroes—they are just ordinary people in an ordinary town. But perhaps Mr. McCloskey wanted to remind his readers of those famous, ancient men and to suggest that the adventures of ordinary people today are also worth writing books about.

When he wrote the story that follows, "Nothing New Under the Sun (Hardly)," Mr. McCloskey also had some other works of literature in mind. As you will see, the mysterious stranger reminds the people of Centerburg of two famous fictional characters. Have you heard about Rip Van Winkle, the character created by the writer Washington Irving? One day Rip Van Winkle fell asleep in the Catskill Mountains and slept for twenty years. When he woke up, he was an old man with a long beard and old-fashioned clothes. He returned to his village, but of course no one knew him.

Another fictional character that is important in McCloskey's story is the Pied Piper. He was a traveling musician. The mayor of Hamelin, Germany, hired the Pied Piper to rid the town of rats. The Piper played so well that the rats followed him in a swarm. But all the children of the town followed him too—never to return home. When you read "Nothing New Under the Sun (Hardly)," you will see why the people of Centerburg thought the mysterious stranger might be Rip Van Winkle or the Pied Piper.

Nothing New Under the Sun (Hardly)

by ROBERT McCLOSKEY

After the County Fair, life in Centerburg eases itself back to normal. Homer and the rest of the children concentrate on arithmetic and basketball, and the grownups tend to business and running the town in a peaceful way. Election time still being a month away, the Democrats and the Republicans are still speaking to each other. The Ladies' Aid hasn't anything to crusade about at the moment, and Uncle Ulysses hasn't bought any new-fangled equipment for his lunchroom recently. There is nothing for people to gossip about, or speculate on, or argue about.

There's always the weather, the latest books and movies, and ladies' hats. But, of course, that doesn't provide nearly enough to talk and think about for a whole month until election time. Uncle Ulysses, the sheriff, and the men around the barbershop usually run out of things to talk about toward the middle of the month. Sometimes during the mornings the conversation is lively. Like today, the sheriff came in beaming and said, "Well, I put on long ullen wonderwear—I mean woolen underwear, this morning."

"Soo?" said Uncle Ulysses. "Guess I'll have to get mine out of mothballs this week."

"Humph," said the barber, "I wouldn't wear woolen underwear for anything on earth. It *itches!*"

Well, that was something to argue about for almost an hour. Then the subject changed to woolen socks, to shoes, to overshoes, to mud, to mud in roads, to mud in barnyards, barns, and chicken coops. Then there was a long pause. Only ten-thirty by the town hall clock, and conversation had already dwindled to nothing at all. Nothing to do but look out of the barbershop window.

"There goes Doc Pelly," said the barber, "I wonder who's sick?"

"Colby's wife is expectin' a baby," said Uncle Ulysses. "I'll ask Aggy this noon. She might know about it."

"There's Dulcey Dooner," said the sheriff.

"He hasn't worked for three years," added the barber disapprovingly.

A few children came into view. "School's out for lunch," pronounced the sheriff.

The door opened, and Homer came in saying, "Hello, everybody. Uncle Ulysses, Aunt Aggy sent me over to tell you to stir yourself over to the lunchroom and help serve blue-plate specials."

Uncle Ulysses sighed and prepared to leave. The sheriff cupped a hand behind his ear and said, "What's that?" Uncle Ulysses stopped sighing, and everybody listened.

The noise (it was sort of a rattle) grew louder, and then suddenly an old car swung into the town square. The sheriff, the barber, Uncle Ulysses, and Homer watched it with gaping mouths as it rattled around the town square once — twice — and on the third time slowed down and shivered to a stop right out front of Uncle Ulysses' lunchroom.

It wasn't because this car was old, old enough to be an *antique*; or because some strange business was built onto it; or that the strange business was covered with a large canvas. No, that wasn't what made Homer and the sheriff and Uncle Ulysses and the barber stare so long. It was the car's *driver.*

"Gosh, what a beard!" said Homer.

"And what a head of hair!" said the barber. "That's a two-dollar cutting job if I ever saw one!"

"Could you see his face?" asked the sheriff.

"Nope," answered Uncle Ulysses, still staring across the square.

They watched the stranger untangle his beard from the steering wheel and go into the lunchroom.

Uncle Ulysses promptly dashed for the door, saying, "See you later."

"Wait for me!" the sheriff called. "I'm sort of hungry."

Homer followed, and the barber shouted, "Don't forget to come back and tell me the news!"

"O.K., and if I bring you a new customer, I get a commission."

The stranger was sitting at the far end of the lunch counter, looking very shy and embarrassed. Homer's Aunt Aggy had already served him a blue-plate special and was eyeing him with suspicion. To be polite, Homer and Uncle Ulysses pretended to be busy behind the counter, and the sheriff pretended to study the menu — though he knew every single word on it by heart. They just glanced in the stranger's direction once in a while.

Finally Uncle Ulysses' curiosity got the best of him, and he sauntered down to the stranger and asked, "Are you enjoying your lunch? Is everything all right?"

The stranger appeared to be very embarrassed, and you could easily tell he was blushing underneath his beard and all his hair. "Yes, sir, it's a very good lunch," he replied with a nod. When he nodded a stray wisp of

beard accidentally got into the gravy. This made him more embarrassed than ever.

Uncle Ulysses waited for the stranger to start a conversation but he didn't.

So Uncle Ulysses said, "Nice day today."

The stranger said, "Yes, nice day," and dropped a fork. Now the stranger *really was* embarrassed. He looked as though he would like to sink right through the floor.

Uncle Ulysses quickly handed the man another fork, and eased himself away, so as not to embarrass him into breaking a plate, or falling off his stool.

After he finished lunch, the stranger reached into the pocket of his ragged, patched coat and drew out a leather money bag. He paid for his lunch, nodded good-bye, and crept out of the door and down the street with everyone staring after him.

Aunt Aggy broke the silence by bouncing on the marble counter the coin she had just received.

"It's good money," she pronounced, "but it looks as though it had been *buried* for *years!*"

"Shyest man I ever laid eyes on!" said Uncle Ulysses.

"Yes!" said the sheriff. "My as a shouse, I mean, shy as a *mouse!*"

"Gosh what a beard!" said Homer.

"Humph!" said Aunt Aggy. "Homer, it's time you started back to school!"

By midafternoon every man, woman, and child in Centerburg had something to gossip about, speculate on, and argue about.

Who was this stranger? Where did he come from? Where was he going? How long was his beard and his hair? What was his name? Did he have a business? What could be on the back of his car that was so carefully covered with the large canvas?

Nobody knew. Nobody knew anything about the stranger except that he parked his car in the town parking space and was spending considerable time walking about town. People reported that he paused in his walking and whistled a few bars of some strange tune, a tune nobody had ever heard of. The stranger was shy when grownups were near, and he would cross the street or go around a block to avoid speaking to someone. However, he did not avoid children. He smiled at them and seemed delighted to have them follow him.

People from all over town telephoned the sheriff at the barbershop asking about the stranger and making reports as to what was going on.

The sheriff was becoming a bit uneasy about the whole thing. He couldn't get near enough to the stranger to ask him his intentions, and if he *did* ask, the stranger would be too shy to give him an answer.

As Homer passed by the barbershop on his way home from school, the sheriff called him in. "Homer," he said, "I'm gonna need your help. This stranger with the beard has got me worried. You see, Homer, I can't find out who he is or what he is doing here in town. He's probably a nice enough fellow, just an individualist. But, then again, he might be a fugitive, in disguise or something." Homer nodded. And the sheriff continued, "Now, what I want you to do is gain his confidence. He doesn't seem to be afraid of children, and you might be able to find out what this is all about. I'll treat you to a double raspberry sundae."

"It's a deal, Sheriff!" said Homer. "I'll start right now."

At six o'clock Homer reported to the sheriff. "The stranger seems like a nice person, Sheriff," Homer began. "I walked down Market Street with him. He wouldn't tell me who he is or what he's doing, but he did say he'd been away from people for a great many years. He asked me to recommend a place for him to stay, and I said the Strand Hotel, so that's where he went just now when I left him. I'll have to run home to dinner now, Sheriff, but I'll find out some more tomorrow. Don't forget about that raspberry sundae," said Homer.

"I won't," replied the sheriff, "and, Homer, don't forget to keep me posted on this fellow."

After Homer had gone, the sheriff turned to the barber and said, "We don't know one blessed thing about this fellow except that he's shy, and he's been away from people for quite a spell. For all we know he might be a fugitive, or a lunatic, or maybe one of these amnesia cases.

"If he didn't have so much hair I could tell in a second what kind of a fellow he is," complained the sheriff. "Yep! Just one look at a person's ears and *I* can *tell!*"

"Well," said the barber, "*I* judge people by their *hair*, and I've been thinking. This fellow looks like somebody I've heard about, or read about somewhere. Like somebody out of a book, you understand, Sheriff?"

"Well, yes, in a way, but I could tell you definite with a good look at his ears!" said the sheriff. "Here comes Ulysses. Let's ask him what *he* thinks."

Uncle Ulysses considered a second and said, "Well, I judge a person by his *waistline* and his *appetite*. Now I'm not saying I'm right, Sheriff, because I couldn't tell about his waistline under that old coat, but judging from his appetite, I'd say he's a sort a person that I've read about somewhere. I can't just put my finger on it. Seems as though it must have been in a book."

"U-m-m," said the sheriff.

Just then Tony the shoe-repair man came in for a haircut. After he was settled in the barber chair, the sheriff

142

asked him what he thought about the mysterious stranger.

"Well, Sheriff, I judge everybody by their *feet* and their *shoes*. Nobody's worn a pair of gaiters like his for twenty-five years. It seems as though those shoes must have just up and walked right out of the pages of some old dusty book."

"There!" said the sheriff. "*Now*, we're getting somewhere!"

He rushed to the phone and called Mr. Hirsh of the Hirsh Clothing Store, and asked, "Say, Sam, what do *you* think about this stranger? . . . Yes, the one bith the weard, I mean beard! . . . uh-huh . . . storybook clothes, eh? . . . Thanks a lot, Sam, good night."

Then he called the garage and said, "Hello, Luke, this is the sheriff talking. What do you make of this stranger in town . . . Yes? . . . literature, eh? Durned if I kin see how you can judge a man by the car he drives, but I'll take your word for it. Good night, Luke, and thanks a lot."

The sheriff looked very pleased with himself. He paced up and down and muttered, "Getting somewhere! Getting somewhere at last!" Then he surprised everyone by announcing that he was going over to the *library!*

In a few minutes he was back, his mustache twitching with excitement. "I've solved it!" he shouted. "The librarian knew right off just what book to look in! It's *Rip Van Winkle!* It's Rip Van Winkle this fellow's like. He must have driven up into the hills some thirty years ago and fell asleep, or got amnesia, or something!"

"Yeah! That's it!" agreed the barber along with Uncle Ulysses and the shoemaker.

Then Uncle Ulysses asked, "*But* how about that 'what-ever-it-is' underneath the canvas on the back of his car?"

"Now look here, Ulysses," shouted the sheriff, "you're just trying to complicate my deduction! Come on, let's play checkers!"

Bright and early the next morning the Rip-Van-Winklish stranger was up and wandering around Centerburg.

By ten o'clock everyone was referring to him as "Old Rip," and remarking how clever the sheriff was at deducing things.

The sheriff tried to see what was under the canvas, but couldn't make head or tail of what it was. Uncle Ulysses peeked at it too and said, "Goodness only knows! But never mind, Sheriff. If anybody can find out what this thing is, Homer will do the finding!"

That same afternoon after school was dismissed, Uncle Ulysses and the sheriff saw Homer strolling down the street with "Old Rip."

"Looks like he's explaining something to Homer," said the sheriff.

"Homer'll find out!" said Uncle Ulysses proudly. Then they watched through the barbershop window while the stranger took Homer across the square to the parking lot and showed him his car. He lifted one corner of the canvas and pointed underneath while Homer looked and nodded his head. They shook hands and the stranger went to his hotel, and Homer headed for the barbershop.

"Did he talk?" asked the sheriff the minute Homer opened the door.

"What's his name?" asked Uncle Ulysses.

"What is he doing?" asked the barber.

"Yes, he told me everything!" said Homer. "It sounds just like a story out of a book!"

"Yes, son, did he get amnesia up in the hills?" asked the sheriff.

"Well, no, not exactly, Sheriff, but he did *live* in the hills for the past thirty years."

"Well, what's he doing here now?" the barber demanded.

"I better start at the beginning," said Homer.

"That's a good idea, son," said the sheriff. "I'll take a few notes just for future reference."

"Well, to begin with," Homer started, "his name is Michael Murphy—just plain Michael Murphy. About thirty years ago he built himself a small vacation cabin out in the hills, some place on the far side of the state forest reserve. Then, he liked living in the cabin so much he decided to live there all of the time. He packed his belongings on his car and moved out to the hills."

"He cided ta be a dermit?" asked the sheriff.

"Not exactly *a hermit*," Homer continued. "But yesterday was the first time that he came out of the hills and saw people for thirty years. That's why he's so shy."

"Then he's moving back to civilization," suggested Uncle Ulysses.

"That comes later," said Homer. "I've only told as far as twenty-nine years ago."

"Can't you skip a few years, son, and get to the point?" demanded the sheriff.

"Nope! Twenty-nine years ago," Homer repeated firmly, "Mr. Murphy read in an almanac that if a man can make a better mousetrap than anybody else, the world will beat a path to his house—even if it is way out in the hills.

"So-o-o he started making *mousetraps*."

There was a pause, and then the sheriff said, "Will you repeat that again, son?"

"I said, Mr. Murphy started making *mousetraps*. He made good ones too, the very best, and when one of Mr. Murphy's traps caught a mouse, that was the end of that mouse for all time."

The sheriff forgot all about taking notes as Homer continued, "But nobody came to buy the traps. But that was just as well, you see, because twenty-eight years ago Mr. Murphy began to feel *sorry* for the mice. He came to realize that he would have to change his whole approach. He thought and thought and finally he decided to build mousetraps that wouldn't hurt the mice.

"He spent the next fifteen years doing research on what was the pleasantest possible way for a mouse to be caught. He discovered that being caught to music pleased mice the most, even more than cheese. Then," said Homer, "Mr. Murphy set to work to make a *musical* mousetrap."

"That wouldn't hurt the mice?" inquired Uncle Ulysses.

"That wouldn't hurt the mice," Homer stated. "It was a long, hard job too, because first he had to build an organ out of reeds that the mice liked the sound of, and then he had to compose a tune that the mice couldn't possibly resist. Then he incorporated it all into a mousetrap. . . ."

"That wouldn't hurt the mice?" interrupted the barber.

"That wouldn't hurt the mice," Homer went on. "The mousetrap caught mice, all right. The only trouble was, it was too big. What with the organ and all, and sort of impractical for general use because somebody had to stay around and pump the organ."

"Yes, I can see that wouldn't be practical," said Uncle Ulysses, stroking his chin. "But with a small electric motor. . . ."

"But he solved it, Uncle Ulysses! The whole idea seems very practical after you get used to it. He decided since the trap was too large to use in a house, he would fasten it onto his car, which he hadn't used for so long anyway. Then, he could drive it to a town, and make a bargain with the mayor to remove all the mice. You see he would start the musical mousetrap to working, and drive up and down the streets and alleys. Then all of the mice would run out of the houses to get themselves caught in this trap that plays music that no mouse ever born can possibly resist. After the trap is full of mice, Mr. Murphy drives them past the city limits, somewhere where they can't find their way home, and lets them go."

"Still without hurting them?" suggested the barber.

"Of course," said Homer.

The sheriff chewed on his pencil, Uncle Ulysses stroked on his chin, and the barber ran his fingers through his hair.

Homer noticed the silence and said, "I guess the idea *is* sort of startling when you first hear about it. But, if a town has a water truck to sprinkle streets, and a street-sweeping truck to remove dirt, why shouldn't they, maybe, just hire Mr. Murphy's musical mousetrap once in a while to remove mice?"

Uncle Ulysses stroked his chin again and then said, "By gum! This man Murphy is a genius!"

"I told Mr. Murphy that *you* would understand, Uncle Ulysses!" said Homer with a grin. "I told him the mayor was a friend of yours, and you could talk him into anything, even hiring a musical mousetrap."

"Whoever heard of a misical moostrap!" said the sheriff.

"That doesn't hurt the *mice!*" added the barber, as

Homer and Uncle Ulysses went off arm in arm to see the mayor.

It scarcely took Uncle Ulysses and Homer half an hour to convince the mayor that Mr. Murphy's musical mouse-trap should be hired to rid Centerburg of mice. While Uncle Ulysses chatted on with the mayor, Homer dashed over to the hotel to fetch Mr. Murphy.

Homer came back with the bearded inventor and introduced him to the mayor and to Uncle Ulysses. The mayor opened a drawer of his desk and brought out a bag of jelly beans. "Have one," he said to Mr. Murphy, to sort of break the ice and to make his shy visitor feel at home. Mr. Murphy relaxed and answered the mayor's questions without blushing too much.

"How do we know this *thing of a jig* of yours will do what you say it will?" asked the mayor.

Mr. Murphy just whistled a few bars, "*Tum tidy ay dee,*" and a couple of mice jumped right out of the mayor's desk!

"Of course," Homer explained, "the mice come *quicker,* and get *removed* when the mousetrap plays that tune through the streets. Mr. Murphy guarantees to remove every single mouse from Centerburg for only thirty dollars."

"It's a bargain!" said the mayor. "I wondered where my jelly beans were disappearing to!" And he shook hands with Mr. Murphy. Then he proclaimed Saturday as the day for de-mousing Centerburg. By this time everyone knew that the shy stranger's name was Michael Murphy, but people still spoke of him as Rip Van Winkle (Rip for short), because of the sheriff's deduction. Everybody talked about the musical mousetrap (that didn't hurt the mice) and the mayor's de-mousing proclamation.

148

The children, especially, were looking forward to the great event. They watched with interest while Mr. Murphy went over his car and his musical trap to be sure everything was in perfect working order. Homer and Freddy and most of the other children were planning to follow the trap all around town Saturday and see the mice come out and get caught in Michael Murphy's musical trap.

"Gosh, Homer," said Freddy, "let's follow him until he lets them loose out in the country! That *will* be a sight, seeing all those mice let loose at once!"

"Well, Freddy, I've been thinking it might not be a good idea to follow the mousetrap past the city limits," said Homer, to Freddy's surprise.

"You know, Freddy, I've been over at the library reading up on mice and music—music can do funny things sometimes. It can soothe savage beasts and charm snakes and *lots* of things. If we're going to follow this musical trap till the mice are let loose, we better make some plans."

Homer and Freddy spent all Friday recess period making plans. They decided that all the children should meet in the schoolyard before the de-mousing started on Saturday. They arranged a signal, thumbs up, if everything was going along all right; and thumbs down if anyone was in trouble.

"It's just to be on the safe side," Homer explained.

Saturday dawned a beautiful crisp fall day, fine weather for the grand de-mousing of Centerburg. Mr. Michael Murphy came forth from the Strand Hotel, and after carefully slinging his long gray beard over his shoulder, he cranked his car and warmed up the engine. He carefully removed the canvas covering from the musical mousetrap and ever so painstakingly arranged the spiral ramps and runways so that no mouse, no matter how careless, could stub a toe or bump a nose. He then climbed behind the steering wheel, and the musical mousetrap was under way!

A loud cheer arose from the crowd of children as Mr. Murphy yanked a lever and the reed organ started to play. Even before the cheering stopped the mice began to appear!

Through the streets of Centerburg rolled Mr. Michael Murphy and his musical mousetrap. The mice came running from every direction! Fat, doughnut-fed mice from Uncle Ulysses' lunchroom, thin mice from the churches, ordinary mice from houses and homes, mice from the stores, and mice from the town hall.

They all went running up the ramps and runways and disappeared in Michael Murphy's musical mousetrap. The children followed behind enjoying the whole thing almost as much as the mice.

After traveling down every street in town, the procession came to a stop in front of the town hall, and the mayor came out and presented Mr. Murphy with his thirty-dollar fee — thirty bright, crisp new one-dollar bills.

Just as the mayor finished counting out the bills into Mr. Murphy's hand, the sheriff stepped up and said, "Mr. Murphy, I hope this won't embarrass you too much, in fact, I hate to mention it at all, but this here misical moostrap, I mean mousetrap of yours, has got a license plate that is thirty years old . . . A *new* license will cost you just exactly thirty dollars."

Mr. Murphy blushed crimson under his beard. "It's the law, you know, and *I* can't help it!" apologized the sheriff.

Poor Mr. Murphy, poor *shy* Mr. Murphy! He handed his thirty dollars to the sheriff, took his new license plates, and crept down the city hall steps. He climbed into his car and drove slowly away toward the edge of town, with the musical mousetrap playing its reedy music. The children followed along to see Mr. Murphy release all of the mice.

"I really hated to do that, Mayor," said the sheriff as the procession turned out of sight on Route 56A. "It's the law you know, and if I hadn't reminded him, he might have been arrested in the next town he visits."

There's no telling how this de-mousing would have ended if the children's librarian hadn't come rushing up shouting, "Sheriff! Sheriff! Quick! *We guessed the wrong book!*"

"What?" shouted the sheriff and the mayor and Uncle Ulysses.

"Yes!" gasped the children's librarian, "not *Rip Van Winkle,* but *another* book, *The Pied Piper of Hamelin!*"

"And almost every child in town is followin' him this very minute!" the sheriff yelled.

The sheriff and the librarian and the mayor and Uncle Ulysses all jumped into the sheriff's car and roared away after the procession. They met up with the children just outside the city limits. "Come back! Turn around, children!" they shouted.

"I'll treat everybody to a doughnut!" yelled Uncle Ulysses.

The children didn't seem to hear, and they kept right on following the musical mousetrap.

"The music must have affected their minds," cried the librarian.

"Sheriff, we can't lose all these children with election

time coming up next month!" mourned the mayor. "Let's give Murphy another thirty dollars!"

"That's the idea," said Uncle Ulysses. "Drive up next to him, Sheriff, and I'll hand him the money."

The sheriff's car drew alongside the musical mousetrap, and Uncle Ulysses tossed a wad of thirty dollar bills onto the seat next to the shy Mr. Murphy.

"Please don't take them away!" pleaded the librarian.

"Come, Murphy, let's be reasonable," shouted the mayor.

Mr. Murphy was very flustered, and his steering was distinctly wobbly.

Then the sheriff got riled and yelled at the top of his lungs, "*Get 'em low! Get 'em go! Let 'em go!*"

And that's exactly what Mr. Murphy did. He let them go. He pulled a lever, and every last mouse came tumbling out of the bottom of the musical mousetrap. And *such a sight* it was, well worth walking to the city limits to see. The mice came out in a torrent. The reedy organ of the musical mousetrap stopped playing, and the squeaking of mice and the cheering of children filled the air.

The torrent of mice paused, as if sensing direction, and then each Centerburg mouse started off in a straight, straight line to his own Centerburg mousehole. Mr. Murphy didn't pause. He stepped on the gas, and the musical mousetrap swayed down the road. The mayor, the children's librarian, the sheriff, Uncle Ulysses, and the children watched as it grew smaller and smaller and finally disappeared.

Then Uncle Ulysses remembered the children. He turned around and noticed them grinning at each other and holding their thumbs in the air. They paid no attention whatever when they were called!

"That music has pixied these children!" he moaned.

"No, it hasn't, Uncle Ulysses," said Homer, who had just come up. "There's not a thing the matter with them that Doc Pelly can't cure in two shakes! Just to be on the safe side, Freddy and I asked Doc Pelly to come down to the schoolyard this morning and put cotton in all the children's ears. You know, just like Ulysses, not you, Uncle Ulysses, but the ancient one—the one that Homer wrote about. Not me but the ancient one."

"You mean to say Doc Pelly is mixed up in this?" asked the mayor.

"Yes, he thought it was awfully funny, our being so cautious."

Uncle Ulysses laughed and said, "Round 'em up, and we'll all go down to the lunchroom for doughnuts and milk."

"Sheriff," said the mayor, "with election time coming next month *we* gotta put our heads together and cook up a good excuse for spending sixty dollars of the tax-payers' money."

Understanding What You've Read

1. Many authors bring humor to their stories by having their characters use silly or exaggerated ways of speaking. Find sentences spoken by the sheriff that show such use of humor.
2. Why did everyone call the stranger "Old Rip"?
3. What did the Pied Piper of Hamelin do for the city of Hamelin, Germany? What did the people of Centerburg expect Mr. Murphy to do for them? How was what happened in the story unexpected?
4. The humor in a story can depend on a misunderstanding by one character of something another one said. What did the sheriff mean on page 155 when he said, "Let 'em go!"? What did Mr. Murphy think he meant?
5. How is the ending of this story different from the ending of *The Pied Piper of Hamelin*? How does this add to the humor of the story?

Writing

1. Use word play to rewrite the following sentences as the sheriff might say them.

   a. Come back! Come back!
   b. A stitch in time saves nine.
   c. Homer, my boy, you really saved the day.

2. Pretend you are a reporter for the Centerburg newspaper. Write a humorous paragraph in which you tell what happened the day Michael Murphy drove his musical mousetrap through Centerburg.

More Books to Make You Laugh

Paddington on Stage: Plays for Children by Michael Bond and Alfred Bradley. Houghton Mifflin, 1977. Some of the funniest adventures of the popular bear called Paddington are presented here in play form.

McBroom and the Great Race by Sid Fleischman. Little, 1980. Here's an exaggerated tale of a race between a rooster and a jackalope.

Centerburg Tales by Robert McCloskey. Viking, 1951. Here are more stories about Uncle Ulysses, the sheriff, and Homer's other friends.

Lentil by Robert McCloskey. Viking, 1968. When the town finds itself in an embarrassing situation, Lentil and his harmonica save the day.

Homer Price by Robert McCloskey. Viking, 1971. This book follows Homer through several adventures, including a holdup.

Ghosts I Have Been by Richard Peck. Viking, 1977. Blossom finds that she has supernatural powers that upset life in her hometown.

Black and Blue Magic by Zilpha Keatley Snyder. Atheneum, 1966. Marco is clumsy, so when he receives the gift of wings, it leads to black and blue magic.

Part 3
Expressions

Understanding the Parts of a Book

Suppose you want to find breakfast cereal in a super-market. You can walk through the whole store looking for the cereal. Or you might look for signs that tell you what is on the shelves. These signs can help you find your way to the break-fast cereals.

A book, like a supermarket, is laid out in an orderly way. Most nonfiction books have guides to help you know what is in them. This lesson will tell you about the useful guides you can find in most books.

Using a Table of Contents

In the beginning of most books there is a **table of contents.** This is a list of the major topics—by chapter—that appear in the book. It shows the page on which each chapter begins. It also shows how the writer has organized the major ideas. Look at this table of contents from the book *A Book for Dog Lovers.*

As you can see from this table of contents, the author has organized the book into four *parts*. What are these four parts? Within each part, there are *chapters*. The numerals on the right are the page numbers on which each chapter begins. How is this book, *Blazing Trails*, organized? Check its table of contents. How is your science book organized?

Which chapter in *A Book for Dog Lovers* tells you about famous dogs? Most of the time, you can tell what a chapter is about from its title. But sometimes you can't. What do you think Chapter 12 in Part II of *A Book for Dog Lovers* is about? You can't tell if you don't already know that the spinoni Italiani is a miscellaneous breed of dog.

Using an Index

The table of contents tells you that Chapter 5 is about hounds. But suppose you want to know only one thing about hounds—what a bloodhound looks like. The **index** can help you now.

An index is an alphabetical list of names and *topics*. It is much more detailed than a table of contents. Sometimes there are *subtopics* under each topic. These are listed in alphabetical order, too.

Look at the entry for *Bloodhound* in the first column of the index below. On the first line are listed all of the pages on which *bloodhound* is mentioned in a general way. You might find the answer to your question about what a bloodhound looks like on one of those pages. But perhaps you can find an answer more quickly by looking at the subtopics. Read down the list of subtopics under *Bloodhound* until you come to the line that says *"description of, 45."* That entry shows where to find the answer to your question—on page 45.

Using a Bibliography

Another useful part of many books is a **bibliography.** This is a list of books and their authors. Some bibliographies include magazines, newspapers, and other sources, as well as books. In some books there is only one bibliography. It comes near the end of the book before the index. In other books, you may find a bibliography at the end of each part or chapter.

Some bibliographies list only the sources from which information or articles included in the book were taken. Other bibliographies list books suggested for further reading. The bibliographies in this book are of this type. You'll find one on page 94. What are all the books listed there about? The title *Books About Living Things* tells you what all the books are about. Which books do you think you'd like to read?

The Introduction and the Glossary

THE INTRODUCTION   Some books have an **introduction.** It comes just before the first chapter of the book. Sometimes an introduction is titled "To the Reader." It may tell you about the purpose of the book or why or how the author wrote the book. It may explain special things you will find in the book. Turn to page xvi of this book. What does the introduction **To the Reader** tell you?

THE GLOSSARY   In addition to a table of contents, an index, and a bibliography, many books contain a **glossary.** A glossary is a special dictionary. Words that are used in the book and that may be new to you are listed here. The glossary usually appears near the end of the book. Look at page 551 in this book. Notice how a glossary is like a dictionary.

Try This

1. In what part of a book will you find each of the things below?

   a. a list of books you might like to read
   b. an alphabetical list of topics and subtopics
   c. a list of the chapter titles in the book
   d. an explanation of the purpose of the book
   e. an alphabetical list of special words and their meanings

2. Will you find each of the following parts of a book in the front or the back of a book?

   a. glossary   c. table of contents
   b. index   d. introduction

3. Answer the following questions about *Blazing Trails*.

   a. On which page does a Skills Lesson about using the library begin?
   b. What is the general topic of all the selections in the first part of *Blazing Trails*?
   c. Where in *Blazing Trails* can you look to learn how to pronounce *Sacajawea*?

4. In what ways are the glossary for *Blazing Trails* and a dictionary alike? In what ways are they different?

5. Look at the table of contents for *Blazing Trails*. How many bibliographies are listed? On what page is the bibliography for this unit? What kinds of information are given in this bibliography?

165

VOCABULARY STUDY

Antonyms

"I've done it, Dr. Lens!"

"You're joking."

"No. I'm quite **serious**."

"Can I touch it?"

"Well, OK, but be careful. One false move and you'll destroy what it took me years to **create**."

"Ooo. It tickles."

"It's supposed to tickle. It's a smile-maker, remember? I'm calling it Chuckle-O."

"Chuckle-O! Ha ha ha ha ha ha ha . . . . That's a good one! Ha ha ha ha ha ha. . . . Funniest thing . . . ha ha ha . . . I ever . . . ha ha ha . . . heard . . . ha ha ha ha ha."

"Dr. Lens! Please! You're too excited. **Calm** yourself."

"Aw, come on, Dr. Mirror. Let yourself go. Touch Chuckle-O. Ha ha ha ha ha! It's fantastic! Ha ha ha ha!"

"You're going to wear it out if you keep this up. Give me back my Chuckle-O!"

"Never! Ha ha ha ha. You'll have to fight me for it!"

"How can we fight if you're laughing?"

"We'll fight when the battery runs down. Hee hee hee hee. By the way, why did you invent Chuckle-O?"

"Because we fight too much, and I don't like to fight."

"Gee. Neither do I. Are you thinking what I'm thinking?"

"Yes. I think I'll get another battery for Chuckle-O."

Word Play

1. Match each word in Column 1 with its antonym, or opposite, in Column 2 and its correct definition in Column 3.

1	2	3
serious	destroy	make; invent
create	excited	sincere; not joking
calm	joking	peaceful; quiet

2. Give an antonym for each of the words below. Then make up sentences using the antonyms.

a. chuckle   b. false   c. smile   d. funny   e. laugh

Suppose you had a book on games. What part of the book would guide you to the pages about marbles? How would you find out if the book had a chapter on games played in ancient Rome?

How are the games you play like those played in other countries or long ago? Take a walk along . . .

A STREET OF GAMES

by Dina Brown Anastasio

Close your eyes and picture a street. It can be any kind of street, anywhere in the world. It must, however, be big enough for many groups of children to gather and play. All of a sudden the street begins to come alive. Children of all ages form small groups in the middle of the street.

Who are these children? Well, since we are pretending anyway, let us pretend that they are children from different parts of the world. We might even carry our pretending one step further and say that some of these children also lived a long, long time ago.

What a gathering we have imagined! In front of an old red building, a group of very young children are trying to decide what to play. The group includes a child who lived in ancient Rome, one who lived in England a long time ago, a child from China, and several children who live in the United States today. They seem to be trying to find a game that they all know. At last they decide. They will play hopscotch. They all know this game.

They begin by drawing the diagram, and already there is disagreement. Most of the children agree that the diagram should look somewhat like a ladder.

One of the American children prefers that it look like a snail. But he is outvoted.

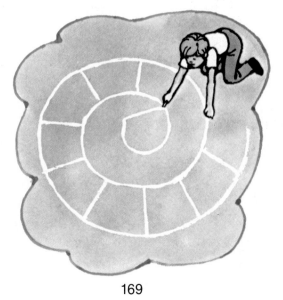

They begin to draw the ladder. But how many squares? Most of the Americans agree that there are eight squares in hopscotch.

"No, it's nine," says the girl from Rome. "I am the oldest, and I say that there are nine squares. If you don't believe me, look in the old Forum in Rome. The diagram is still there, scratched into the pavement."

"That's wrong," says a boy from England, who is also very old, but not quite as old as the girl from Rome. "There are twelve squares in hopscotch."

They argue for a little while. Then they decide to try it each way. They play the first game using eight squares.

"Now add a 'HOME,' " says a girl from Maine. "You have to have a place to rest before heading back to 'START.' "

Most of the Americans agree. But the others do not. The boy from England wants to rest in "LONDON." The girl from China wants to rest in the "PUBLIC HOUSE." And the girl from ancient Rome doesn't want to rest at all.

The arguments continue, and the players begin to wonder if they'll ever play. After they have chosen their stones, they argue about what to call them. "It's a tor!" "A potsie!" "A puck!" "A dump!" "A scotch!" "A pick!"

"Oh, what does it matter?" says a boy from Chicago. "Call it whatever you like! Let's just play!"

And so they begin. Some throw their stones into the squares, and some kick it. But it is hopscotch just the same.

Down the street, a tug of war is taking place. There are no arguments this time, for everyone plays the game the same way. However, when you ask the children to tell you the reason for the game, you get many different answers.

For instance, the Eskimo boy tells you that it is a contest to find out whether there will be a mild or a cold winter. When winter is approaching in an Alaskan town, he says, everyone who has a summer birthday takes one end of the rope. Those with winter birthdays pull the other end. If the summer birthdays win, the winter will be mild.

The Korean and Japanese children tell you that a tug of war is not a game. They tell you that it is a very serious contest indeed. One village pulls against another. It is believed that the winning village will have the best harvest.

In the middle of the block, three children are talking. One is a cave boy. The other boy lived near the Amazon River

171

long before Christopher Columbus was born. The girl is from Kansas City. She is throwing a rubber ball up in the air.

"I could teach you how to play ball," she is telling the others. "And then we could play something, maybe baseball, basketball, lacrosse, or even just catch."

The boy from the Amazon reminds her that it was his people who invented the ball.

"They took some gum from the rubber tree," he says, "and formed it into a ball. Lacrosse and basketball?" he adds. "Why, we were playing those games long before the English came to America."

The cave boy laughs and says, "Baseball indeed! We were playing baseball with a stick and a rock before either of you were born."

Farther down the block some older children are playing marbles in the dirt next to the street. A boy from ancient Rome tells the others that he used to use nuts instead of marbles. "Later," he says, "my parents bought me marbles made of glass." Someone else says that she played the game with beans.

Each of the children seems to want to play a different marble game. A boy from Africa wants to play marble golf. He makes four small holes in the ground. Then he uses a stick to roll his marbles from behind a starting line toward the holes. Other players, in turn, do the same. And the player who fills the most holes is the winner.

A girl from Denver then shows the others how she plays marbles. She draws a circle in the dirt with a stick. Then she puts a marble in the center. Everyone else adds a marble to the center of the circle.

The girl then places her knuckles on the ground outside the circle and shoots another marble, called a "shooter." She tries to shoot some of the marbles out of the circle. If she misses, she leaves her shooter where it is and shoots it from that spot on her next turn. If she shoots some marbles out of the circle, she keeps them.

Or does she? A boy from Paris doesn't seem to agree.

"It's all for fun," he says. "You can't keep my marbles."

173

At the far end of the block, a boy from Spain watches a sewerball game. He guesses that the players are from a city, for it is rare to find three sewer covers on the same corner anywhere else.

The boy wonders if other children play sewerball in Paris, or Rome, or Tokyo. He watches carefully. He is trying to learn the rules so that he can teach them to his friends back in Madrid, Spain.

And this is perhaps the way most of us learn how to play the games of childhood. A sister or brother shows us how to jump hopscotch squares without stepping on the lines. A friend teaches us sewerball and stickball. We pass the rules from one person to another, from one country to another, and from generation to generation. Yes, we make some changes. But the games themselves never really change.

Understanding What You've Read

1. Why do the players disagree about hopscotch?
2. Why do the Korean and Japanese children say that tug of war is not a game?
3. How do we learn to play games?

Applying the Skills Lesson

In which part of a book about sports would you find each of the following items? (Refer to the Skills Lesson if you need help.)

1. an entry that gives the way to pronounce *lacrosse* and a definition of this word
2. the page number on which a chapter on different ball games begins
3. a list of books about sports and games

Suppose you had a book about musicians. What two parts of the book would guide you to pages giving information about José Feliciano?

A guitar, a song—and an adventure in courage. Here is . . .

Feliciano!

by Richard B. Lyttle

José Feliciano is the second of eight sons born to a family of farmers in Puerto Rico. When José was five, his family moved to New York City.

The Feliciano children were full of spirit and good fun. But because José was blind, his parents overprotected him, so he was cut off from much of the fun. He had to learn to amuse himself. Very early in life, the radio and its music became important to him. When he was six, he learned how to play the concertina.

Popular singers were José's heroes. He saw the life of a singer as a way to become independent. But because he was blind, José could not read music. He had to learn by ear. And he did have a natural talent. By the age of nine, he had learned to play the guitar. He made his first public appearance before he was ten years old.

Later, in high school, José was an expert mimic. He delighted his classmates by copying the styles and voices of well-known singers. But these performances did not satisfy him. If he was to become independent, he would have to start singing for pay.

With his guitar in a large paper sack, José began making the rounds of the coffee houses in New York. After entering a coffee house, he would ask the manager if he could play a few songs. Most managers said they had no time to listen to José.

José would then ask if he could at least tune his guitar before leaving. Even the busiest manager could not turn down that request. Of course, the guitar would always be in fine tune. José would pull it out from the paper sack. Then he would play so well that the manager and all of the customers were at once delighted.

José was seventeen when he took his first paying job in a Detroit nightclub. When he returned to New York, a music critic for the *New York Times* wrote that everyone who wanted to see the birth of a star should watch Feliciano.

In July 1964, he appeared on national TV for the first time. At about the same time, RCA released his first album. It seemed he was really on his way.

Most of his reviews were good. But one critic said José's voice sounded too much like the voices of other singers. José agreed. His high school performances as a mimic had slowed the development of a style that was all his own.

In 1966, José went on tour in Latin America. There he sang his songs in Spanish. He was a great success. Better still, the songs in his native tongue proved to be just what he needed to build a special style.

Pictures and stories about Feliciano appeared in magazines. José wore success well and lost nothing of his touch in working with an audience.

He continues to work hard and is now widely known in the United States and other countries.

Besides playing the guitar and singing on TV, he has acted on many TV shows.

Of course, José thinks of music as an ideal career for the blind.

"If you are blind," he says, "and have talent as a musician, you probably can make it if you really give it everything you've got and make sure that it is the only thing on your mind."

Anyone who has heard José Feliciano knows he gives his music everything he's got.

Understanding What You've Read

1. Why did José Feliciano make music his career?
2. How did José learn music?
3. How did José feel when a music critic said that his voice sounded too much like the voices of other singers?
4. How do you think José's success might have affected his relationships with other people?

Applying the Skills Lesson

In which part of a book about music and musicians would you find information on the items below? (Refer to the Skills Lesson if you need help.)

1. whether the book had information on José Feliciano
2. whether the book had a chapter on guitar music
3. how to pronounce *concertina* and a description of this instrument
4. a list of books from which the author got information
5. why the author wrote the book

TEXTBOOK STUDY

Understanding the Parts of a Textbook

When you get a new book, it's a good idea to look at each part of it. The table of contents will help you if you want to know what general topics are covered in a book. The index will help you find specific information. The glossary and bibliography will give you other kinds of information.

As you study the table of contents and the index that follow, refer to the sidenotes. Try to answer the questions in them.

The Table of Contents in Science

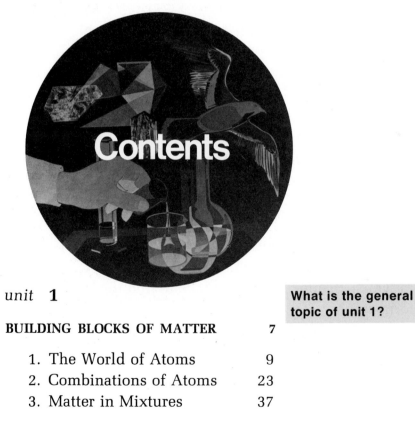

Contents

What is the general topic of unit 1?

179

—Understanding Your Environment
Silver Burdett

On which pages will you find a chapter about the inside of the Earth?

Building Skills

Answer the following questions about the table of contents that begins on page 179 and ends above.

1. Which unit is all about plants?
2. How many chapters are there in each unit?
3. In which chapter would you look to find the following information?

   a. what plants do not carry seeds
   b. how water travels through a plant
   c. what kinds of animals lived long ago
   d. what an atom is

A Mathematics Index

The words in boldface are *topics*. How many subtopics are given for equal ratios?

Which page teaches you how to make an estimate in addition?

This is called a *cross-reference*. It refers you to another entry. What is that entry?

— *Mathematics Around Us*
Scott, Foresman

Building Skills

Answer the following questions about the index above.

1. Suppose you want to learn about adding equations. What pages would give you this information?

2. On what page is there information about even numbers?

Understanding Topical Organization

Once there was a parrot named Polly (of course!). Polly knew how to say many different things. She might have said: "Polly wants a cracker! Nice day today! Joan's a good girl! Rain tomorrow! Rain tomorrow!" Polly didn't know anything about *topical organization*.

Authors—unlike parrots—have to understand topical organization. They can't go from the topic of crackers to the topic of the weather to the topic of Joan and then back again to the weather. If an author does that, he or she won't be understood. Good readers have to understand topical organization, too. If you don't understand the order in which an author is presenting ideas, you can become just as confused as you would be if you tried to have a serious talk with Polly.

Finding Topics

You know that a table of contents shows the organization of the major topics in a book. Like a book, a chapter or an article may be organized by topics.

The title of a chapter or article sometimes gives you an idea about its major topic. But sometimes the title alone is not enough. Here is the title of an article. You would need to look at the article itself to find out that it is about the Smithsonian Institution.

"America's Attic"

Smithsonian Institution Building, Washington, D.C. Sometimes called The Castle.

Within many chapters and articles, you will see **headings.** These words are usually printed in boldfaced type. When you are reading or studying a chapter or an article, it's a good idea to look at the title and the headings before you begin to read. This is called **previewing.** Previewing gives you an idea of the topics that will be covered. Previewing also helps you see how the topics relate to one another. If you previewed the headings in the article titled "America's Attic," here is what you would find:

title ⟶ "America's Attic"
heading ⟶ The Museum of History and Technology
heading ⟶ The National Air and Space Museum
heading ⟶ The Art Museums
heading ⟶ The Natural History Museum
heading ⟶ The Rest of the Museum

How is the article organized? As you can see from the headings, the article is organized according to the different museums that make up the Smithsonian Institution.

Milestone Hall, National Air and Space Museum

When There Are No Headings

Not every chapter or article has headings. But you can be sure that the author has organized his or her ideas in some way. Read the following article in which there are no headings. The sidenotes will help you see how the author has organized the topics of the article.

The Arlington Symphony Orchestra, Arlington, Virginia

The Orchestra

The orchestra is made up of a group of musicians playing together. Most orchestras are large and have many people playing different instruments. The instruments are grouped by "families." There is the *string* family, the *woodwinds,* the *brass,* and the *percussion.* There are also *keyboard* instruments that belong to more than one family.

This paragraph introduces the article. What topics do you think will be covered later in the article?

What is the first topic covered in this article?

The strings are the largest family in the orchestra. They make up more than half of it. The family members are the violin, the viola, the cello, and the bass. They are played by the drawing of a bow across their strings.

The topic changes here.

The woodwind family is made up of the flute, the oboe, the clarinet, and the saxophone. This family is only a small part of the orchestra.

What topic is the author dealing with now?

The brass family is known for the brilliance of its sound. Among its family members are the trumpet, the trombone, and the French horn. They are not heard as often as the strings, but you know they're "alive" when you hear them!

The topic of this paragraph is the *percussion family*.

What do you think the members of the percussion family are? Its members are all instruments that are played by being "struck." This includes the drums and many others.

This paragraph and the next have the same topic. The topic of both paragraphs is *keyboard instruments*.

What about the piano? To which family does it belong? It belongs really to both the percussion and the string families. It is a keyboard instrument with felt hammers that strike metal strings to make its sounds.

The organ is also a keyboard instrument. It sometimes joins the orchestra. However, the organ is not used as often as the piano.

It is truly a wonderful experience to hear all these families of the orchestra working together.

The last paragraph summarizes or ties all the topics together.

Try This

1. Below is a list of five topics covered in the article you just read. The order of topics is mixed up. Put them in the same order as they appeared in the article.

   a. the brass family
   b. the string family
   c. keyboard instruments
   d. the woodwind family
   e. the percussion family

2. The following headings are for an article titled "How to Improve Your Writing." The headings are out of order. Put them in the order that would make sense in the article.

   a. Handing In the Perfect Paper
   b. Editing Your Writing
   c. Getting It All Down Quickly
   d. Locating the Facts
   e. Typing a Clean Copy

Etymologies

"Do you sell sentences?"

"No, not finished sentences. But we do sell sentence kits. You can make your own original sentences. We're having a sale on imported word kits. I'll give you a good price on a starter kit — with three terrific words."

"Only three words? What can I do with three words?"

"Plenty. See for yourself. Each word kit comes with its own etymology. An etymology is the history, or origin, of a word. Here's the French word **ballet**. It originally came from the Italian *ballo*, meaning 'dance.'"

"Ballet is a dance form using gestures and actions to tell a story, isn't it? I can make a nice sentence with the word *ballet*. What else is in the kit?"

"The word **mimic**, meaning 'to imitate,' from the Greek word for actor — *mimos*."

"Gee, I don't know. Is it possible to imitate something in a ballet?"

"Sure. In *Firebird*, a ballerina imitates the movements of a bird. The kit also contains a nice Latin word."

"I knew it. Here's the catch!"

"No! The word is **origin**, meaning 'parentage.' *Origin* comes from the Latin *originis*, meaning 'that in which something has its beginning.' You'll make many original sentences with this kit. By the way, what are you planning to do with the sentences?"

"They're for a display rack in our dad's store. He sells punctuation. Here, have a comma with our compliments."

Word Play

1. Each of the words below is related to one of the words in boldface in the story. Match each word with its meaning.

   ballerina — use gestures and actions rather than words

   mime — not existing before; new; first

   original — a female ballet dancer

2. The Greek word *geo* means "earth." Look up three words beginning with *geo-* in a dictionary and use each one in a sentence.

As you read, notice how the author has organized the different topics in this selection. The headings will help you to understand this organization.

Some sea animals make beautiful homes that you can turn into . . .

Shell Treasures

by Katherine N. Cutler

Shellcraft is the art of using shells to make many attractive things. The first step in this popular hobby is finding sea shells to work with. The second step is turning these objects of nature into objects of art.

Animal Houses

What is a sea shell? It is the house of a soft-bodied animal called a mollusk. The animal has built the shell to protect itself. (You may not realize that shells you've found once held living animals.)

How does the mollusk make its shell? Wrapped around the body of the animal is a sac called a mantle. Inside the mantle are cells that make lime. The shell is made from this lime.

Each kind of mollusk makes its house in a different shape. Some shells are round; some are spiral. Some are smooth and glossy. Others are rough and ridged.

From earliest times people have admired these animal houses. That is why collecting shells has been popular through the ages.

Different Kinds of Shells

Some shells are found only in certain parts of the world. Other shells seem to be everywhere. The warmer the water in which a shell is found, the brighter its color seems to be. Shells from calm waters are thinner than those found where there are high seas and a pounding surf.

Most of the shells you find fall into two classes. They are called *bivalves* and *univalves.*

Bivalves are shells that have two parts joined together by a hinge. (The prefix *bi-* means "two.") Clams and oysters are examples of these. Sometimes you will find only one half of a bivalve. You can recognize it by the hinge mark.

Scallop

Univalves are made in one piece. (The prefix *uni-* means "one.") Cones, sundials, and cowries are some kinds of univalves.

Cone

Trumpet

Kitten's Paw

Shell Names

When you want to know the names of the shells you are gathering and using, you can look in a shell-identification guidebook. There are several of these books. You can find them at most bookstores or in your library.

All shells have family names which almost always come from Latin. They also have common names that are generally used. And they may have descriptive nicknames.

One example is a shell known generally as a jingle shell. Its family name is *Anomia*. Because there is a tiny print like a baby's foot in the center of it, its nickname is "baby's foot shell." Most books list a shell under both the common name and the family name. Sometimes, but not always, you can find it under the nickname.

Sundial

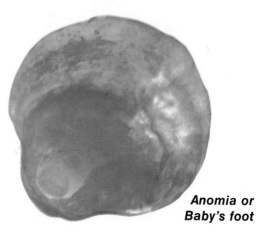

Anomia or Baby's foot

Collecting Shells

You can make many things with shells that you collect. When you are looking for shells, try not to take ones that house live animals. The animals inside may have come into shallow water to breed, and you would be destroying more than the parent animal.

While it is fun to look for shells at any time, it is best when the tides are at their highest and lowest. This happens when the moon is either crescent or full. High tides bring in more shells. Low tides show greater areas of beach.

As you start out to gather shells, take a good-sized bag to hold your treasures. Wear sneakers or beach shoes, for it is easy to cut a bare foot on a piece of glass or broken shell. To avoid a sunburn, wear a hat and a thin shirt.

Shells are not always lying on the open beach. Sometimes you find the ones you treasure most by poking in the dry seaweed at the tide line. You might turn over a broken plank or move a small rock. Replace rocks you turn over so that sea life will not be disturbed.

You may say, "But how can I make things with shells? I don't live near any beaches where there are shells." This shouldn't trouble you, for there are many ways to get them. There are many interesting snails in inland ponds and rivers. If you let people know you are interested in shells, you will find that friends will bring some home to you after they go to beaches. They may also give you shells they have at home. Often there are boxes of shells for sale in gift shops and craft shops. There you can buy little packages of shells.

Gluing the Shells

You will need very little equipment. The most important thing is the proper glue. Be sure it is safe to use and clear enough to see through when it dries. It should also be easy to wipe up without causing any damage if it spills. Besides glue, you will need a water-color paintbrush and some tweezers.

To glue single small shells, make a puddle of glue on a piece of paper. Use the tweezers to draw the shell through the glue, and put the shell in place. When you want to cover a large space with shells, paint glue over all of the space. Then stick the shells directly on the glue.

Things You Can Make

Here are some ideas for things you may want to make from shells. Of course, you'll also want to make your own shell designs.

Underwater Scene in a Jar: You will need a jar with a top. Put sand in the bottom of the jar. Shake it so that the sand forms drifts. Place different shells and pieces of coral in the sand. (A piece of coral, if you have one, makes a good center of interest.) When you have finished, fill the jar

with water. Add two tablespoons of laundry bleach. This will keep the water clear. Replace the jar top.

Mobile: Shells on a mobile are balanced so that they move gently in the slightest draft. You can enjoy their beauty from all sides as they turn. Use driftwood or whatever else you like for the bar. Thin wire, heavy thread, or nylon fishing line can be tied to the middle of the bar and fastened to something so that it balances.

Choose shells of different shapes and colors. Make a small hole in each, then thread them to the bar.

Owl: Use a pine cone with a firm, pointed stem end for the owl's body and head. On the top end, glue round, white shells for the eyes and pointed shells for the ears and beak. Make the owl look alive by putting tiny, dark, round shells in the center of the "eyes" for the pupils. Make the back and folded wings by overlapping the shells. Glue two small shells to the stem end for the feet.

Then make a puddle of glue on a branch and hold the owl in place until the glue takes hold.

Shell Display: Make a wall decoration for your room. Find a piece of driftwood or weathered wood that has an interesting shape. Glue shells to it, following the shape of the wood.

Anyone who becomes interested in shells will have many hours of pleasure. It is not only great fun to use shells imaginatively, but it also gives pleasure to your family and friends when you share these things with them.

Understanding What You've Read

1. What is a sea shell?
2. When is the best time to collect shells at the beach? Why?
3. How can a shell-identification guidebook be useful?

Applying the Skills Lesson

1. Find a paragraph in the selection that *introduces* the topics that will be covered. Find a paragraph that *summarizes* or ties together all the topics.
2. Below is a list of the topics of some paragraphs covered in this selection. In what order did the topics appear?

   a. how to collect shells
   b. what shells are
   c. what you can make with shells
   d. how shells are named
   e. bivalves and univalves
   f. how to glue shells

TEXTBOOK STUDY

Understanding Topical Organization

Textbooks usually organize information by topics. As you read the following selections from textbooks, look for ways in which the author organizes the information. Sometimes headings may help you to see the organization more clearly. The sidenotes will also help you. Refer to them as you read.

Understanding Topical Organization in Social Studies

Look at the headings. Into how many parts is this selection divided?

In the Northeast

Much of the land in the Northeast is taken up by cities and metropolitan areas. In its northern and western parts are much forest and woodland. These regions are used for lumbering and recreation. The rest of the section has mixed pasture and farmland. Farmers here grow fruits and vegetables and keep dairy cattle.

In the South

Notice that this paragraph talks about the land and products of the South. What is the topic of the paragraph on the Northeast? What is the topic of the paragraph on Alaska and Hawaii?

More people live in this part of the United States than in any other region. The mixture of land here is much like that of the Northeast. There is some little-used mountain and woodland here. The rest is mixed farmland and pasture, but this section produces a

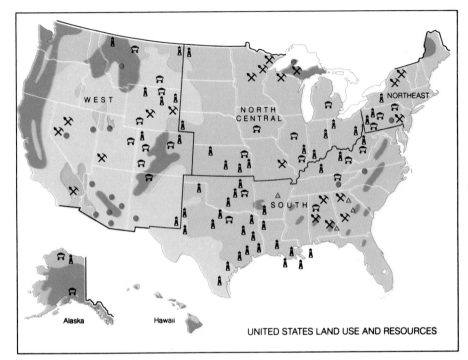

UNITED STATES LAND USE AND RESOURCES

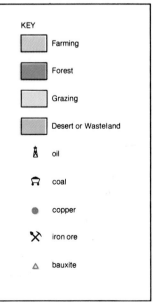

KEY

Farming

Forest

Grazing

Desert or Wasteland

oil

coal

copper

iron ore

bauxite

wider variety of crops than the Northeast. There is general farming, poultry-raising, and dairying. Also, farmers here grow a great deal of cotton and tobacco, as well as nuts and fruits.

Why do you suppose the variety of crops is so much greater here? What sort of climate does it have?

In the North Central Section

These states have the best farmland in the United States. It lies in a thick belt across the lower part of the section, supplying wheat, corn, and livestock in abundance. Just above this is an area of rich dairyland and general farming. The northernmost part is unfarmed forest.

In the West

Along the Pacific Coast there is much rainfall in the north, and less in the south. But in the valleys, especially the Valley of California and the Willamette River Valley, there is excellent soil. Every kind of farming is found here, even cotton growing. Otherwise, in this region, crops are grown in very tight areas where water is available for irrigation. But cattle are raised everywhere.

In Alaska and Hawaii

Alaska has mostly forest land and frozen plain, but some cattle are raised in the south. The long summer, too, allows some vegetables to be grown. Hawaii has lots of mountains and forest, but some grasslands, where cattle are raised. Along the coasts are strips of farmland as good as that in any other part of the United States. Sugar cane and fruits grow in Hawaii.

— The United States
Houghton Mifflin

Building Skills

1. What is the general topic of the selection you just read?

   a. products from land in the United States
   b. rainfall in the United States
   c. the size of the United States

2. How has the author organized the general topic?

   a. by the kinds of products grown in the United States
   b. by the different geographical areas in the United States
   c. by the different climates in the United States

Understanding Topical Organization in Science

Why Rocks Look Different

For one thing, different rocks have different minerals in them. Rocks that have different minerals in them usually look different. Here are two igneous rocks that have different minerals in them. ● The gray one is basalt

The title gives you a clue to the general topic.

This symbol and the ones that follow tell you to stop reading and look at the picture that has the same symbol by it.

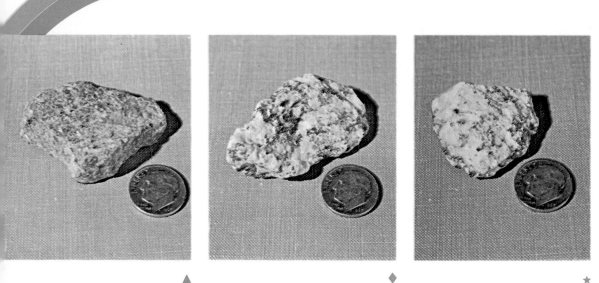

▲ ◆ ★

and the black one is obsidian. In what other ways besides color do they look different?

For another thing, rocks may look different even when they have the same minerals. For instance, two rocks may have different *amounts* of the same mineral. This piece of granite has in it a good deal of pink feldspar. ▲ Other granite rocks with just a little feldspar in them do not look pink. ◆ Notice that this granite rock contains a lot of a black mineral called hornblende. The lighter-colored piece of granite here has hornblende in it too — but only a little. ★

Here is another reason why rocks may look different. Some of the minerals in a rock may have well-formed

This is one reason rocks look different. What other reasons does the author give?

crystal faces. For example, this is the mineral quartz. ◈ A crystal of quartz has eight sides. Each of these sides is a crystal face. Observe the crystal faces.

—*Concepts in Science:* Purple
Harcourt Brace Jovanovich

◈

Building Skills

1. What is the general topic of the selection you just read?

   a. igneous rocks
   b. why rocks look different
   c. minerals in rocks

2. Below are two lists of topics. Which one shows how the author organized this selection?

1	**2**
Rocks that have different minerals in them	Basalt and obsidian
Rocks that have different amounts of the same minerals in them	Three kinds of granite
Rocks that have crystal faces	Quartz

Using Outlines to Help You Read

Suppose you are going camping. There are many things you'll need to take along on your trip. When it comes time for you to start packing, how will you remember all the things you wanted to take? One way is to list them. Your list might look like the one on page 205.

An organized list like this helps you remember to pack what you need to take with you. You can also make a list to help you remember and understand what you read. When you make an organized list of the information in a chapter or article, it's called an **outline.**

Topics and Subtopics

In an article or in a chapter of a book, there are usually several major topics. Often, a major topic includes a number of smaller topics. The smaller topics are called **subtopics.** The major topics in the list of things to take on your camping trip are *Equipment, Clothing,* and *Supplies and Other Things.* What are the subtopics in the list?

The Framework of an Outline

Here is the framework of an outline that includes two major topics and several subtopics.

(Title)

I. _____(major topic)_____
  A. _____(subtopic)_____
  B. _____(subtopic)_____
II. _____(major topic)_____
  A. _____(subtopic)_____
  B. _____(subtopic)_____
  C. _____(subtopic)_____

Two subtopics are covered under major topic I. How many are covered under major topic II? Notice that the outline uses Roman numerals and capital letters to show a series of topics.

The Roman numerals show the major topics. The capital letters show the subtopics.

In topical organization, each major topic includes any subtopics that come under it. The author's thoughts move in an orderly way from one topic to another. It is easy to see this in the organization of an outline like the one below.

Life in the Desert

I. Animal life
   A. Camel
   B. Desert rat
II. Plant life
   A. Cactus
   B. Grasses
   C. Sagebrush

Making an Outline

Read the following article. Think about how you would make an outline from it.

Some Places of Historical Interest in America

New York City has many places of historical interest. In the Wall Street area of lower Manhattan, you'll find narrow cobblestone streets. These streets were first used over three hundred years ago. Wall Street itself was almost as busy—and as well known—during colonial days as it is today.

Brooklyn Heights and the Battery are two places in New York City that were important during the Revolutionary War. You can still see why if you visit them. Each gives a wonderful view of the harbor, Staten Island, and New Jersey.

Not more than a few hours' drive from Manhattan is Valley Forge, Pennsylvania. Millions of people have visited here over the years to see the place where Washington's troops spent their unforgettable, terrible winter.

Missouri, too, has some places of historical interest. In St. Joseph you can see the stables that housed the Pony Express horses. Hannibal, Missouri, is remembered as the place where Mark Twain's fictional characters, Tom Sawyer, Becky Thatcher, and Huckleberry Finn, grew up.

What are the major topics covered in the article? Three places are mentioned. Here is what your outline of only the major topics will look like:

I. New York City
II. Pennsylvania
III. Missouri

Pony Express stables, St. Joseph, Missouri

*Cobblestone street,
New York City*

*Home of Washington's troops,
Valley Forge, Pennsylvania*

Home of Mark Twain, Hannibal, Missouri

What subtopics were covered in the paragraphs about New York City? You can list them in this way:

I. New York City
   A. The Wall Street area
   B. Brooklyn Heights and the Battery

How many places in Pennsylvania are mentioned in the article? Only one—Valley Forge—is talked about. So *Valley Forge* is a separate major topic.

II. Valley Forge, Pennsylvania

How many places in Missouri are mentioned? Can you see why the next stage of your outline will look like this?

III. Missouri
   A. St. Joseph
   B. Hannibal

Now you can put the pieces of the outline together. Remember to write the title—*Some Places of Historical Interest in America*—above the whole outline.

How do you choose a title for your outline? The title should state the *general topic* of the chapter or article that you are outlining. Sometimes the title of the chapter or article may be the same as the title of your outline. Other times you may have to make up a title for your outline.

Try This

Read the article on pages 211 and 212. Then outline it. Your outline should show two major topics. One of the major topics has three subtopics. The other has four subtopics. Remember to give a title to your outline.

Sculpting is the art of shaping or arranging things in space. There are a number of different methods of sculpting. One of them, *carving*, is cutting away pieces of something from a large piece. Wood, stone, marble, ivory, and bone can be carved into beautiful shapes. If you want to try carving, a large bar of soap would be a good material to try first.

Wood

Ivory

Snow

Stone

Modeling means making a model from something soft. Clay, wax, and some kinds of soft plastic can be modeled. To model something, artists use their hands and fingers and perhaps some simple tools. Often the clay or wax shape that an artist makes is not finished art. A plaster mold may be made around the shape. Then hot metal is poured by the artist into the mold. After that, the metal is left to cool in the shape of the mold. The cooled, hard metal shape is called a "casting."

Constructing is a third kind of sculpting. This means putting things together. A piece of metal may be attached to other pieces of metal to make a design. Glass, wood, wire, and other things can also be used in constructing.

Artists sometimes talk about a sculpture's "visual qualities": mass, plane, color, and texture. *Mass* means how light or heavy a piece appears to be. Some light pieces *look* heavy. Some heavy pieces *look* light. Mass is not the same thing as real weight.

Plane has to do with curved surfaces and flat surfaces on a piece. Think of a sculpted figure of a person with a body that looks like a box (flat planes). Now think of a snowman (all curves). Think of a real person (a mixture of curves and flat surfaces).

Color is important in creating a mood. Think of a sculpture of a horse painted purple. Now think of a horse sculpted in white marble. How does color affect the "moods" of the two sculptures?

Texture means how rough or smooth something is. Think of a tiger carved in hard, smooth stone. You may get feelings of the tiger's beauty and speed. Now think of a tiger constructed from rusty old car parts. You may get feelings of the tiger's strength and fierceness.

VOCABULARY STUDY

Getting Meaning from Context Clues

The evil Professor Crum sat in the glow of a flickering candle and wrote in his diary.

Dear Diary,
There hasn't been much to do between evil deeds, so I've taken a part-time job. I work in a health food store. It's a popular place. We get a lot of **customers**. Most of the people who come to buy are good and kind, so you can imagine why I feel uncomfortable.

I'm in charge of the juice **section**. It's the busiest part of the store. All day long I have to squeeze avocados and mangos to make fruit drinks. I try hard to start **arguments** with the people by squirting them. But instead of fights, all I get is smiles. I didn't realize there were so many nice people in the world. I may have to raise my rates on evil deeds, or I'll never make a living.

Word Play

1. Find the words or phrases in the diary that tell you what the boldfaced words mean. These words or phrases are context clues. Make up a sentence using each of the boldfaced words.
2. Look up *avocado* in the glossary. Then write a sentence using the word with context clues to show its meaning.

213

As you read, think about how you would outline this selection. Notice that it tells you about three groups of theater workers: people who give directions to others; people in charge of things used in a play; people who perform.

It's fun to be in an audience watching a play. Think what it would be like to . . .

START YOUR OWN THEATER

by Karleen Schart Sabol

One of my friends is twelve years old. She and her friends started a theater in her barn. You can start your own theater, too. You don't need a barn, of course, but you do need a play.

Go to the library and get several books of plays. Pick out one that you like. If the book says anything about *royalties*, you may have to pay to put the play on. The royalty is the money that you pay to the author, or playwright, for the right to use his or her play. There are lots of plays, however, for which you don't need to pay royalties. These are said to be "in public domain." You can ask your librarian to help you find one of these. (Or better still, you can write your own play.) When you do decide on the play you want, make enough copies of it so that everyone working on the play can have one. These copies are called *scripts*.

Your play will need a *producer*. This person organizes the whole thing. He or she makes sure you have a place where you can present your play. This can be almost anywhere. My friend's barn is great, but you can also use a garage, a cellar, or a room that nobody uses much. Even a lawn or sidewalk will do. Just make sure you have enough space for the actors to move around (the stage). You'll also need a place where the actors can get ready or wait when they aren't acting. And, of course, you'll need room for the audience to sit.

The producer also chooses some of the other people who work to put on the play. And if you need any money to put on your play, he or she thinks of ways to earn it. In other words, the producer is the boss. So make sure you get someone who will stick with the job.

A *director* is needed to stage your play. At rehearsals, he or she tells the actors when and where and how to sit, stand, and move while they're on the stage. This is called giving them their *blocking*. The director also helps the actors figure out the best ways to say their lines so the parts they're playing will seem real.

You need a *stage manager* to help the director. The stage manager keeps what is called a master script. In it, he or she writes all the instructions given by the director. This means that every actor's blocking is marked. Every *entrance cue* (when an actor comes onstage) and *exit cue* (when an actor goes offstage) is marked. All the *technical cues* (when the lights go on or off, when it's time for a sound effect, and so on) are marked. Then, if any questions come up during a rehearsal, the stage manager has the answers ready in the master script. During the actual performances, the stage manager runs the show.

A *set designer* is also needed. This person first reads the play. Then he or she decides what the set should look like. Whatever your play is about, the set should show where the action is taking place. This can be done very simply. But it is a good idea to check the library for books about how to build sets.

What about the wardrobe for your play? Someone is needed to be in charge of the wardrobe. This person gets together all the clothes, or costumes, to be worn in your play. Sometimes, if you put on a modern play, you can wear your own clothes. But even if you do, you'll need someone to make sure they are just right for the play. If your play calls for old-fashioned clothing, the wardrobe

person finds out what kind of clothes to make, buy, rent, or borrow. There are books in the library that show what kinds of clothes people have worn in different times and places. If the costumes get ripped and need to be sewn, the wardrobe person is the one to repair them. If they get dirty, the wardrobe person has to clean them. He or she must make sure that all costumes are ready before the play goes on.

Technicians are needed to get lights and sound effects for your play. The lighting can be very simple. The most important thing is having enough light so the audience can see what's happening onstage.

The sound can be handled in a number of ways. You can check your library for records of sounds (train whistles, thunder, screams). Or you can use a tape recorder to record your own sounds. If you have enough people in your theater group, you can let someone stand offstage, banging pans or doing bird calls or making any other sounds that might be needed.

The stage manager tells the lighting and sound technicians

when any effects are needed. But it's up to the technicians to figure out the best ways to get these effects. (A warning: Don't touch any electrical wiring if you aren't sure what you're doing. Find a grown-up who knows about electricity to help you.)

A *property* (or *prop*) person also is important for your play. A sofa on the stage is a prop. So is a telephone, a picture on the wall, a handkerchief, or anything else used in the play. The prop person decides (with the director's help) what is needed. Then he or she makes, borrows, or buys all the props. The person in charge of getting props works closely with the set designer. Together they make sure that large pieces of furniture match the set. The prop person must also check before each performance to make sure all props are where they belong on the stage.

Now that you know about the producer, director, stage manager, and others, can you guess who is still missing? It is the people to act in your play! You should hold tryouts. At a tryout, everyone who wants to be in your play reads some of the lines of the part he or she wants to play. Then the director and producer, and sometimes

the stage manager, decide who is best for each part. Each actor needs his or her own script and should read the whole play carefully. Of course, the actors need to memorize their own lines and their cues. Each of the actors should have a good, strong voice and lots of energy.

When you have everyone and everything you need, figure out when you want to put the play on. You may need from three weeks to a month for rehearsals, and maybe longer. The best times for performances are usually in the afternoon or in the early evening on weekends.

It's up to you whether or not to charge admission. My friend and her group don't charge anything. But they do pass around a hat for donations. And they always get enough money to pay expenses for the play they are doing and to start putting on another one.

What if you don't have enough interested friends to put on your own plays? You can go to your nearest professional or community theater. Ask if you can be an apprentice. You will work very hard, but it's a good way to learn about theater. And you'll have lots of fun, too. Whatever you do, enjoy it—and good luck!

Understanding What You've Read

1. What is a *royalty*?
2. What are some of the jobs of the producer?
3. What are two things the author suggests you can do if you want to learn more about the theater?

Applying the Skills Lesson

Make an outline of the selection you have just read. Your outline should show three major topics. (Hint: See the skills note at the top of page 214.) The subtopics are the different jobs mentioned in the selection. Remember to give your outline a title that states the general topic of the selection.

TEXTBOOK STUDY

Outlining Information

Sometimes you will find it easier to remember what you read if you make an outline of it. Think about what the general topic is. The general topic includes all the subtopics. When there are headings, use them to help you find the general topic and subtopics.

The sidenotes point out things to consider when outlining information. Refer to them as you read the selections. Try to answer the questions in them.

Outlining Information from Science

What is the general topic of this selection?

Mosses

Have you ever noticed tiny green plants growing in the shade near buildings or on trees? If so, you may have been looking at small plants called *mosses.*

If you were previewing this selection, would you expect to find information under this heading about where mosses grow?

What are mosses like? If you ever pulled mosses from the ground, you know they have roots that are not like those of other plants. Little hairs at the base of the stem hold the plant upright. These hairs take in water and minerals.

Mosses do not have stems or leaves that are like those of other plants, either. The tubes found in the roots, stems, and leaves of bigger green plants are missing in mosses. These tubes carry water, minerals, and food through the bigger plants. In mosses, these things pass from cell to cell.

Where are mosses found? You could look for mosses in almost any cool, wet, shady place. They can be found in the woods. They can be found on the banks of streams and ponds. Even if a stream or pond dries up, mosses can live through long, dry spells. They start growing again when water returns.

On your outline, you might turn this heading into a statement: Where mosses are found. How would you turn the other two headings into statements of the topic?

Why are mosses important? People at flower shops often pack flowerpots with mosses. They do this because mosses hold water for a long time. Gardeners also mix mosses with their soil. They make the soil good for plants to grow in. Some mosses are dried and burned as fuel.

Mosses are also good soil builders. Their rootlike parts grow into the cracks of rocks. This helps break up the rocks to form soil. What other ways do you know of that plants help form soil?

—*Exploring Science:* Green Book
Laidlaw Brothers

Building Skills

Make an outline of the selection you just read. Use Roman numerals and capital letters. Remember to give your outline a title.

Outlining Information from Social Studies

Along the western coast of a map of South America you will find the country of Peru. Now look at the map below. You can see that Peru is divided into three regions. They are so

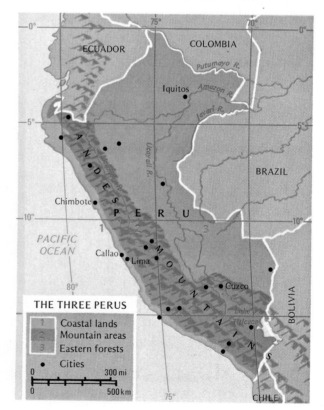

THE THREE PERUS

1 Coastal lands
2 Mountain areas
3 Eastern forests
• Cities

0   300 mi
0   500 km

different from one another that some people speak of the three Perus. The first Peru is the narrow strip of desert that runs the whole length of the country along the coast. Almost no rain falls here, but there are about forty small rivers that flow through the desert. Near these rivers are Peru's large cities and towns. Among them is the capital city of Lima. Look at the map again. What other cities can you find in the first Peru?

To the east of the desert rises the second Peru. It is the Andes, the highest mountains in the Western Hemisphere. In this second Peru, several miles above the sea, the air is chilly most of the year. Few things grow here.

The third Peru is on the other side of the Andes. There the land drops down sharply. That region is mostly rain forest. Very few people live in the third Peru.

—People in the Americas
Silver Burdett

Do you expect that the author will organize this section into three topics? What three topics do you think the author will now talk about?

This is the second major topic. What Roman number will you give it on your outline?

Building Skills

Make an outline of the selection you just read. Remember to use Roman numerals and capital letters. Give your outline a title.

Using the Library

PHILADELPHIA PUBLIC LIBRARY

ESTABLISHED 1731

"Nice building. But what are we going to put in it?"

As you know, Ben Franklin put *books* into his library. But in today's libraries (often called "media centers"), you'll find a lot more than books. You can find films, picture and pamphlet files, magazines, and newspapers. You can find records, tapes, and "talking books." In some libraries you can use a *microfilm* room. Large books or long articles are put on film. When you want to see what a book or article says, you run the film through a microfilm machine. Some of today's libraries even move around on wheels.

Of course, today's libraries have mostly books, books, and more books. How do you go about finding the book you want among the thousands that line the shelves? Usually the best place to start is the **card catalogue.**

The card catalogue is simply a set of small drawers. In them are cards that give information about the books in the library. There are three kinds of cards: *author cards, title cards,* and *subject cards.* Suppose you don't have a special book or author in mind. You're just looking for books on a certain subject. Then the subject cards are for you. If you already know the name of the book you want or the author's name, use the title or author cards.

Look at the three cards that follow. Pay attention to the notes under each card. They will help you understand how to read a catalogue card.

AUTHOR CARD

```
 J
413
Kra    Kraske, Robert.
          The story of the dictionary/by Robert Kraske. —
       1st ed., illustrated with photos. — New York: Har-
       court Brace Jovanovich [1975]

          67 p.: ill.

       Bibliography
          Includes Index.
          SUMMARY: Traces the history of the dictionary and de-
       scribes what goes into the making of this second most popular
       book in the English language.
```

Each nonfiction book in the library has a *call number.* The call number is on the top left-hand part of the card. The *J* means this book can be found in the juvenile or children's area of the library. To find this book on the shelves, you'd only have to find the section of the library with books that have call numbers in the 400's.

Both fiction and nonfiction books have title cards. If you were looking for the title card for *The Story of the Dictionary*, you'd look in the drawer marked *S*. The words *A*, *An*, and *The* are not considered when title cards are filed.

Suppose you did not know the title or author of this book, but wanted a book about dictionaries. You might look under the subjects *English Language*, *Words*, or *Dictionaries* in the card catalogue.

Now suppose you wanted to know about the Braille system. You can see that the subject is listed at the top of the following card. Information about a book that is on the *Braille System* follows the subject listing.

SUBJECT CARD

```
  J      Braille System.
371.9
  Nei    Neimark, Anne E.
              Touch of light; the story of Louis Braille [by]
         Anne E. Neimark. Illustrated by Robert Parker. [1st
         ed.] New York: Harcourt Brace Jovanovich [1970]

         186 p. illus.
            SUMMARY: The life of the nineteenth-century Frenchman
         who invented a system of reading for the blind.
            Bibliography.
```

Not all catalogue cards have a summary like the one above. Why is such a summary useful?

TITLE CARD

> J   Touchmark.
> F
> Law   **Lawrence, Mildred.**
>   Touchmark/by Mildred Lawrence; illustrated by
>   Deanne Hollinger. — 1st ed. — New York: Harcourt
>   Brace Jovanovich [1975]
>   184 p.: ill.
>   SUMMARY: An orphaned girl living in pre-Revolutionary
>   Boston longs to be apprenticed to a pewterer.

The letter F means you should look for this book on the fiction *shelves*. Fiction books do not usually have call numbers. These books are arranged in alphabetical order by the author's last name. The *Law* under the letter F on the card shows the first three letters of the author's last name.

Fiction books also have author cards. If you were looking for another fiction book by Mildred Lawrence, you'd look in the drawer marked *L* and find Lawrence by using alphabetical order.

Try This

Answer the following questions about the book on the subject card on page 226.

1. Is this book fiction or nonfiction?
2. Who is the author of this book?
3. What is the title of this book?
4. What is the call number of this book?

Using Reference Books

Very often you'll want to check a fact from your reading. Or you may want more information about something you've read. The **reference books** in your library may help you. Following are descriptions of some reference books that you might need to use many times during your school years.

ENCYCLOPEDIAS   A **general encyclopedia** is a book or a set of books that contains information about many subjects. A general encyclopedia has hundreds of articles about science, history, well-known people, art, sports, and many other subjects. The articles in an encyclopedia are usually arranged in alphabetical order.

In addition to general encyclopedias, there are **specialized encyclopedias.** These books contain information on only one subject. In your library you might find a sports encyclopedia and a medical encyclopedia. You also might find an encyclopedia of art and many other kinds of encyclopedias.

DICTIONARIES   There are many kinds of dictionaries in a library. On page 229 are entries from two kinds of dictionaries you might want to use some day.

sixty, *a.* and *n.* Soixante. *About sixty,* une soixantaine (de).

sizable [ˈsaizəbl], *a.* D'une bonne grosseur; de la grosseur voulue (par les règlements).

—The New Cassell's French Dictionary
Funk & Wagnalls

Anderson, Marian. 1902– American concert contralto, b. Philadelphia. Began singing career (1924); appeared on concert stage in Europe; recital in New York (Dec. 30, 1935), subsequently appearing successfully throughout U.S. Awarded Spingarn medal (1939).

—By permission.
From *Webster's Biographical Dictionary* © 1980 by G. & C. Merriam Co., Publishers of the Merriam-Webster Dictionaries.

ATLASES   An **atlas** is a book of maps. There are many different kinds of maps in an atlas. There are also, at the back of an atlas, tables listing important geographical facts, such as the highest mountains in the world. If you want to know what the longest river in the world is or what the major products of a certain country are, an atlas is a useful tool.

ALMANACS   How much rain fell in your state last year? What is the birthday of your favorite TV star? What is the population of Hawaii? What is the most popular book in the English language? An **almanac** may give you answers to these and many, many other questions. Almanacs are books of information. They come out every year. So they are useful sources of up-to-date information. Next time you're in the library, look at this year's almanac. You'll be surprised at how many different kinds of facts can be listed in one book.

Try This

1. What reference book would you use to answer each of the following questions? You may find that more than one book would give an answer to some of the questions.

   a. Who was Marie Curie?
   b. How high is Mount Everest?
   c. What does the Spanish word *caballo* mean?
   d. How is glass made?
   e. What are the major products of Chile?
   f. What states border New Jersey?

2. In which reference book would you probably find the following information?

   a. a map of Europe
   b. the year Babe Ruth was born
   c. the yearly rainfall in South Africa
   d. the pronunciation of *platitude*
   e. the origin of the Olympic Games

VOCABULARY STUDY

Multiple Meanings

Zigmore's

The Before-and-After Cream
—That Really Works

Just squirt it on a word and BLAM! The meaning changes!

When **Staff** used our product, he changed from a "rod" into a "group of employees" almost overnight!

Before   *After*

The B & A Cream worked even faster for **Rare**. At nine o'clock **Rare** was "undercooked." By nine-thirty, with a little help from our miracle product, she was "hard to find." (We're still looking for her.)

Before   *After*

But B & A's biggest success story is **Mantle**. **Mantle** began life as a "cloak." Now, after just one application, she is "one of the layers of the inside of the Earth."

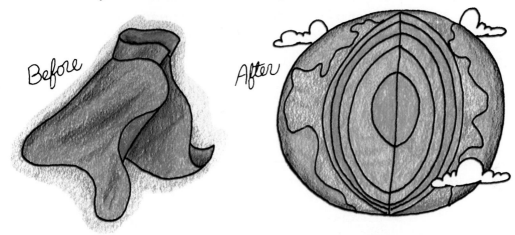

Before

After

So, if you're a word who wants twice the meaning for half the cost, buy Zigmore's Before-and-After Cream. Join the thousands of words who spent their change to make a change.

Zigmore's—$4.98 at supermarkets everywhere.

Word Play

1. For each word in boldface, try to make a sentence that uses the word twice, once for each of the two different meanings of the word. It can be a silly sentence.
2. Use a dictionary to see if you can find a third definition for each word in boldface. Make a sentence with each word using this third meaning.

Newspapers and TV aren't the only places you'll see Charlie Brown and Snoopy. Most libraries have books about them. In the selection below, look for clues to help you know how to find such books in your library.

How did Charles Schulz get his ideas for Lucy and Linus? What parts of Snoopy's personality are based on a real dog's? Charles Schulz is here to tell you about his . . .

Life with the Li'l Folks

by Charles M. Schulz

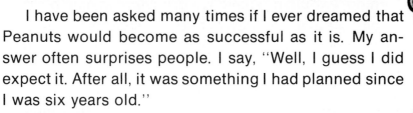

I have been asked many times if I ever dreamed that Peanuts would become as successful as it is. My answer often surprises people. I say, "Well, I guess I did expect it. After all, it was something I had planned since I was six years old."

When I was in grade school, I was a great fan of all the Disney characters. I also enjoyed Popeye and

235

Wimpy very much. I used to decorate my loose-leaf binders with drawings of Mickey Mouse, the Three Little Pigs, and Popeye. Whenever friends in class saw these drawings, I would be asked to draw them on their notebooks as well. I used to buy every comic magazine that came out and study the different ways of drawing.

My dad loved to read the comic strips. We talked about them together and worried about what was going to happen next to some of the characters. On Saturday evening, I would run up to the drugstore at nine o'clock. I'd buy the two Sunday Minneapolis papers. The next morning, I got the two St. Paul papers. So we had four comic sections to read.

Several years later, I became a delivery boy for one of our town's printing firms. I used to pass the windows of the St. Paul *Pioneer Press* and look in. There I saw the huge presses and the Sunday funnies tumbling down across the rollers. I wondered if I would ever see my own comics on these presses.

My mother also encouraged me in my drawing but, sadly, never lived to see any of my work in print.

When I was thirteen, we were given a black-and-white dog. Spike was a mixed breed and a little larger than the beagle Snoopy is supposed to be. On Saturday evenings, just before nine, he always put his paws on my dad's chair to let him know it was time to get in the car and drive up to the store to buy those newspapers. When I decided to put a dog in Peanuts, I used the general appearance of Spike, with similar markings.

I had decided that the dog in the strip was to be named Sniffy. Then one day, when I was walking past a newsstand, I glanced down at the rows of comic magazines. There I saw one about a dog named Sniffy. So I had to go back to my room and think of another name. Before I even got home, I remembered my mother once saying that if we ever had another dog, we should name it Snoopy.

I never wanted to have Snoopy talk. But it became important that he do some kind of thinking. When Snoopy began to think, he took on a personality that was very different from any other cartoon dog's. He was a little smarter than the kids in the strip. But he did suffer a few defeats—you might say, at his own paws. However, most of the time he won out over the kids.

In my childhood, sports were pretty important to my friends and me. I have always tried to use my own knowledge of games in my sports comic strips. Anytime I had crushing defeats in sports, I transferred my frustrations to poor Charlie Brown.

During my senior year in high school, my mother

showed me an ad that read: "Do you like to draw? Send in for our free talent test." This was how I first knew about Art Instruction Schools, Inc. It was and still is in Minneapolis. Even though I could have taken my drawings there in person, I did all the lessons by mail because I was not that proud of my work.

When I was just out of high school, I started to send cartoons to most of the major magazines. But I received only rejection slips. Several years later, I again tried to sell my work. I visited several places in the Twin Cities to try to get a job in an art department. One day, with my sample comic strips in hand, I visited the offices of Timeless Topix comic magazines. The art director seemed to like my lettering. He gave me several comic-book pages that had already been drawn by others but with the balloons left blank. He told me that I should fill in the words. This was my first job.

Soon after I took the job at Timeless Topix, I was also hired by Art Instruction Schools. My job at the school was to correct some of the lessons. There I met many people who did much to help me in my later work. I learned how important it is to draw properly—whether it be a shoe, a doghouse, or a child's hand. Cartooning,

PEANUTS

Copr. 1950 by United Feature Syndicate, Inc.

after all, is simply good design. A good cartoon comes from learning how to design a human hand *after* knowing how to draw it properly.

Some of the people who worked at Art Instruction Schools with me have remained friends all of these years. I have used the names of several people in Peanuts. Charlie Brown was named after my very good friend, Charlie Brown, whose desk was across the room. I remember the day he came over and first looked at the little cartoon face that had been named after him. "Is that what he looks like?" he asked sadly. The characters of Linus and Frieda were also named after friends of mine who were teachers.

I used my spare time, after correcting lessons, to work on my own cartoons. I sold fifteen of them to the *Saturday Evening Post.*

It was an exciting time for me because I was doing just what I wished to do. One day I sold a page of little cartoons that I had drawn and titled "Just Keep Laughing." In one of them was a small boy who looked like Schroeder sitting on the curb with a baseball bat in his hands. He was talking to a little girl who looked like Patty. I made more drawings of little kids. Then I sold

By Schulz

Copr. 1950 by United Feature Syndicate, Inc.

them as a weekly feature called "Li'l Folks" to the St. Paul *Pioneer Press.* Later, the name Li'l Folks was changed to Peanuts.

When Peanuts began in 1950, there were only four characters: Patty, Charlie Brown, Shermy, and Snoopy. I was not sure which one would become the lead. But the personalities soon took care of that. The good lines were given to Charlie Brown or to one of the new characters. After the year 1950, Charlie Brown turned into the loser he is known as today.

When Lucy came into the strip she was a very tiny girl with round eyes. Later I cut the circles in half. She and her brother, Linus, now are the only ones to have tiny half-circles on each side of their eyes.

Lucy's personality was based on that of our oldest daughter, Meredith. We called Meredith a "fussbudget" when she was very small. Linus came from a drawing that I made one day of a face almost like the one he now has. I showed it to a friend of mine whose name was Linus Maurer. He thought it was kind of funny, and we both agreed it might make someone new for the strip. It also seemed that Linus would fit very well as Lucy's younger brother.

I have always believed that you can make the characters do things you want them to. But the characters themselves should give you ideas. The more you can tell one character from another, the better the comic strip will be. Readers can then believe that the characters are real.

To create something out of nothing is a wonderful experience. To take a blank piece of paper and draw characters that people love and worry about is very satisfying. I hope very much that I will be allowed to do it for many years to come.

Understanding What You've Read

1. When did Charles Schulz become interested in comics?
2. How did Schulz's parents help him?
3. From what sources did Schulz get some of his ideas for his comic characters?

Applying the Skills Lesson

1. The selection you just read came from the book *Peanuts Jubilee* by Charles Schulz. How would you find the title card for this book in the card catalogue? How would you find the author card? Under what subjects might you look for other books about comic characters?

2. In which reference books would you find the information asked for in the lettered items below? Choose your answers from the following list of reference sources.

   biographical dictionary   atlas
   dictionary   general encyclopedia

   a. where St. Paul, Minnesota, is
   b. Charles Schulz's date of birth
   c. the meaning of the word *frustration*
   d. general information on comics and cartoons

What reference books would quickly give you information about Maria Tallchief? As you read, think of other ways the library can help you.

Betty Marie Tallchief spent many years of hard work developing her talent. One day the whole world would see her as ...

Truly a Ballerina

by Tobi Tobias

To celebrate her twelfth birthday, Betty Marie Tallchief gave a concert. For the first half she played the piano, and for the second half she danced. That concert, she said, showed how she felt inside. She was split in half between the two things she loved most. One day she would have to choose between them.

By the time she was seventeen, Betty Marie realized what she wanted more than anything else. It was to be a dancer. Her mother understood how much she wanted to dance. She allowed her to go to New York City. Many important dance groups work in New York. There, Betty Marie hoped to find a job in a ballet company.

Betty Marie found a place with the Ballet Russe [roōs] de Monte Carlo. The company traveled from city to city, giving performances. Betty Marie danced so well that people began to notice her. Soon she was given some solo parts.

Ballet life was often hard, though, and Betty Marie was sometimes unhappy. She kept to herself at first, and many people in the company thought she was unfriendly. Some of them were jealous because she was doing so well. Betty Marie missed her family, too. She wrote long letters home.

Still she went on trying, working hard, and learning. Finally, the director of the Ballet Russe, Sergei Denham [ser·gā′ den′əm], asked her to stay on in the company. Of course, she said yes.

Then Mr. Denham decided that she should have a beautiful stage name. So Betty Marie became "Maria." But she refused to change Tallchief. She was proud of her American Indian name.

Maria Tallchief soon had an exciting chance. George Balanchine joined the Ballet Russe. Mr. Balanchine was a well-known choreographer. He also taught dancers. If he picked out a young woman and trained her, she might become a great ballerina.

Maria caught Mr. Balanchine's eye at once. Her dancing was fast and brilliant. She could jump up and beat her long, shapely legs together eight times in the air. She could turn in the air and land on the points of her strong toes. Her balance was sure. Her leaps were sharp and high. Her turns were quick and powerful!

Day after day, Mr. Balanchine worked with Maria. He was a gentle, patient teacher. But he often asked her to perform steps that seemed impossible. She tried over and over again, until she could do what he wanted. Soon she was dancing better than ever before.

Maria Tallchief in the Nutcracker ballet.

After some time, Mr. Balanchine asked Maria to be his wife. She was twenty-one when they were married.

After a short stay in Paris, Mr. Balanchine went back to work at his own studio in New York, the School of American Ballet. He formed a company called Ballet Society with dancers he had trained there. In time, this group would grow into the New York City

Maria Tallchief and George Balanchine rehearse.

Ballet and become one of the best ballet companies in the world. Maria joined this company as its leading dancer when she was twenty-two.

Mr. Balanchine created many wonderful ballets for his company, especially for Maria. One of them was *Firebird*. Maria danced the part of a beautiful, wild bird with magic powers.

Mr. Balanchine set very difficult steps for her. They made the audience gasp with wonder and surprise. Maria flashed across the stage. She flew, she whirled, she slashed through space like a flaming arrow. *Firebird* proved that Maria was truly a ballerina. She was not just a fine dancer, but one of the best in the world.

Understanding What You've Read

1. Why did Maria's mother let her go to New York City?
2. What was ballet life like for Maria when she was dancing with the Ballet Russe?
3. How did George Balanchine help Maria to become a better dancer?

Applying the Skills Lesson

In which reference books would you find the numbered items below? Choose your answers from the following list of reference sources.

atlas	dictionary
biographical dictionary	specialized encyclopedia
general encyclopedia	of dancing

1. how far Fairfax, Oklahoma, is from New York
2. George Balanchine's date of birth
3. information about the history of ballet
4. information about well-known dancers

TEXTBOOK STUDY

Learning to Use Sources of Information

Sometimes you may need to learn more about something you have read in one of your textbooks. If your library skills are sharp, they can save you a lot of time as you gather information. While reading the first selection, think about what sources you could look in to find out more about the information in them. Use the sidenotes to help you.

Using the Library to Learn More in Language Arts

A Book to Read

How would you find this book in the library? Under what letter in the card catalogue would you look for the title?

TITLE: *A Child's World of Stamps*
AUTHOR: *Mildred DePree*
PUBLISHER: Parents' Magazine Press

Whether you are a stamp collector or not (yet), you can have fun on a "tour of the world" by way of the postage stamp. Along with bright, enlarged pictures of stamps, this book presents poems, stories, and interesting facts from all parts of the globe that make stamps come to life.

For example, with a stamp showing an African elephant, you will learn that one of these beasts eats over fifty kilograms of leaves and grass each day. You will see and learn about parrots from South America, pandas from China, and puffins from Scotland.

Some countries have issued stamps to honor certain folk heroes. A stamp from the Middle East shows Sinbad the Sailor being carried away by an enormous bird. What folk hero do you think the United States has placed on a stamp? Johnny Appleseed.

How can you find out what *folk heroes* are? What reference source would help you?

—Language for Daily Use: Purple
Harcourt Brace Jovanovich

Building Skills

1. What reference source might help you find out who Johnny Appleseed and Sinbad the Sailor are? Under what topic would you look to find the information on these folk heroes?
2. Which of the following three reference sources might you use to learn about the hobby of stamp collecting?

   a. a specialized encyclopedia of stamps
   b. an atlas
   c. a biographical dictionary

Using the Library to Learn More in Social Studies

There are no sidenotes for this selection. Read it and then answer the questions that follow.

The Air Above Us

Air is an ever-present resource in our natural **environment.** But people usually take it for granted.

What does air do? For one thing, it moves. When it moves, we call it wind, and we can feel it on our skin.

The sun's heat warms air and causes it to rise. Then cooler air rushes in to take its place. This happens at the equator. It also happens over large land areas. When the sun strikes dry

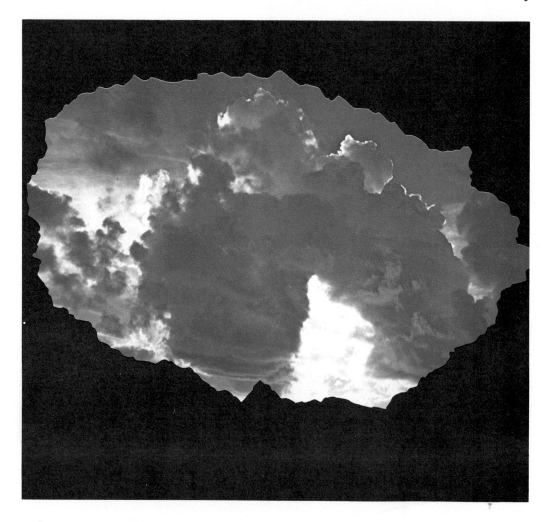

land, the land becomes hotter than the surrounding water. Here, too, air rises. The movement of air, up and down and from place to place, brings changes in the weather.

Why does air move? Air has weight just like anything else. Warm air is lighter than cold air. It has low weight, or low air pressure. Cold air is heavier; it has high weight or high air pressure. Differences in temperature cause differences in the pressure or weight of air. These pressure differences make the wind blow and the weather change.

— The United States
Houghton Mifflin

Building Skills

1. What reference book would tell you what the word *environment* means and how to pronounce it?
2. Below is a list of topics you might find in a general encyclopedia. Which would give you a great deal of information about air? Which would give you some information about air? Which would give you very little or no information about air?

Air
Environment
Weather
United States History

Books About Expressions

Backyard Vacation: Outdoor Fun in Your Own Neighborhood by Ann Cole, Carolyn Haas, and Barbara Naftzger. Illustrated by Roland Rodegast. Little, 1980. Ideas for summer vacation activities are listed in this book.

Chinese and Japanese Crafts and Their Cultural Background by Jeremy Comins. Lothrop, 1978. Many photographs and drawings help tell the story of the beautiful crafts of two rich cultures.

American Indian Music and Musical Instruments by George S. Fitcher. McKay, 1978. You'll find out about the songs and instruments of many different Native American cultures.

What Can She Be? A Newscaster by Gloria Goldreich and Esther Goldreich. Lothrop, 1973. Barbara Lamont is a television newscaster. You'll find out how she and other television newspeople do their jobs.

The Story of Stevie Wonder by James Haskins. Lothrop, 1976. This is about Stevie Wonder's life and how he writes and performs his music.

I Can Cook Cookbook by Sophie Kay. Illustrated by Bill Sanders. Ideals, 1980. This collection of recipes is an easy introduction to cooking.

How to Be a Clown by Charles R. Meyer. McKay, 1977. Here is information about the history of clowning. You'll also find out how to do some of the things that today's circus clowns do to make people laugh.

Part 4

The Poet's Way

UNDERSTANDING AND APPRECIATING LITERATURE

Imagery and Comparisons in Poetry

from

OLIPHAUNT

by J. R. R. TOLKIEN

Grey as a mouse,
Big as a house,
Nose like a snake,
I make the earth shake,
As I tramp through the grass;
Trees crack as I pass.

Authors often use **imagery** — words that appeal to one or more of your senses — to help you imagine and understand more clearly the things they are describing.

Understanding Imagery and Comparisons in Poetry

Read the poem in the cartoon. How does the poet describe Oliphaunt? How does imagery help in the poet's description? The poet uses imagery that helps you *see, hear,* and *feel* an elephant-like animal walking through the jungle. Which word appeals to your sense of touch? Which word appeals to your sense of hearing? You would feel the earth *shake* beneath your feet and hear the trees *cracking* if you were in the jungle with Oliphaunt. How does J. R. R. Tolkien describe Oliphaunt? He tells you that it is "grey as a mouse," and "big as a house," and that it has a "nose like a snake."

The imagery that describes Oliphaunt is based on **comparisons**. How is Oliphaunt like a mouse? They are the same color, gray. How is Oliphaunt like a house? They are both about the same size—big. How is Oliphaunt's nose like a snake? They are shaped the same.

Similes and **metaphors** are two kinds of comparisons. Similes use the word *like* or *as* in their comparisons. Metaphors use just the word *is* or another form of the verb *to be* to link the two things that are being compared.

Read the following sentences. Which ones contain similes? Which contain metaphors?

1. The fresh carrot tasted as sweet as honey.
2. The moon was a silver balloon.
3. The wind is a galloping pony.

Sentence 1 uses a simile. Sentences 2 and 3 use metaphors.

What two things are compared in each sentence? Sentence 1 compares a carrot and honey. Which of your senses does this comparison appeal to? Carrots and honey both *taste* sweet. Sentence 2 compares the moon to a silver balloon. What does this comparison appeal to? This comparison appeals to your *sight*. A full moon may have the same color and shape that a silver balloon does. Sentence 3 compares the wind to a galloping pony. What sense does this comparison appeal to? This comparison appeals to two of your senses. The wind can move so quickly that it *feels* like a pony rushing by. The wind can also *sound* like a pony galloping by. Sometimes comparisons, as well as other kinds of imagery, can appeal to more than one of your senses at the same time.

255

Personification is another kind of comparison. When authors use personification, they describe an object or animal by giving it human characteristics or qualities. Look for personification in this poem about the seasons.

Pencil and Paint

by ELEANOR FARJEON

Winter has a pencil
For pictures clear and neat,
She traces the black tree-tops
Upon a snowy sheet,

But autumn has a palette
And a painting-brush instead,
And daubs the leaves for pleasure
With yellow, brown, and red.

What two things are given human qualities in "Pencil and Paint"? The poet describes winter and autumn as if they were two artists at work. Which of your senses does the imagery in this poem appeal to? This poem uses color words to appeal to your sense of sight. What colors do you see in winter? What colors do you see in autumn? The colors of winter are described as the *black* of the trees and the *white* of the snowy ground and sky. The colors of autumn are described as *yellow*, *brown*, and *red*.

Authors use imagery, or special comparisons, to create descriptions that appeal to your senses. Three kinds of imagery are *simile, metaphor,* and *personification.* Remember, a *simile* compares one thing to another by using the word *as* or *like* to link the two things being compared. A *metaphor* compares one thing to another by using the verb *is* or another form of the verb *to be.* A metaphor does not use *as* or *like* in stating a comparison. *Personification* helps you see something in a new way by giving it human characteristics.

You can use similes, metaphors, and personification as tools to help you more fully understand and enjoy literature and the world around you.

Try This

Read the following poem; then answer the questions.

A Modern Dragon

by ROWENA BASTIN BENNETT

A train is a dragon that roars through the dark.
He wriggles his tail as he sends up a spark.
He pierces the night with his one yellow eye,
And all the earth trembles when he rushes by.

1. What is a train compared to in the poem's first line? Is this comparison a simile, metaphor, or personification?
2. Which word in the first line of the poem appeals to your sense of hearing?
3. Which of your five senses does the imagery in the second and third lines of the poem appeal to?
4. Which of your senses does the imagery in the poem's fourth line appeal to? Which word creates the sensory image?

Writing

1. Write at least three sentences that use personification. Here are some things you might want to write about as if they had human qualities.

    the wind   a dinosaur   a car

2. Write a poem or a paragraph to describe riding in a car, bus, train, or plane. What do you see, hear, smell, taste, or touch? Use similes or metaphors.

As you read "The Poet's Way," notice how the poets use different kinds of imagery to make comparisons.

Look around you. What do you see? Now listen. What do you hear? What do you smell, taste, and touch? The poems that follow use sensory imagery to make some interesting comparisons.

The Whales Off Wales

by X. J. KENNEDY

With walloping tails, the whales off Wales
Whack waves to wicked whitecaps.
And while they snore on their watery floor,
They wear wet woolen nightcaps.

The whales! the whales! the whales off Wales,
They're always spouting fountains.
And as they glide through the tilting tide,
They move like melting mountains.

Autumn Leaves

by EVE MERRIAM

Down
    down
        down
Red
    yellow
        brown
Autumn leaves tumble down
Autumn leaves crumble down
Autumn leaves bumble down
Flaking and shaking,
Tumbledown leaves.

Skittery
Flittery
Rustle by
Hustle by
Crackle and crunch
In a snappety bunch.

Run and catch
Run and snatch
Butterfly leaves
Sailboat leaves
Windstorm leaves.
Can you catch them?

Swoop,
Scoop,
Pile them up
In a stompy pile and
Jump
    Jump
        JUMP!

Glory, Glory ...

by RAY PATTERSON

Across Grandmother's knees
A kindly sun
Laid a yellow quilt.

Check

by JAMES STEPHENS

The Night was creeping on the ground!
She crept and did not make a sound,

Until she reached the tree: And then
She covered it, and stole again

Along the grass beside the wall!
—I heard the rustling of her shawl

As she threw blackness everywhere
Along the sky, the ground, the air,

And in the room where I was hid!
But, no matter what she did

To everything that was without,
She could not put my candle out!

So I stared at the Night! And she
Stared back solemnly at me!

261

Comma in the Sky

by AILEEN FISHER

A comma hung above the park,
a shiny punctuation mark;
we saw it curving in the dark
the night the moon was new.

A period hung above the bay,
immense though it was far away;
we saw it at the end of day
the night the moon was full.

I Go Forth to Move About the Earth

by ALONZO LOPEZ

I go forth to move about the earth.
I go forth as the owl, wise and knowing.
I go forth as the eagle, powerful and bold.
I go forth as the dove, peaceful and gentle.
I go forth to move about the earth
      in wisdom, courage, and peace.

Understanding What You've Read

1. Find at least one example of personification in the first stanza of "The Whales Off Wales" (page 258). What simile is used in the second stanza?
2. Which stanza of "Autumn Leaves" (page 259) uses imagery that appeals mostly to your sense of hearing? Find at least three words in this stanza that tell you how autumn leaves sound.
3. In "Comma in the Sky" (page 262), what two things does the poet compare the moon to? What do these comparisons tell you about the moon?

Writing

1. "Glory, Glory . . ." (page 260) compares sunlight to a yellow quilt. Write a sentence that uses another metaphor for sunlight.
2. "The Whales Off Wales" (page 258) is a funny poem because of the imagery and because of the poet's use of personification. The poet gives the whales human characteristics: they snore and they wear woolen nightcaps. Write your own paragraph or poem about an animal. Use at least one simile and one example of personification. You may wish to write about one of the following animals:

   A seal giving itself a bubble bath
   A monkey chatting with a friend

The following poems are all about things people like to do. You will see how poets use similes, metaphors, and personification to help you feel what it is like to take a bike ride, camp out under the stars, ski down a hill, and watch an exciting basketball game.

On Our Bikes

by LILLIAN MORRISON

The roads to the beach
            are winding
   we glide down
            breeze-whipped
 curving
         past hills of sand
   pedal and coast
          through wide smell of the sea
           old familiar sunfeel
     windwallop.

Race you to the water's edge!

Open Range

by KATHRYN and BYRON JACKSON

Prairie goes to the mountain,
   Mountain goes to the sky.
The sky sweeps across to the distant hills
And here, in the middle,
   Am I.

Hills crowd down to the river,
   River runs by the tree.
Tree throws its shadow on sunburnt grass
And here, in the shadow,
   Is me.

Shadows creep up the mountain,
   Mountain goes black on the sky,
The sky bursts out with a million stars
And here, by the campfire,
   Am I.

 Skiing

by ROSE BURGUNDER

Fast as foxes,
buzzy as bees,
down the slope
on our silver-tipped skis—

early in the morning
Roseanna and I
far from our house
on the hilltop fly.

A snowbird's yawning,
the sky's all pink,
somewhere in the valley
the lights still blink.

No one's awake
but us, and a bird.
The day's too beautiful
to speak a word.

Foul Shot

by EDWIN A. HOEY

With two 60's stuck on the scoreboard
And two seconds hanging on the clock,
The solemn boy in the center of eyes,
Squeezed by silence,
Seeks out the line with his feet,
Soothes his hands along his uniform,
Gently drums the ball against the floor,
Then measures the waiting net,
Raises the ball on his right hand,
Balances it with his left,
Calms it with fingertips,
Breathes,
Crouches,
Waits,
And then through a stretching of stillness,
Nudges it upward.

The ball
Slides up and out,
Lands,
Leans,
Wobbles,
Wavers,
Hesitates,
Exasperates,
Plays it coy
Until every face begs with unsounding screams—

And then

   And then

      And then,

Right before ROAR-UP,
Dives down and through.

Understanding What You've Read

1. Find at least one example of imagery in "On Our Bikes" (page 265) that appeals to your sense of touch. Find an example of imagery in the same poem that appeals to your sense of smell.
2. In "Skiing" (page 267), what does the poet compare the skiers to? Are these comparisons similes, metaphors, or personification?
3. What are some of the words in "Foul Shot" (pages 268–269) that compare a basketball to a person?

Writing

1. Use comparisons to write three sentences or a short poem about one of the following sports. Use imagery that appeals to your senses of smell, touch, and sight.

   swimming   baseball   running

2. The imagery in "Open Range" appeals mostly to your sense of sight. Think about what it would be like to go camping. Then write your own paragraph or poem. Use imagery that tells what you would hear, taste, or smell.

Get ready to meet a snopp, a dream woman, and a ghost. Look for the imagery and comparisons the poets use to help describe the imaginary characters and create the mood in each of the narrative poems that follow.

The Snopp on the Sidewalk

by JACK PRELUTSKY

It was lying on the sidewalk
like a gray old ragged mop,
but the second that I saw it,
I was sure I'd found the snopp.

It did not move a fiber
of its long and shaggy hair,
as if seeming not to notice
that I stood and watched it there.

At first I thought, "I'll touch it,"
and then I thought, "I won't,"
but when again I thought, "I will,"
the snopp said softly, "Don't."

271

This startled me so greatly
that I turned to run away,
but as I started down the street,
the snopp called after, "Stay."

I asked, "What do you want of me,
for snopp, I cannot guess?"
The snopp, still never stirring,
only answered me with, "Yes."

I did not understand this
so I tried once more to go,
but I'd barely started homeward
when the snopp said sweetly, "No."

And so I stayed that day and night,
and yes, I stayed a week,
and nevermore in all that time
did either of us speak.

At last I said, "Oh snopp, dear snopp,
I really have to go."
The snopp showed no emotion
as it whispered only, "Oh."

I headed home, not looking back,
afraid to ever stop.
I knew that if I paused but once
I'd never leave the snopp.

But the snopp remains within my mind,
I'm sure it always will—
that strange thing on the sidewalk
that I'm certain lies there still.

The Dream Woman

by PATRICIA HUBBELL

Early in the morning
Before the lights are on,
The dream woman scurries
Uptown and down.
Leaping in my window
She rushes to my bed,
Grasps at my dream
And wrings it from my head.
Quickly, quietly, she stuffs it in her bag,
Snaps shut the clasp
And runs from my side.
Out at the window,
Down a film of air,
The dream woman hurries
Lest the dawn appear.

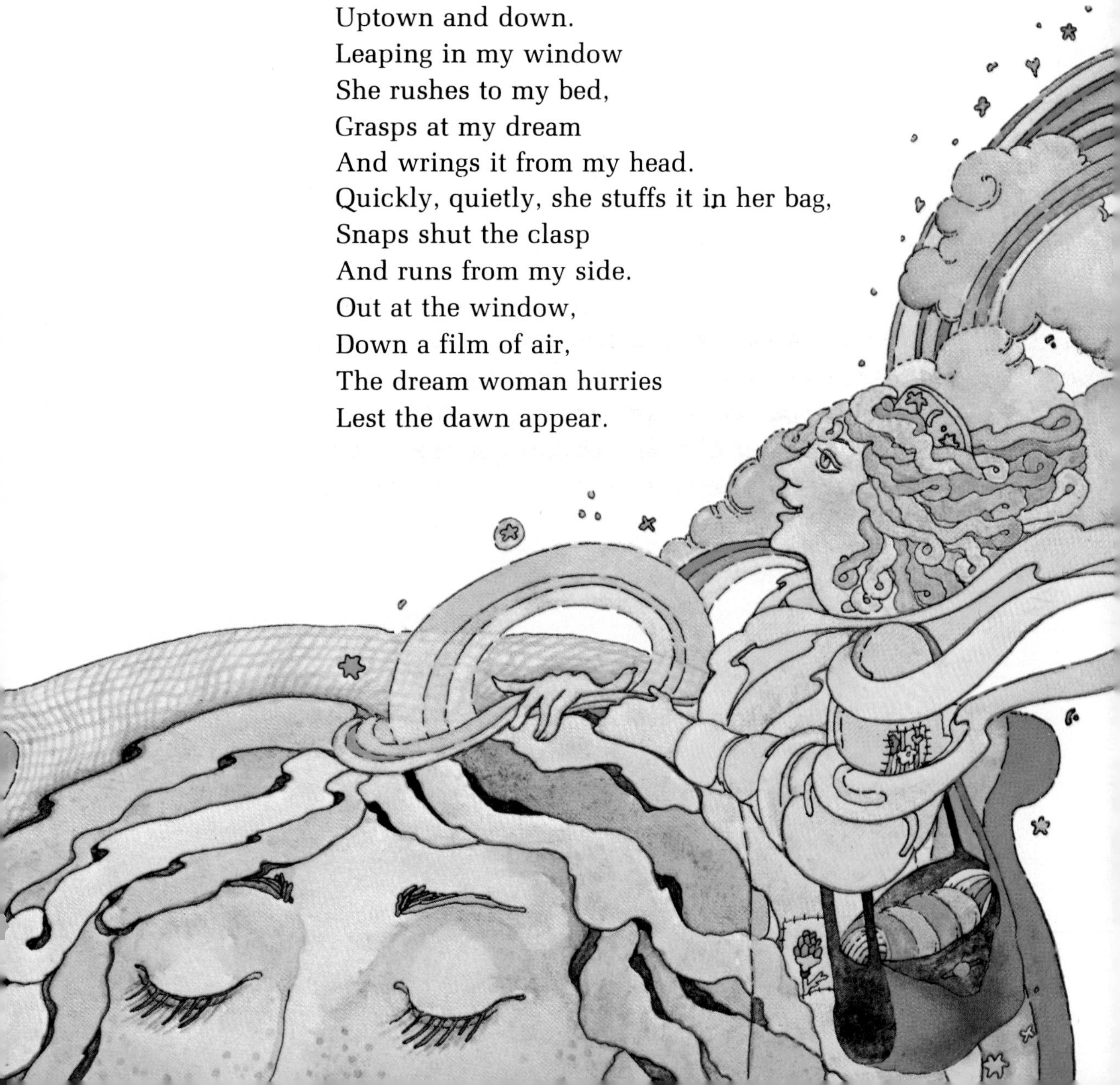

When her bag is piled high
With dreams sad and gay,
She hurries to her home
To spin them all away.
She sits beside her spinning wheel,
She sits beside her loom,
And spins without ceasing
From morning until noon.

She gathers up the dreams
From her small black bag,
Shuffles them and sorts them
By color and by size,
Piles up the pink dreams,
Irons out the black,
Dyes a little white one
To match another scrap;
Gets out the darning needle,
Mends one that's torn,
And adds a slight embellishment
To one that's worn.

275

Nancy Hanks

by ROSEMARY BENÉT and STEPHEN VINCENT BENÉT

If Nancy Hanks
Came back as a ghost,
Seeking news
Of what she loved most,
She'd ask first
"Where's my son?
What's happened to Abe?
What's he done?"

"Poor little Abe,
Left all alone
Except for Tom,
Who's a rolling stone;
He was only nine
The year I died.
I remember still
How hard he cried.

"Scraping along
In a little shack,
With hardly a shirt
To cover his back,
And a prairie wind
To blow him down,
Or pinching times
If he went to town.

"You wouldn't know
About my son?
Did he grow tall?
Did he have fun?
Did he learn to read?
Did he get to town?
Did you know his name?
Did he get on?"

Understanding What You've Read

1. In the first stanza of "The Snopp on the Sidewalk" (page 271), what does the poet compare the snopp to? What does this tell you about the snopp?
2. What does the dream woman do with the dreams she gathers? What does the poet compare dreams to? Which of your senses does the imagery in the poem appeal to most?
3. Look at the third stanza of "Nancy Hanks" (page 276). What words show that Nancy was worried about Abe's being poor and feeling cold?

Writing

1. Write at least three sentences about an imaginary animal. Use similes to help you describe it. You may wish to use one of the following imaginary animals:

   a babbit   a flouse   a prump

2. Write a paragraph or a narrative poem about an imaginary person. Use similes, metaphors, and personification in your descriptions. You may wish to use one of the following people:

   The Star Hanger   The Mountain Builder
                  The Ocean Mover

More Poems to Read

Four Corners of the Sky selected by Theodore Clymer. Little, 1975. Native American poems, chants, and oratory from many cultures are beautifully illustrated.

Straight On till Morning: Poems of the Imaginary World selected by Helen Hill, Agnes Perkins, and Althea Helag. T. Y. Crowell, 1977. This book includes poems of magic and mystery.

On Our Way: Poems of Pride and Love selected by Lee Bennett Hopkins. Knopf, 1974. Here are poems by twenty-two black poets, including Gwendolyn Brooks, Nikki Giovanni, and Langston Hughes.

Piping Down the Valleys Wild edited and introduced by Nancy Larrick. Delacorte, 1968. This book includes popular poems of many moods.

The Moment of Wonder: A Collection of Chinese and Japanese Poetry collected by Richard Lewis. Dial, 1974. Here is a book of beautiful, imaginative poems.

As I Walked Out One Evening: A Book of Ballads selected by Helen Plotz. Greenwillow Bks., 1976. Here are 130 ballads of the English-speaking world.

Laughing Time compiled by William Jay Smith. Delacorte, 1980. This collection of poems is bound to make you laugh.

How Beastly! A Menagerie of Nonsense Poems by Jane Yolen. Collins, 1980. These poems are all about imaginary animals.

Part 5

Learning About America's Past

Finding the Topic and Main Idea
of a Paragraph

What do the pictures above have in common? Did you say that the animals are all members of the cat family? Good! Now figure out what all the sentences in the following paragraph have in common.

Many famous authors are better known by their pen names than by their real names. You may know that "Mark Twain" was a pen name used by Samuel Clemens. But did you know that "Lewis Carroll," author of *Alice in Wonderland,* was really a mathematician named Charles Dodgson? "Dr. Seuss," the author of books for young people, is really Theodor Geisel.

All the sentences in the paragraph said something about *authors' pen names*. If you recognized this, then you recognized the **topic** of the paragraph. The topic of a paragraph is what all or most of the sentences are about.

Finding the Stated Main Idea of a Paragraph

Do you remember what the **main idea** of a paragraph is? It's the most important thing the paragraph says about the topic.

You find the topic of a paragraph by asking yourself (and answering) this question: What are most of the sentences in this paragraph about? You find the main idea by answering this question: What is the most important thing that the paragraph *says* about the topic?

Read the paragraph below. First decide what its topic is. Then look for the most important idea in the paragraph.

Wind-chill gives a truer measure of cold weather than temperature alone does. A temperature of −7°C on a day when winds are only eight kilometers per hour gives a wind-chill of −9°C. But on that day, if the wind begins to blow at sixty-four kilometers per hour, wind-chill makes it feel more like it's −30°C.

It's easy to see that the topic of the paragraph is *wind-chill*. Each sentence says something about this topic. What is the most important thing the paragraph says about wind-chill? Notice that the main idea is stated in the first sentence: "Wind-chill gives a truer measure of cold weather than temperature alone does."

A main idea may also be stated in the last sentence of a paragraph. Find the topic and main idea in the following paragraph.

The first kind of energy used for transportation most likely was water. Perhaps someone fell into a rushing river and held on to a floating log. This might have given the person the idea of making a raft. Sometime after that, someone had the idea of "catching" the wind—in sails. Perhaps a few hundred years later someone decided to hitch an ox to a cart. Animal power was born. Until about four hundred years ago, water, wind, and animal power were the only kinds of energy that people used for transportation.

What is the topic of the paragraph?

1. energy for transportation
2. the first raft
3. animal power

Is every sentence about the first raft? No. Does every sentence tell you about animal power? No. But every sentence says something about *energy for transportation.* Which sentence in the paragraph states the most important idea about the topic?

You have seen that a main idea can be stated in the first or the last sentence of a paragraph. But remember, a main idea can also be stated somewhere in the middle of a paragraph.

Try This

Read each of the following paragraphs. State the topic of each. Then find the sentence that states the main idea in each paragraph.

1.   What happened in 1611? What causes tides? Who won medals in the 1976 Olympics? You can find the answers to these and other questions in an almanac. An almanac may even list such things as the speeds of the fastest animals in the world. Where can you look to find facts about your home state? You guessed it — in the almanac!

2.   The National Zoo in Washington, D. C. is part of the Smithsonian Institution. It is best known as the home of the two giant pandas, Ling-Ling and Hsing-Hsing [shing'shing']. Lincoln Park in Chicago has more visitors than any other American zoo. More than 4 million people visit Lincoln Park each year. Visitors to New York City's Bronx Zoo can see the whole park as they ride above it in an airlift. The St. Louis Zoo's "Cat Country" and sea-life house offer visitors a pleasant way to learn about living things. As you can see, America has many wonderful zoos.

3.   Rebecca Boone was as much a pioneer as her husband, Daniel Boone. Together, they made their home in the wild woods of the American frontier. In 1775 the Boones moved to Boonesboro, a settlement on the Kentucky River. Rebecca and her daughter, Jemima, were the first Caucasian women to see this part of Kentucky.

VOCABULARY STUDY

Synonyms

The not-so-evil Professor Crum sat in the flickering light of a candle and wrote in his diary.

Dear Diary,

I'm sure I **mentioned** that I work part-time in a health food store. I think I said it in my last entry. Well, things have gone from bad to worse. You know how I'm **considered** to be the foulest, most rotten person alive. People have judged me even more horrible than Billy the Kid. But that was yesterday. Today I am on shaky ground. The owner of the health food store says I'm the best juice squeezer this side of the Rockies. And that is a huge, **immense** blow to my evil reputation. What will the world think of me? I'd better do something nasty soon, or I'm finished for good. But don't worry, Diary, because I'm hatching a plan.

Word Play

1. Professor Crum used synonyms to explain the boldfaced words in the diary page above. Reword each sentence below using the *synonym* for each boldfaced word. Remember that synonyms are words that have nearly the same meanings.

   a. Chan is **considered** the best goalie on our soccer team.
   b. Miranda **mentioned** that she was planning to visit.
   c. When Jan baked cookies, she put them too close together on the tray. They melted into one **immense** cookie.

2. Look up *foul*, *horrible*, and *reputation* in a dictionary. Then find a synonym for each word and use the synonym in a sentence.

In many paragraphs in this selection, the main idea is stated in the first or last sentence. Look for the main ideas as you read.

A brave Native American woman wanted to get back to her home. Little did she know that history books would later record her trip and explain the importance of the . . .

Journey of the Tejas Woman

by Kathryn Hitte

Coronado

DeSoto

In the years from 1540 to 1543, two huge parties of adventurers explored much of the land that is now the United States. They were Spanish men who had come to the New World in search of treasure. They had heard tales of great riches to be found north of Mexico—unbelievable riches! Some said there were golden cities there!

Hernando De Soto led one party westward from what is now Florida. Almost at the same time, Francisco de Coronado led *his* men first northward from Mexico and then eastward. Each group was eager to be first to find the trea-

As far as we know, she was a Tejas woman. The Tejas tribe made their home in what is today eastern Texas. It is from their tribal name—which means "Hello, friend"—that the state's name comes.

We know very little about the Tejas Woman. Her story is found in a history of Coronado's journey. It was recorded by Castañeda, who was with

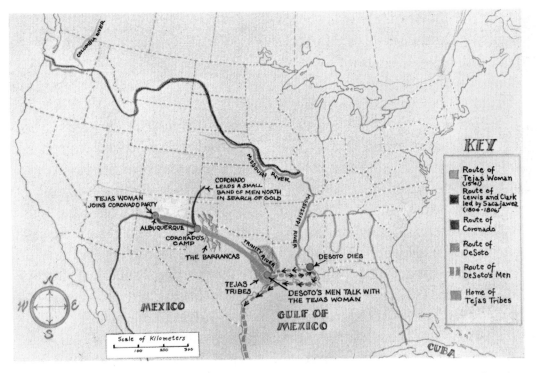

sure. They never met on their journeys. But a Native American woman became a link that joined them.

Coronado. Castañeda did not tell us the woman's name.

Her part in history begins in the land of the Pueblo people of the area now called New Mexico. She was living there, far from her home, when Coronado's party reached this area. How she got there we can only guess.

When Coronado headed east again, several Native Americans went along. The Tejas Woman was one of them.

It was the spring of 1541. Coronado's group of explorers came to vast, treeless grasslands that went on mile after mile. Thousands of buffalo grazed here. The land was so flat, Castañeda wrote, that he could "see the sky under a horse's body."

Did the woman know how close they were coming to her home? We wonder.

The plains ended. A world of rocky cliffs and canyons lay before the explorers. They had reached what the Spanish called the *Barrancas.* Here were steep cliffs of colored rock carved by the winds. Here were many ravines and canyons, deep hollows in the earth. They blocked the way east for many miles.

To Coronado and his men,
the Barrancas brought only problems and discouragement. But they brought joy to the heart of the Tejas Woman.

"She recognized the country," Castañeda wrote. He was a good reporter. As you read his report, you feel that he was not making anything up. The woman had been here before! She must have shown some kind of excitement that Castañeda noticed.

Coronado decided not to try to cross the Barrancas. Instead, he would take a small

We know what the land was like there. We can easily imagine that the Tejas Woman must have known how to make her own way in the wild. She would get water from the rushing streams and shelter from the trees. Fruits and nuts and fish would be her food.

She would come out of the canyons into rolling prairie land—little hills and fields. Then would come forests and the best farmland around. She would be home. Home among the farms and villages of her own people, the Tejas, at last!

We have no facts of her homecoming. We know only what came later. It happened almost exactly one year after the woman left Coronado's party. It concerns those rival gold seekers, De Soto's men.

They had traveled westward, remember. By this time, De Soto himself was dead. His men had journeyed on under a new leader. They were weary and discouraged. They had come a long, long way. But they had found no treasure.

group of horsemen northward and search for the golden cities there. The rest of his party must camp here, near the Barrancas, until he sent them word.

The Tejas Woman may not have understood the talk among the Spanish. But she knew what she saw. She knew what was happening.

According to Castañeda's report, "She fled down the Barrancas." She went eastward through the ravines and canyons—alone.

In the summer of 1542, they reached a Tejas village. There

they learned of a woman who had traveled with others like themselves, other Spaniards. De Soto's men found the woman and somehow talked with her. They were excited by her story. They told it in Mexico afterward.

Think back a minute. What a strange, wild chance that meeting was! Think of the size of the North American continent! How many other ways De Soto's men might have gone! Yet they came *this* way. They reached *this* village, where *this* woman lived. And she remembered names.

Those Spanish names told De Soto's men that she spoke the truth. She gave them a sense of contact with their own people that must have cheered them. And they could guess from her story that their rivals had found no riches, either.

Of what importance, really, is the Tejas Woman's story? She did not play a great part in an explorer's journey, as the Shoshone woman Sacajawea later did. (From 1804 to 1806, Sacajawea led Lewis and Clark on their famous journey.) The Tejas Woman meant little to the Coronado party.

She meant only a bit more to De Soto's men. Yet she is mentioned today in a number of books. She is given a place in American history. Why?

Because of her, the continent was crossed for the first time. Coronado reached what is now western Texas. De Soto's men reached eastern Texas. The woman's journey linked the two. That is a major event in American history.

Because of that crossing, the size of North America could be judged for the first time. After the 1500's, maps of America slowly began to improve, to look more as they should.

Here is a last thought. Of those three journeys that together spanned the continent, only one had a happy ending. The nameless woman of the Tejas people found *her* treasure when she found her home.

Understanding What You've Read

1. Why was the Tejas Woman's journey an important event in United States history?
2. What was the difference between the journey of the Tejas woman and that of Sacajawea?
3. How do we know about the Tejas Woman's journey?

Applying the Skills Lesson

1. Read the first paragraph of the selection on pages 286–287. What is the topic of that paragraph? What is the main idea?
2. What is the topic of the first full paragraph on this page (page 291)? Which sentence states the main idea of that paragraph?

In this selection, some paragraphs deal with the topic of Lady Moody's life in Boston. Other paragraphs deal with the topic of her plans for a settlement. As you read, think about the topic of each paragraph. Look for sentences that state the main idea of the paragraph.

A place where all people could find freedom. In the early 1600's, this was . . .

Lady Moody's Dream

by Dina Brown Anastasio

Lady Deborah Moody looked out at the ocean beyond her town. She remembered the long, slow trip across the Atlantic from England after her husband's death. She remembered arriving in 1640 in Boston, where she hoped to find her dream of complete freedom of religion for all people.

But it was not to be. The leaders of Boston, she soon discovered, were not very different from those in England. Everyone, it seemed, was expected to worship and live according to the wishes of the leaders.

In Boston, Lady Moody wondered if she had made a mistake. She compared her new life to the one she had left behind. She had been a very wealthy woman in England. She had owned acres and acres of land. She had lived in a huge mansion surrounded by gardens and greenhouses. As a child, she had been taught by the best tutors. Later, she had gone to college in Paris.

Nevertheless, during the two years that she lived in Boston, she found things that she had never known in England. She found the joy of sharing hardship and laughter with her neighbors. She lived in a fine stone house near the village green. Every night, her neighbors left their small log homes and joined her in front of the fire in her kitchen. During the day their children gathered in her home, and she taught them to read and write.

Her life was a hard one, and there was a great deal of work to be done. But the work soon proved to be fun. The colonists had learned from the American Indians how to tap the maple sugar trees. Every year, sugar-making time brought with it a party. Corn planting—also learned from the American Indians—was another chance for a party.

But the lack of freedom in Boston finally became too much for Lady Moody. She realized that she must move on.

From Boston, Lady Moody, her son Sir Harry, and several of their friends sailed to Salem, Massachusetts. But again they failed to find the freedom they were seeking.

Once more they set out in search of their dream. They sailed down the New England coast in 1642 and reached the mouth of the Hudson River at what is now New York City. At that time it was a Dutch settlement called New Amsterdam.

One day shortly after their arrival, Lady Moody stood on the tip of New Amsterdam and looked across the river to Brooklyn. At that moment she knew that her search was over at last. She knew that if she could not find the freedom she was searching for, she would make it herself. So she bought a large piece of land in the southern part of Brooklyn, which was then wilderness. She was the first woman ever to buy land in America. She became the first woman to start an American settlement.

Lady Moody chose a name for her settlement—Gravesend. It was the name of the small town in England where, before her husband's death, Lady Moody and her family had spent many happy moments.

Lady Moody did not think of herself as an architect. She had no such training. But she drew up a plan for her town. Three hundred years later, her plan would be put in a museum. She would be known as one of America's first architects.

In Lady Moody's plan, forty triangular lots surrounded a town square. In the square, the settlers and the American Indians could gather to make plans and talk with their neighbors. Near the square there would be a meeting house. There would also be a church where people of all faiths could worship.

Within a few years, the town grew. Houses and crops gleamed in the sunshine. The American Indians' watchful eyes took on many expressions. There were times of anger and times of peace. There were times of misunderstanding and times of understanding. And then there came a time when their eyes began to fill with friendship.

It had taken eighteen years, but Lady Moody's dream had become a reality.

Understanding What You've Read

1. Why did Lady Moody move to Boston?
2. How were Boston's leaders like England's leaders?
3. What was Lady Moody's life like in Boston?
4. How did Lady Moody make her dream come true?

Applying the Skills Lesson

1. The list below states the topics of some of the paragraphs in the selection you just read. Look back at the selection. Find the paragraphs whose topics are listed below.

   a. the paragraph on page 293 about *Lady Moody's life in England*
   b. the paragraph on page 295 about the topic *the name Gravesend*
   c. the paragraph on page 295 about the topic *how Gravesend would look*

2. The main idea of the first paragraph on page 294 is stated. What is the main idea of that paragraph?

TEXTBOOK STUDY

Recognizing Topics and Main Ideas

Since textbooks are written to give information, they are generally arranged to help the reader easily find the main ideas of paragraphs. Often, the main idea of a paragraph is stated.

Think about each paragraph's topic. Then look for the main idea. Use the sidenotes to help you.

Recognizing Topics and Main Ideas in Science

Some kind of plant will grow almost anywhere on the earth. Plants grow in the spaces between the parts of the sidewalks. They grow in window boxes in cities. You would have a hard time finding a place where plants do not grow. Some plants grow in damp soil; some in deserts. Some grow in ponds and streams, while others grow in the ocean. Plants can grow on mountaintops and in the cold of the Arctic.

Plants can grow on many kinds of objects. Perhaps you have seen plants growing on rocks and trees. Plants even grow on old shoes and on animals. Where else have you seen plants growing?

—Understanding Your Environment
Silver Burdett

Ask yourself what all of the sentences in the first paragraph are about. Your answer is the topic of the paragraph.

Notice that the topic of this paragraph is very much like the topic of the paragraph above. What is the difference between the two topics?

Building Skills

1. Below is a list of three topics. Which is the topic of the first paragraph? Which is the topic of the second paragraph? Which is *not* a topic of either of the paragraphs you just read?

   a. objects plants will grow on
   b. where plants will grow
   c. how plants grow

2. The main ideas of the two paragraphs above are stated. In each paragraph, find the sentence that states the main idea.

Recognizing Topics and Main Ideas in Language Arts

This heading is a clue as to what most of the paragraphs are about in this selection.

This first paragraph introduces the topic of *where the names of the settlers' new homes came from.* Which sentence states the main idea?

How Our Language Grows

New Homes — Old Names

Settlers brought their own names from Europe to America, and, naturally, they brought the names of their home towns as well. It probably made them feel more at home in the New World to give a colony the name of a familiar and honored Old World Place.

Many English settlers made their homes on the East Coast. A map of this part of our country will show you a *Boston,* a *London,* and a *Richmond.* All are named for places in England. Settlers often added *New* to the names of their homes. We have *New Boston, New London, New York, New Hampshire,* and *New Jersey.*

As settlers moved westward across America, the same names went right along with them. Pioneers who left the East founded *Richmonds* in eleven Western states. There is a *Philadelphia* in Illinois, Mississippi, Missouri, and Tennessee — all named after the one in Pennsylvania.

English cities are not the only ones to have namesakes in America. There are *Berlins,* named for the German city; *Venices* and *Romes* named for cities in Italy; *Athenses* and *Spartas* named for Greek cities. Russian settlers in Idaho named a city *Moscow.* *Lima,* Ohio, was named for the city in Peru. A city in Illinois is named for *Cairo,* Egypt.

This sentence states the main idea of the paragraph. How many examples are given to support this idea?

— Language for Daily Use: Purple
Harcourt Brace Jovanovich

Building Skills

1. State the topic of the second paragraph, the third paragraph, and the fourth paragraph in the above selection.
2. Find the sentence that states the main idea of the third paragraph in the above selection.

Understanding Unstated Main Ideas and the Details in a Paragraph

"I'm going to a place that has sharks, tigerfish, seahorses, whales, starfish, and a cafeteria!"

The girl in the cartoon is giving you a lot of details about where she's going. Where do you think she's going? An aquarium? A pet store? The circus? From the *details*, you should be able to tell that she's going to an aquarium.

A **detail** is a piece of information. In a paragraph, it may be a word, a group of words, or a whole sentence. When the main idea of a paragraph is stated, the other sentences are usually details that support or explain the main idea. Look for details that support the main idea in the following paragraph.

In the early 1800's, Oregon was claimed by four nations. Spain said that Balboa's discovery of the Pacific Ocean gave Spain the right to settle Oregon. England said that Oregon was English land because Sir Francis Drake had sailed along

Oregon's coast in 1579. A Russian sailor named Bering had explored the northern Pacific Ocean in the 1700's. Russia therefore claimed rights to both Alaska and Oregon. The United States based its claim to Oregon on the explorations made by Sacajawea and Lewis and Clark from 1804 to 1806.

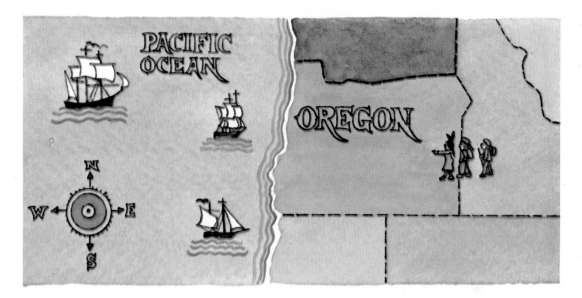

The main idea of the paragraph is stated in the first sentence: "In the early 1800's, Oregon was claimed by four nations." How do the other sentences support this idea?

When the Main Idea Is Not Stated

In many paragraphs, the main idea is not stated in one sentence. But you can state the main idea yourself if you understand what all the details add up to. You can find an unstated main idea in the same way you found the main idea of the cartoon on page 300. You added up the details and were able to figure out that the little girl is going to an aquarium.

The main idea of the following paragraph is not stated.

Use the details in order to figure out the paragraph's main idea. Remember, the main idea is the most important idea about the topic of a paragraph.

For many years, most Americans lived in small towns or on farms. As late as 1880, only two people out of every ten lived in a city. By 1920, however, half the people in the United States lived in cities. Today more than seven out of ten Americans are city-dwellers.

Each sentence tells where Americans lived at a special time in our history — in 1880, 1920, and today. Each sentence gives a detail that contributes to the main idea. Which of the following sentences states that main idea best?

1. For many years, most Americans lived in small towns or on farms.
2. Since 1880, the United States has changed from a nation of country-dwellers to a nation of city-dwellers.
3. Today many people live in cities.

Read sentence 1 again. Does this sentence tell you anything about where Americans live today? No. It tells you only about the way things were in the past. It is a detail. Why is sentence 3 only a detail? The paragraph tells you that Americans have moved from the country to cities over the years. Therefore, sentence 2 best states the main idea.

Try This

In each of the following paragraphs, the main idea is not stated in one sentence. First find the topic of each paragraph. Then think of what the paragraph *says* about that topic. Notice the details that support the main idea.

1. In 1608, France sent many families to settle in "New France" in America. Holland also sent settlers to America. The Dutch settlement of New Amsterdam was started in 1624. From 1580 until the early 1600's, many English people also tried to start colonies in America.

What is the topic of the paragraph?

a. English settlements in America
b. European settlements in America
c. French settlements in America

What is the main idea of the paragraph?

a. France, Holland, and England tried to build American colonies in the late 1500's and early 1600's.
b. Early settlements in America were successful.
c. From 1580 until the early 1600's, many English people tried to start colonies in America.

2. Lara tries to get enough sleep each night. She makes sure that she gets the right kinds of food. She avoids eating sweets or too much of any one kind of food. Lara also makes a point of getting lots of fresh air and exercise.

What is the topic of the paragraph?
a. what Lara likes to eat
b. what Lara does every day
c. how Lara takes care of her body's needs

What is the main idea of the paragraph?
a. Lara is an interesting person.
b. Lara does things to keep healthy.
c. Lara tries to get enough sleep at night.

3. Cities are interesting places to many people. For example, New York has many museums, art galleries, theaters, and restaurants for people to enjoy. It also has great landmarks like the Empire State Building, the Statue of Liberty, the United Nations headquarters, and Rockefeller Center. Some people even find riding New York's subways interesting.

What is the main idea of the paragraph?
a. New York is an interesting place.
b. Cities are interesting places to many people.
c. New York's subways are interesting.

VOCABULARY STUDY

Suffixes

The Suffix Song

Oh, I'm a famous suffix
And my meaning is "without."
I'll take away most anything,
Of that there is no doubt.
A **treeless** forest has no trees
To rustle, shake, or bend;
And **endless** is the word we use
For things that have no end.
There's scoreless, matchless,
Worthless, priceless,
Nameless, "with no name";
And airless, careless, toothless, hairless,
Blameless, "with no blame."
The twelve words I have shown you
Should be enough to guess
My spelling and identity,
I'm L-E-S-S, *-less*!

Word Play

1. In the paragraph below, replace each phrase in parentheses with a boldfaced word from the song above.

   Our new baseball team can't decide on a name for our team. So we are playing (with no name). We thought of the "Pine Cones," but half the team wanted a tree on the shirt and half wanted the shirt (with no tree). We're all thinking of names for the team, but our list is (with no end). I think we should be called Teamless.

2. Make a sentence for each word with the *-less* suffix, or ending, in the song.

In many of the paragraphs in this selection, the main idea is not stated. You can state the main idea yourself. First find the topic. Then use the details to figure out the main idea.

The Peddler's Pack

by Charlotte MacLeod

If you lived two hundred years ago, you might wonder what you'd find in . . .

Have you ever heard someone say, "I'm waiting for my ship to come in"? Before the American Revolution, colonists were always waiting for their ships to come in because they were not supposed to manufacture anything for sale. Their British rulers wanted them to buy goods made in England. The only way to buy a piece of cloth or a pan or a printing press or even a pin was to order it from the "old country." When a ship docked, everybody would run to the waterfront and barter with the sailors for whatever had been brought on the voyage.

As time went on and more colonists came, towns around the waterfront got too crowded. People began moving away from the seaports. In the vast wilderness, they found plenty of places to settle.

Now, however, they were too far away to trade with the ships for the many things they needed. They had no stores in which to shop. They had no neighbors to lend them a tool or a dish or a pinch of salt.

Still, the settlers didn't have to go entirely without the manufactured articles that made life a little bit easier. Some brave and clever young people decided to become peddlers. They went to the ships and bought everything they could from the sailors. Then, with big packs on their backs, they walked into the wilderness looking for customers.

Peddlers could make a great deal of money if they weren't afraid of danger and hard work. Most of the time there were no roads to follow. A peddler had to rely on the sun and stars to guide the way. He had to hope he would be lucky enough to find a settlement. When a peddler did find one, the people gathered around him. He told them news of the outside world. Perhaps he carried a message from a friend or relative. For a while, he joked and told stories. Then he opened his pack and began to trade.

In early times, it didn't much matter what the peddler showed the settlers. They needed so many things that there was always a customer for every item in his pack. Even a needle or thread was a treasure.

Everyone wanted to buy, but few had money—partly because the colonists were forbidden to make their own coinage. So instead of nickels and dimes and dollar bills, the settlers might offer the peddler food grown on their farms, yarn spun from their sheep, or skins of animals.

Sometimes, a peddler might use a river as his "expressway." Poling a raft was often better than cutting a path through swamps and thickets. Still, travel by water could be hard and dangerous. The peddler might be caught in a

storm and swept overboard with his precious cargo.

Picture a tired peddler poling a heavy raftload of goods he hoped to trade along the riverbank. How happy he must have been to find a farmhouse. Perhaps he would say, "If you help me, I will stay and keep a store. Settlers will come to trade and be your neighbors. You can build a school."

Soon, news of the store would spread up and down the riverbank. People would ask, "Does the storekeeper have much to sell?" Others would reply, "Yes, he has a whole raft of things."

The next time you hear someone talk about having a whole raft of stuff, remember that this was the way peddlers helped to start new cities and towns.

As more and more settlers moved into the wilderness, more and more peddlers shouldered packs to trade with the growing population. In time, the townspeople built roads. Peddlers could use pack horses, mules, or wagons to bring in more merchandise than they could carry on their backs.

When the United States won independence from Great Britain and there were no more restrictions on manufacturing, factories sprang up everywhere. Peddlers no longer had to rely on the ships for goods. Many peddlers worked for single factories, carrying only one kind of merchandise.

When the tin peddler came down the pike, the metal pots and pans in his wagon rattled and banged together loudly. People heard him coming long before they caught sight of his horse. Cloth peddlers had special wagons built to carry bolts of material on long rollers. Customers could climb up and look at all the different patterns before choosing the one they liked best.

By this time, America had its own coinage. Customers could pay in money instead of animal skins or homespun yarn. But many purchases were still made by barter. A peddler didn't mind if someone chose to pay for a new skillet with a dozen fresh eggs and a loaf or two of home-baked bread. The peddler just ate the food along the way, saving the cost of dining at an inn.

As the factories grew, so did the peddlers' wagons. Largest of

them all was the Conestoga wagon, made in Conestoga, Pennsylvania. It could carry up to six tons of merchandise. Its high, rounded top looked like a ship's sail in the distance. The wagons were soon nicknamed "prairie schooners." When you picture covered wagons, you probably think of the westward journeys of the pioneers. But it was the demand for bigger and better freight carriers that caused the first Conestogas to be built.

By the end of the nineteenth century, prairie schooners sailed the plains no more. Railroad trains had changed the peddler's way of life.

Today, salesmen and saleswomen may travel thousands of miles in a week by airplane and automobile. Many sell more in one day than an old-time peddler sold in a lifetime. But they are still carrying on one of our country's earliest and most colorful professions.

Understanding What You've Read

1. Why was the arrival of a ship from England an exciting event for the colonists?
2. How did the settlers pay for the peddler's goods?
3. Name the different ways in which peddlers traveled with their goods.
4. Why were the Conestoga wagons built?
5. Why were Conestogas called "prairie schooners"?
6. What does a peddler's pack remind you of?

Applying the Skills Lesson

1. Read the first full paragraph in the right-hand column on page 309. Which of the three sentences below best states its main idea?
   a. Some peddlers sold only things made of metal.
   b. Some peddlers sold only cloth.
   c. Some peddlers carried only one kind of merchandise.

2. State the topic of the second paragraph in the right-hand column on page 309. Then state the main idea of that paragraph.

There are many details in this selection. By noting how they are related, you can find the main ideas.

In Massachusetts in the 1760's, young Paul Cuffe was finding out everything possible about ships. He had one dream—to learn . . .

THE SECRET OF THE SEA

by Lavinia Dobler *and* Edgar A. Toppin

A boy stood on a windy shore in southern Massachusetts. He was spellbound by the restless ocean.

The sea seemed to give Paul Cuffe strength and courage. When the waves rose high in the air with a roar, Paul was sure the ocean was trying to tell him something he should know. Other times, when the sea was as calm as glass, he looked far away to the horizon. What was beyond?

Paul Cuffe lived on Cuttyhunk Island, about seven miles from the Massachusetts coast. Paul was the seventh child of the ten children.

In 1766, when Paul was almost eight years old, his parents bought land in Dartmouth, Connecticut. Six years later, when Paul was thirteen, his father died. Paul and his brother John took on much of the responsibility for the farm.

Caring for his family and managing the farm made Paul older than his years. It also meant a great sacrifice — his dream of getting an education. But more than ever, he was determined to find out about ships. Whenever he had a free moment, he hurried to the shore to study them.

Paul never forgot the day he had his first lesson in navigation. He had looked forward to it eagerly. But when the teacher started explaining the use of mathematics to figure position and direction, Paul was lost. As soon as the lesson was over, Paul walked out of the room, his head down, his feet dragging. He went back to the farm. His sister was waiting at the door.

"Paul, tell me about the lesson," she asked.

Her brother looked at her, pain written on his face. "It was all as dark as midnight," he said.

"After a while you will understand it," his sister said to comfort him.

"I hope so," he said, "because someday I am going to sea!"

At the age of sixteen, part of Paul's dream came true. This was in 1775, the first year of the American Revolution.

Paul worked on a ship bound for the Gulf of Mexico. On his second trip, he sailed to the West Indies. On his third voyage, in 1776, when he was seventeen years old, Paul was captured by the British. He was in prison in New York City for three months.

While behind bars, Paul made up his mind that when he was set free he would study harder than ever. He was determined that someday he would own a ship. He couldn't afford to buy a ship, but one day he might build one.

When the British released him from prison, Paul went to Westport, a village in Massachusetts. He farmed and studied, never forgetting his dream.

Three years later, in 1779, while the British and the American colonists were still at war, Paul built a boat. His brother David helped him.

Paul was certain he could make money by having his own boat. He planned to trade with the people of Connecticut.

But there were many difficulties. The sea was often rough with storms. There was constant trouble with pirates. During the American Revolution, there were no patrols protecting the coast, so pirates were able to menace all the ships on the Atlantic seaboard.

If Paul had not had his dream and his intense love for the sea, he would not have made it. His drive kept him going while others without such a goal would have given up.

One day in 1780, Paul set out to sea in the boat that he and David had built. But, loaded with valuable cargo, it was lost in a bad storm that raged along the Connecticut coast. Paul somehow made it back to shore.

Paul built a second boat. The day he launched it, Paul's heart beat fast. He wasted no time sailing it out into the bay.

Unfortunately, luck was not with him on this journey. Pirates seized his boat.

There are no records telling how Paul Cuffe finally reached land. He escaped from the pirates and probably swam to shore.

When Paul finally got back to his home town, he considered giving up the plan to trade along the seacoast. Whenever he glanced at the water and the rolling waves, though, they held the same fascination for him as they had when he was a boy. He began to build another boat. He was able to borrow money to buy a cargo.

Even though the route was still dangerous, Paul dared to take the risk. He started bravely for Nantucket, some sixty miles southeast of Westport.

Pirates chased him.

As he tried desperately to get away, his boat hit a rock. This time, however, the pirates did not capture him or his boat. Even though the boat was

badly damaged, Paul finally got back to Westport. He wasted no time, working night and day to repair the boat. Later he sailed to Nantucket with his cargo.

Some months later, Paul bought a boat. He also found a good sailor who was willing to be his crew. By the time the Revolutionary War ended in 1783, the pirates were forced to seek other waters. Paul soon started to make large profits.

The year 1783 was important to Paul for another reason. He married Alice Pequit [pek'it], a woman who belonged to the same Native American tribe that Paul's mother belonged to.

The Cuffes had six daughters and two sons. By 1797, Paul was very successful. With profits from his trading, he bought a large farm on the Westport river.

In 1797, when he and his family settled in Westport, they found no schoolhouse or teacher in the neighborhood. Paul was troubled, for he wanted his children to have a good education. He could now afford to educate them, for his trading business was very successful.

Paul used his own money to pay for a schoolhouse to be built on his farm. Then he offered the school to the people of Westport. He also paid the teacher's salary and all the expenses of operating the school.

Paul Cuffe's first years of shipbuilding and sailing the seas were hard. He worked, and he succeeded. A less determined young person would have given up many times. But Paul Cuffe did not! Between the years 1793 and 1806, Paul's fleet grew to include six ships.

In 1817, Paul's health began to fail. He died at his home in Westport on September 9 of that year. Almost a hundred years later, in 1913, Cuffe's great-grandson put up a monument at the grave. Cut into the stone are these words:

In the memory of Captain Cuffe,
Patriot, Navigator, Educator, Philanthropist,
Friend.

Understanding What You've Read

1. Why did Paul have to sacrifice his dream of getting an education?
2. How did Paul plan to make money with the first boat he built?
3. Why did Paul decide to risk building a third boat?
4. What things happened in 1783 that began to change Paul's fortune for the better?

Applying the Skills Lesson

1. Read the sixth paragraph on page 313. Use the details from that paragraph to state its main idea in one sentence.
2. Read the fifth paragraph on page 317. Which of the following sentences best states the main idea of that paragraph?

    a. Paul had a schoolhouse built on his farm.
    b. Paul paid a teacher to work in a schoolhouse.
    c. Paul gave Westport a schoolhouse and paid the operating costs and the teacher's salary.

TEXTBOOK STUDY

Using the Details to State a Main Idea

In some paragraphs in textbooks, the main idea is stated. In other paragraphs, you have to examine the details and then discover the main idea yourself. Sometimes you'll find the most important details in only two sentences. Other times, you'll have to use details from many sentences in order to state the main idea. As you read the following selections, refer to the sidenotes. They will help you find the important ideas.

Finding the Main Idea in Social Studies

All air contains some water, usually in droplets too small to be seen. When air is warm, it can hold a lot of invisible moisture. If the air grows cooler, the water in it becomes visible. Above us, we see the moisture as clouds. Around us, it appears as fog or mist. (Have you ever ridden an airplane into a white, fleecy cloud? Instant dirty, gray fog!)

> The details in this paragraph help explain what a cloud is. What is a cloud?

Suppose the cloudy air becomes still cooler. Then it will let go its moisture as rain, snow, or sleet. We call this **precipitation.** What could cause air suddenly to grow cooler? For one thing, being pushed upward, away from the warm earth. This happens when winds move against a range of high mountains.

> The details in this paragraph tell you why it rains or snows. What causes precipitation?

—*The United States*
Houghton Mifflin

Building Skills

1. What is the main idea of the first paragraph in the selection you just read?

   a. A fog is a kind of cloud.
   b. A fog or cloud is visible moisture in cool air.
   c. From the inside, a white cloud looks gray.

2. What is the main idea of the second paragraph?

   a. Clouds can be pushed upward from the earth.
   b. Precipitation is rain, snow, or sleet.
   c. Precipitation happens when a cloud becomes cooler.

Finding the Main Idea in Language Arts

Pitch

This paragraph gives directions. It does not have a main idea that you can state.

Study the musical staff below. Then sing the melody softly to yourself.

TWIN – KLE, TWIN – KLE, LIT– TLE STAR! HOW I WON – DER WHAT YOU ARE.

The next two paragraphs have stated main ideas. What details explain the main idea in each paragraph?

The rising and falling of your voice when you sing is called **pitch.** Look at the musical staff again. Notice the notes that are written near the top of the staff. They are sung in a high pitch.

Notice the notes that are written near the bottom of the staff. They are sung in a low pitch.

The rising and falling of your voice when you speak is also called pitch. The words in the sentences below are printed like the notes on a musical staff. Say each sentence softly to yourself. Listen to the pitch of your voice rise and fall.

1. I watched t^{ele}v$_{isi}$$_{o}$$_{n}$.

2. Did you bring the p o^{p}$^{corn?}$

—*Discovery in English*
Laidlaw Brothers

Building Skills

State the topic of the second and third paragraphs. Then state the main idea of each of those paragraphs.

Getting Information from Pictures and Diagrams

A country schoolhouse, 1880.

What can you learn from this picture? Look again! You can learn more than you think.

Books, magazines, and newspapers are made up of more than words (called the **text**). The text works together with different kinds of **graphic aids** to help you learn.

Pictures are one kind of graphic aid. Pictures include photographs, drawings, paintings, and cartoons. Pictures give you details that explain the text. Or they give you information that you will not find in the text. Read the following paragraph. Look for details that are given both in the paragraph and in the picture above.

In the 1800's, most country schoolhouses had only one room and one teacher. The schoolhouse was not comfortable at all. Children sat on long, hard, wooden benches. Some children walked more than sixteen kilometers each day—from home to school and back—even in the worst weather.

Below is a list of details. Which details came only from the text? Which came only from the picture? Which appeared in both the text and the picture?

1. In the 1800's, most country schoolhouses had only one room and one teacher.
2. The schoolhouse was not comfortable.
3. Children sat on long, hard, wooden benches.
4. Some children walked more than sixteen kilometers each day—from home to school and back—even in the worst weather.
5. In cold weather, the schoolroom was warmed by a small stove.
6. To keep warm, some children wore their outer clothing indoors.

You can get the information in sentences 2 and 3 from either the text or the picture. You can get the information from sentences 1 and 4 only from the text. Notice that the information in sentences 5 and 6 is not in the text. You could learn these details only from the picture.

Above or below many pictures, you will see a **caption.** A caption, like a title, tells about the picture. Look at the photograph of the blacksmith on page 324. What details does the caption give?

Country blacksmith, around 1895. Before cars came into general use, every town had a blacksmith, or "smithy." In addition to shoeing horses, some blacksmiths made farm tools and carriage equipment. The town blacksmith often served as a dentist.

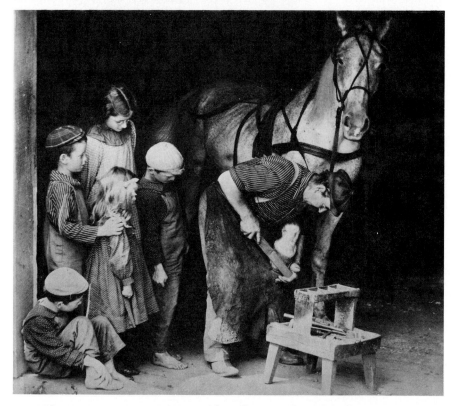

When you turn to a page that has a picture, don't just look at the picture — *study* it! Use details from the picture (and the caption, if there is one) to help you understand the text.

Diagrams

A **diagram** is a special kind of graphic aid. It is always a drawing and often has a caption above or below it. Look at the three diagrams that follow. Read the captions and the notes. Use both to help you understand the diagrams.

The Earth

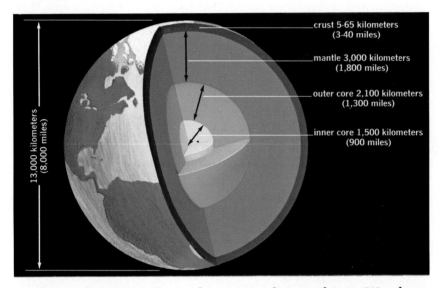

crust 5-65 kilometers
(3-40 miles)

mantle 3,000 kilometers
(1,800 miles)

outer core 2,100 kilometers
(1,300 miles)

inner core 1,500 kilometers
(900 miles)

13,000 kilometers
(8,000 miles)

Some diagrams show the parts of something. Words connected by lines to parts of a diagram are called labels.

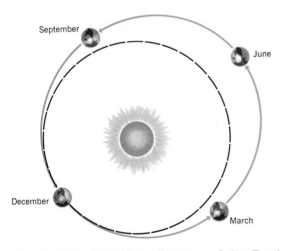

September

June

December

March

Some diagrams show how something changes.

The Earth's Orbit. The distance of the Earth from the sun changes during the year. The shape of the Earth's orbit around the sun is a slightly flattened circle, called an **ellipse.**

How does this caption help you understand the diagram?

325

Another kind of diagram shows you how to do something or how to make something.

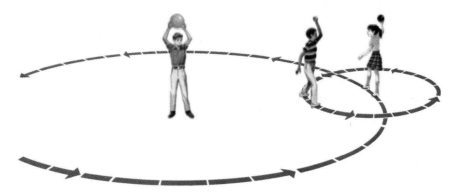

Model of the Sun, Moon, and Earth. You can use three people to make a "living" model of the sun, the moon, and the Earth. Which movement takes less time — the movement of the Earth around the sun or the movement of the moon around the Earth?

Try This

1. Read the paragraph below.

The Earth is made up of layers. The outside, or *crust*, is from 5 to 65 kilometers thick. Under the crust is the *mantle*, which is 3,000 kilometers thick. The *outer core*, which comes between the mantle and the *inner core*, is 2,100 kilometers thick. The inner core is extremely hot. Scientists believe it is made up of iron and nickel.

Which of the following details is only in the diagram *The Earth* on page 325? Which detail is in the paragraph above but not in the diagram?

a. The diameter of the Earth from the North Pole to the South Pole is 13,000 kilometers.

b. The Earth's inner core is made up of iron and nickel.

2. Read the following paragraph. Study the picture. What details can you find only in the picture? What can you find only in the paragraph? What can you find in *both* the picture and the paragraph?

The country store was a popular place in a nineteenth-century town. The store provided a meeting place where people shared the local news. Townspeople could buy almost anything they needed at the country store. There was clothing for men, women, and children. There were tools and seeds for farmers. And there were books, toys, and candy for children.

Prefixes Meaning "Not"

Word Play

Tell what each of these words means: *unfortunately, uncertain, undamaged*. Then use each word in a sentence.

What details do you get from the picture of the ghost town that you cannot get from the text? What details does the text give that the pictures do not? A good reader *reads* both the text and the graphic aids.

They were born when gold was discovered in the West. But after a few years, most of them had become . . .

GOLDEN GHOSTS

Based on a story
by Robert Silverberg

A few crumbling buildings stand beside an unpaved road overgrown with sagebrush. One building was once a bank. There, weary miners stood in line to deposit their new wealth. Another building was a grand hotel. Some dimly seen lines in the ground mark the foundations of houses never built. A narrow path winding into the mountains leads to the mines whose gold made this town sprout overnight.

331

No one has ever counted the ghost towns of the American West. Many have been completely destroyed by time and the weather.

No western state is without its ghost towns. They were places of dreams which grew from mining camps that sprang up during the great gold rushes of the 1800's. They grew with sudden, furious energy. They lived for ten or twenty years and then faded and died.

Not every mining town met the same sort of death. Some did not die at all. In some places, the mines are still going strong: places like Butte [byo͞ot], Montana, and Globe, Arizona. These have become modern cities, very much alive.

In some of the other early mining towns, the mines have played out. But other industries have taken their place.

In Virginia City, Nevada, and Tombstone, Arizona, many buildings of the gold-rush days are well protected for visitors.

The true ghost towns are wholly deserted or perhaps lived in by one or two families. Bodie, California, and Bullfrog, Nevada, belong in this class.

There are also places where nothing at all remains, except perhaps the stump of a building or the shadowy outlines of what were once streets. Some ghosts of this sort are Silver Reef, Utah, and Charleston, Arizona.

These ghost towns remind us of the mining booms that began in 1849 in California. People from all over the world set out toward the Sierra Nevada in search of quick wealth. Some of those who went west in '49 made great fortunes. Most did not.

Panning for gold.

An 1850's gold-rush town — San Francisco.

Towns sprang up and grew like mushrooms while the mining was good. But they often died as easily as they had been founded. Again and again, when there was a strike of gold somewhere, miners arrived and a busy camp was born.

Then came those who hoped to grow rich serving the miners. There were bankers and storekeepers, surveyors and engineers. Presto! A mining camp became a town. Within three or four years, twenty tents turned into a city with an opera house, a hotel, and a row of busy shops.

Then the flow of treasure from the earth slowed down. Or someone came into town with tales of even easier wealth somewhere else. Off the miners went. Perhaps later on, other miners would come and find new treasures there — silver or copper instead of gold. The town would grow again. Some of the mining camps went through perhaps three or four lifetimes this way before becoming ghosts.

Westward, Ho!

The real westward movement began in 1840. Times were hard east of the Mississippi. An endless frontier beckoned to many Easterners. "Oregon fever" and "California fever" sent trains of covered wagons crawling through the immense western lands.

These pioneers were not generally seeking gold. They wanted a place to settle and raise cattle or crops. They thought that beyond the treeless prairie and the great, dry deserts there were rich farmlands free for the taking.

By the mid-1840's, there were about five thousand people in Oregon and about one thousand in California. Most of those in California lived near the lower Sacramento River. There, a Swiss adventurer named John Sutter had built a fort and mill.

In the spring of 1848, a man named Sam Brannan appeared in the little port of San Francisco. He strode down San Francisco's streets, shouting, "Gold! Gold from the American River near Sutter's fort!"

Gold! The word spread, and

Sutter's Mill. In 1848, gold was found nearby.

John A. Sutter.

by 1849 the gold rush was on.

Seeking pay dirt, the "forty-niners" streamed into California to start the great American gold rush. The rush brought great wealth to some but little or nothing to most. It left behind the ghost towns whose ruins stir our imaginations today.

Understanding What You've Read

1. What happened to the old mining camps that sprang up during the gold rushes of the 1800's?
2. What were "Oregon fever" and "California fever"?
3. Why were miners of the late 1840's often referred to as "forty-niners"?
4. What sequence of events created mining towns in the 1800's?

Applying the Skills Lesson

Here are some details from the selection you just read. Which details come only from the pictures or their captions? Which come only from the text? Which come from both the text and the pictures?

1. In the 1850's, gold-rush towns were busy places.
2. Hundreds of gold-mining camps sprang up during the 1800's.
3. In the gold rush, some people panned for gold.
4. Gold was found near Sutter's fort in 1848.

The graphic aids in this selection will help you understand more about life in America in the 1880's. Look for details in the pictures to help you understand the text.

Eat penny candies in the general store. Look at the pictures in your parents' "Wish Book." These are some things you might have done if you were a child in . . .

"Modern" America in the 1880's

by Suzanne Hilton

Painting of a general store and post office.

336

In the 1880's young people were happy that they were growing up in a "modern" world. Let's take a look at what "modern" meant when your great-great-grandparents were your age.

The General Store

For probably the last time in history, there was plenty of space in the United States. Cities were not too large yet. Most people lived in the country.

The general store was the center of country social life. Children always found something new at the store. There were toys and books, trading cards, and colorful posters. At the end of the year there was a new almanac that had new jokes and stories. Then there were the smells— of sour pickles, ground coffee, freshly made soup, and salted fish. Crackers were sold from barrels. Jars of candy made the shelves sing with color. Children with a penny to spend could buy a whole bag of candy. They could buy corn kisses, hearts, gibraltars, cinnamon red-hots, fortune candies, and other candies you may never have heard of. Very few things in the store came already wrapped in small packages. Almost everything had to be measured and put in a paper bag or wrapped in paper.

During the winter, the store was heated by a little stove. A few people were always in the store, just relaxing or playing cards, checkers, or chess. The store was the best place to find out the latest news.

The Wish Book

The general store had almost everything a person needed for country living. But when people wanted something that the store didn't carry, they might turn to what they called the "Wish Book." This was a catalogue that started a whole industry—the mail order business. The idea for it came from a man named Montgomery Ward. The "Wish Book" listed more than four thousand items, including "ready-made" clothing.

Before the War Between the States, tailors thought that everyone was a different size and shape. But uniform makers soon noticed that certain leg and waist measurements generally went together. The "Wish Book" said that the "ready-mades nine times out of ten give you a fit." And they did fit! That's why clothing comes in standard sizes today.

The Weather

In the 1880's people didn't have TV or radio news to tell them what the weather would be like. They did have almanacs which gave the weather forecasts for a whole year. However, they were wrong as often as they were right.

Country-dwellers had their own ways to tell the weather. Fish swimming near the surface of a pond meant rain. People also thought it would rain if frogs croaked more than usual and if the moon was pale with hazy edges. Enough blue sky showing "to make a pair of pants" meant that the clouds would soon disappear. A glowing red moon meant a windy day coming. Everyone knew: "An evening red and a morning gray will set the traveler on his way. But evening gray and morning red will pour down rain on the pilgrim's head."

Travel

In the 1880's, for the first time, people had a little extra time for something called a "vacation." They wanted to see a little of the world beyond the small area they lived in.

"Summer tramps" was the name for people who took a vacation in the summer. It was a brand-new idea, but nothing like a vacation today. There were country inns. But no one could be sure of having a private room. Innkeepers never refused a traveler just because there was no room. They simply woke up people who were happily sleeping and told them to move over for another traveler.

Also, the traveler could not

just point to a spot on the map and say, "I'm going there tomorrow." Sometimes there was no way to get from place to place.

People called railroad travel "going in the cars." Some trains had sleeping cars in which the seats used by day could be turned into beds at night. People could eat in dining cars in some trains. And best of all, trains moved at the amazing speed of forty miles an hour!

Standard Time

The hardest part of going from one place to another was finding out what time the train arrived and what time it left. Standard Time had not been invented yet. There was clock time and there was sun time. Sun time changed every day as the days grew longer or shorter. So clock time was the "right" time, meaning that when it was noon in New York City, it was five minutes before noon in Philadelphia and two minutes before noon in Washington, D. C. That made it exactly 11:30 A.M. in Cleveland, Ohio. And in Albany, New York, it was already one minute and six seconds past noon! The train people became famous for being able to tell passengers exactly what time it was at the very spot in the country where they asked the time.

City Life

Although there was still plenty of open space in the West in the 1880's, the major Eastern cities were becoming very crowded. One look at a large city's streets would show this.

The streets were clogged with horse-drawn carriages. Carriage drivers were allowed to move at only six miles an hour. They were fined $5.00 for driving on the sidewalk.

Cities had public transportation called horsecars, or street railroads. They charged 25 cents for four rides. Horse-drawn hacks, like our taxicabs, cost 75 cents a mile for one passenger and $1.25 for two.

Inventions

A little more than a hundred years ago in the United States was a great time for inventions. One invention that changed the shape and height of the city was the elevator. In 1876, a man named Otis showed this invention at the Philadelphia Centennial Exposition. Within a few years, cities were growing up instead of out.

Department stores were a new idea. Instead of shopping in dozens of small stores, people could find almost everything they needed under one roof. Department stores had a one-price policy. The smaller stores generally charged different prices to different customers for the same item.

In 1876, a new invention—the telephone—was shown in Philadelphia by Alexander Graham Bell. In a year there would be 800

telephones in the United States.

Today most Americans take such things as telephones, department stores, and elevators for granted. We hardly ever stop to think that Standard Time, standard sizes of clothing, and summer vacations were once thought of as new ideas. It gives us reason to wonder: What will people think of our "modern" world of the 1980's a hundred years from now?

Understanding What You've Read

1. What was a general store like in the 1880's?
2. What were some of the ways people forecast the weather?
3. Why were railroad cars considered "modern"?
4. What was meant by a one-price policy in department stores?

Applying the Skills Lesson

1. Look at the picture (page 339) of people on a train in the 1880's. Which of the following details can you learn from the picture only?

   a. Passenger trains were generally comfortable in the 1880's.
   b. In the 1880's, trains moved at forty miles per hour.
   c. Travel by railroad in the 1880's was called "going in the cars."

2. What can you learn about the Philadelphia Exposition from the pictures on page 340 that you cannot learn from the text?
3. What can you learn from the third paragraph on page 337 that you cannot learn from the picture on page 336?

TEXTBOOK STUDY

Pictures and Diagrams

What's the first thing you do when you get a new text-book? Most people leaf through and look at the pictures, diagrams, and other graphic aids. Pictures and diagrams not only make the text more interesting, they also give you the important details to help you understand the text. You'll find many graphic aids in your textbooks, because at times, they explain things better than words alone.

As you read the following selections, look at the pictures or diagrams. They will help you understand the text.

Pictures in Mathematics

The following selection is from a math textbook. The pictures show familiar objects. They help the reader to see the difference between a liter and a milliliter.

Study the text and pictures. Then answer the questions that follow.

Capacity: Liter and Milliliter

A.

One **liter** is a little more than a quart. You can write "1 l" to mean one liter.

B.

This large bottle holds about 19 liters (19 l).

An eyedropper holds about one **milliliter** of liquid.
You can write "1 ml" to mean one milliliter.

A glass of milk is about 250 milliliters (250 ml).

— Mathematics Around Us
Scott, Foresman

Building Skills

1. Why do you think the math book used *familiar* objects in the pictures?
2. If you already knew English measures (quarts and gallons), what details in the pictures of the milk cartons and the bottle would help you understand how English measures relate to metric measures?

Diagrams in Health

When you take a breath, where does the air go? This drawing shows the **respiratory system.** Oxygen is shown by the red dots. Follow its path.

The lungs are made up of thousands of tiny air sacs. This picture

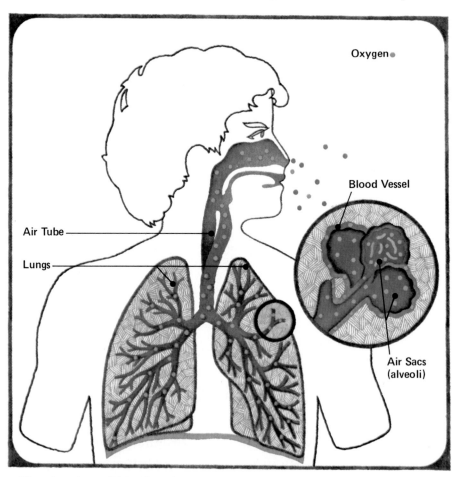

Oxygen

Blood Vessel

Air Tube

Lungs

Air Sacs (alveoli)

The drawing within the circle on the diagram is called an *inset.* **It is a magnified part of the main diagram.**

344

shows some of these air sacs. After the oxygen reaches these air sacs, where does it go? How is it carried all over your body? Your heart and **blood vessels** are your **circulatory system.** Is there any part of your body that does not get oxygen from your blood?

— *Balance in Your Life: Purple*
Harcourt Brace Jovanovich

Notice how the text explains the diagram on page 344.

Building Skills

1. Which of the following titles would best fit the diagram? The text will help you find the answer.

   a. The Circulatory System
   b. The Respiratory System
   c. Oxygen

2. Below are three questions asked in the text. Where would you find the answer to each one: in the diagram, in the text, or in both?

   a. When you take a breath, where does the air go?
   b. After the oxygen reaches these air sacs, where does it go?
   c. How is it carried all over your body?

SKILLS LESSON

Getting Information from Maps and Graphs

Map reading is an important skill that drivers use. It's an important skill for students in school, too. You'll find many maps in your reading. Maps, like pictures and diagrams, are graphic aids. If you can read the maps in your books, you'll be able to understand the text better.

On pages 347 and 348 are three different kinds of maps. As you study them, read the notes above and below the maps. They will help you understand the parts of a map.

Area Map

An *area map* shows cities, bodies of water, mountains, and rivers.

California

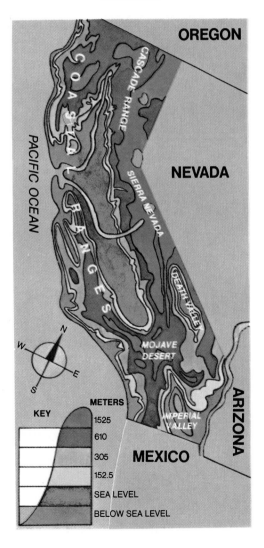

Sacramento is the capital of California. It is marked with a star. How are cities like Los Angeles marked?

A *compass rose* shows direction. When you read a map, north is usually to the top; west is usually to the left of the page.

Topographical Map

A *topographical map* shows what the land is like. What places in California are mountainous? Which places are very low? Refer to the *key*, or *legend*. It shows what the colors mean.

California

347

Information Map

This *information map* shows areas of dairy and wheat farming and industry. Some information maps show such things as the number of people living in different areas. Some show what the weather is like in different places. You must use the key or legend when you study an information map.

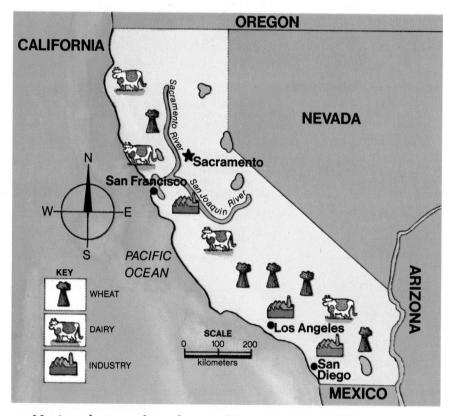

Notice the word **scale** on the map. If you want to figure out how far it is from one place to another, the scale will help you. Use the scale to determine the distance between Sacramento and Los Angeles.

Graphs

Graphs let you see a lot of information all at once. They help you to make comparisons.

Bar Graph

A *bar graph* uses thick dark lines called bars to show comparisons. What is being compared in this graph? Compare the end of each bar to the number on the bottom of the graph. Long Beach is the smallest of the four cities. It had about 359,000 people in 1970. Which of the four cities was the largest in 1970?

Population of Four California Cities, 1970
(in thousands)

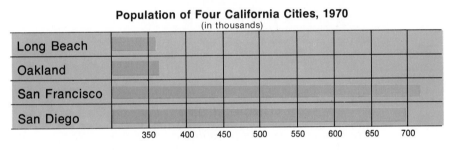

Line Graph

The numbers along the left of the graph are numbers of people. The numbers along the bottom are years. There were about 2.5 million people in Los Angeles in 1960. How many were there in 1970? Is the population expected to rise or go down between 1975 and 1985?

Change in Population of Los Angeles 1950-1985

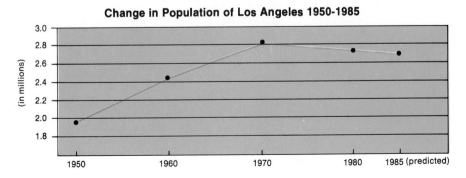

349

Pictograph

A *pictograph* is like a bar graph, but uses pictures instead of bars. How many figures are there next to Pennsylvania? This means there are about 12 million people in that state. About how many people live in New York?

The Four Most Populous States in 1970

New York	🚶🚶🚶🚶🚶🚶🚶🚶🚶🚶🚶🚶🚶🚶🚶🚶🚶🚶
California	🚶🚶🚶🚶🚶🚶🚶🚶🚶🚶🚶🚶🚶🚶🚶🚶🚶🚶🚶🚶
Pennsylvania	🚶🚶🚶🚶🚶🚶🚶🚶🚶🚶🚶🚶
Texas	🚶🚶🚶🚶🚶🚶🚶🚶🚶🚶🚶

NOTE: Each figure stands for 1 million people.

Circle Graph

A *circle graph* is sometimes called a "pie graph." What takes up the most space on this pie graph? What takes up the least amount of space?

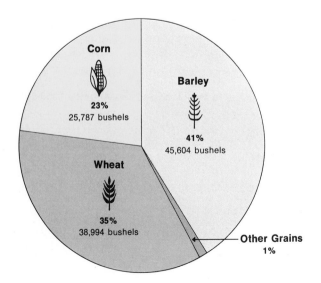

Corn
23%
25,787 bushels

Barley
41%
45,604 bushels

Wheat
35%
38,994 bushels

Other Grains
1%

Time Lines

A **time line** is a kind of graph. The line stands for a long period of time. The line is divided into equal periods of time. The time line below helps you see how a number of events are related in time.

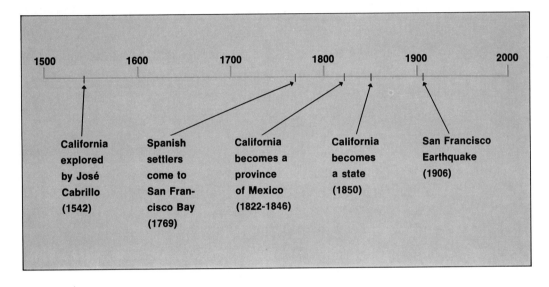

Try This

In the following paragraphs about California, the sentences are numbered. After you read the paragraphs, answer the questions that follow. The questions refer to the numbered sentences.

(1) California is a state on the Pacific coast. (2) It belonged to Mexico from 1822 until 1846. (3) Four years later, California became a state. (4) Although California ranks first among the states in population, it ranks third in land area.

(5) California has both farming and machine industry. (6) The state produces one third of all of America's vegetables. (7) California is well-known for its fruit and nut crops. (8) The state also produces much of the grain used in America, including wheat, barley, and corn.

(9) The largest cities in California are Los Angeles, San Diego, San Francisco, San José, Long Beach, and Oakland. (10) Although the population of large cities like Los Angeles rose in the past, it is expected to remain the same or fall in the next few years. (11) More people are coming to live in California, and the population of one city, San Diego, is increasing.

1. Which graphic aids in this lesson show the information given in sentence 1?
2. Which graph gives the information in sentences 2 and 3?
3. Two facts are given in sentence 4. Which graphic aid shows you that California has the largest population among the states? Does any graphic aid show you that California is the third largest state?
4. Read sentence 5. Which of the three maps shows some of California's industries?
5. Do any of the graphic aids show the information given in sentence 6?
6. Do any of the graphic aids show the information given in sentence 7?
7. Which graph shows the information explained in sentence 8?
8. Do any of the graphic aids give you any of the information that is stated in sentence 9?
9. Sentence 10 explains something shown on the line graph. What does this sentence explain?

Compound Words

Marylou spent three horrible days in Bullfrog. She wanted to go home, but she had only 22¢ and a bag of fruit. She wrote this message to her grandparents:

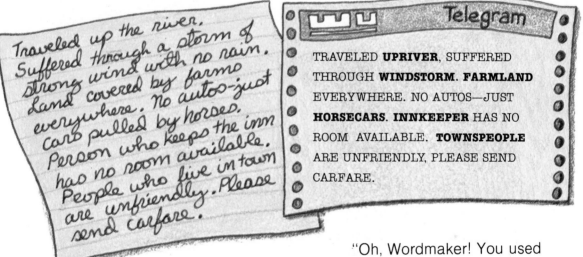

Traveled up the river. Suffered through a storm of strong wind with no rain. Land covered by farms everywhere. No autos—just cars pulled by horses. Person who keeps the inn has no room available. People who live in town are unfriendly. Please send carfare.

Telegram

TRAVELED **UPRIVER**, SUFFERED THROUGH **WINDSTORM. FARMLAND** EVERYWHERE. NO AUTOS—JUST **HORSECARS. INNKEEPER** HAS NO ROOM AVAILABLE. **TOWNSPEOPLE** ARE UNFRIENDLY, PLEASE SEND CARFARE.

"No. It's me! Wordmaker!" exclaimed the strange-looking hero. And he took out a ballpoint pen and changed the message to read:

"That will be 1¢ per word, or 45¢," said the message taker.

"But I only have 22¢," wailed Marylou. Just then she heard a strange noise, like the clicking of a hundred typewriters. "What's that up in the sky? Is it an airplane?"

"Oh, Wordmaker! You used compound words to change my message from 45 words to 22. How can I thank you? Here—take this bag of fruit."

"Thanks. I'm not interested in the apples, but I *would* enjoy that watermelon and those blueberries and that grapefruit and. . . ."

Word Play

1. Find the meaning of each compound word in boldface. Compound words contain two or more shorter words.
2. Try to find the other compound words in the story. Then use each of these compound words in a sentence.

How far did Grace McCance and her family travel in 1885? Where were the railroads at that time? The map in the selection will add information to the text.

Winter blizzards and summer droughts made life hard for the brave . . .

SOD-SHANTY PIONEERS

by Dorothy M. Johnson

After the covered-wagon pioneers went west to seek their fortunes, another frontier opened up. To the prairies of the Dakotas and Nebraska, with their uncertain rainfall and wild windstorms, came the sod-shanty pioneers.

One of them was Grace McCance. She was only three years old at the time her family moved from Missouri to Nebraska, in 1885.

One reason for the great westward movement during the nineteenth century was that people wanted land for farming. There was land in plenty—thousands of square miles of it. Farmers and their families moved westward to claim it.

In 1862, President Abraham Lincoln signed the first Homestead Act. It threw vast stretches open to settlement at a very low cost. Any citizen twenty-one years old or older could file a claim on 160 acres. After five years of working the land, the man or woman could buy it for only $1.25 an acre. This was known as "proving up."

By 1885, pioneers moving to Nebraska traveled by railroad. Grace's father, Charles, sold his only milk-giving cow to pay for moving everything the family owned—household goods, farm tools, three horses, and a mule.

A Tough Beginning

Like most homesteaders on the Great Plains, the McCances lived in a house made of earth. The *soddy* was the typical first home of most people who filed for free land on the prairie. Trees were too scarce to be cut for building log cabins. So the tough prairie sod itself was used for building material. It was cut into neat blocks which were piled up solidly to make thick walls. The roof, supported by planks, was made of sod, too.

The McCances' first soddy was one room only twelve by fourteen feet in size. Compared to many others, however, it was a lovely home. It had a wooden floor, and the side walls were whitewashed. Grace's mother bleached flour sacks to make curtains for the three little windows.

Every drop of water for the family and the animals had to be carried in barrels by wagon from another homestead two miles away, where there was a well with a windmill to run the pump. Another hardship was that, with no cow or chickens at first, the family had no milk, butter, or eggs.

For a field crop, Mr. Mc-Cance raised corn. A kitchen garden provided much of the family's food—onions, beans, watermelons, and sweet corn.

Even very small children had their own work to do. Grace was not yet six years old when her father gave her the job of herding the cows he had bought. It was lonesome work, and she wanted something to keep her mind and hands busy. She begged her mother for some tiny scraps of cloth and learned how to piece quilts. In later years, her beautiful quilts took many prizes and made her famous.

When Grace was six, she had a chance to go to school for three months, walking three miles each way. Schools weren't permanently established. When a teacher and a room could be found, children went to school. If the teacher moved away, there was no longer a school.

Living with the Weather

Farmers always live by the weather. You can't do anything about weather except enjoy it or put up with it, depending on what kind of weather you're having. For Nebraska homesteaders, weather seemed especially bad because there was no shelter or forest in that wide, flat land.

The McCance family adjusted to the weather as well as anybody could. Blizzards—blinding snow whirled by screaming winds—were a peril in the winter. During a blizzard it wasn't safe to go out of the soddy. But it was necessary because the stock had to be fed and fuel had to be brought in for the stove. To get from the house to the barn, it was necessary to have a rope tied between the two buildings. You can hold on to a rope and feel your way along it even when you can't see a thing.

Another kind of prairie wind

is the welcome chinook. It melts snow unbelievably fast so that there is rushing water everywhere. Then there is another peril—floods.

Sometimes children could not get home from school for a day or two because of snow or wind or a flood. There was no way of getting word back to their parents. Everybody simply had to be patient.

Another menace on the prairie was fire, roaring through the wild grass with a howling wind whipping it on. Sometimes buildings, animals,

and even human lives were lost. Grace's father, like other homesteaders, plowed fire guards. These strips of raw earth with no grass on them to burn saved the family more than once.

There was no end to the sudden dangers that weather produced. One warm night in July, a lightning storm struck. Fierce winds blew the roof off the kitchen that had been added to the sod house. Mrs. McCance had a hard time finding enough undamaged food in the mass of mud to prepare breakfast. Many things, blown out across the prairie, never were found at all.

Daily Life

Grace went barefoot except in winter. Once she stepped on a nail, injuring her foot. Even when she couldn't walk, Grace kept busy. She pounded bits of broken dishes and old buffalo bones into a grit that the chickens needed.

Grace's father finally found time to dig a well. Water was brought up by mule power. That is, one of the children would lead an old mule that pulled the heavy bucket up from the well. Mr. McCance no longer had to haul water from two miles away. But the family still had to be careful not to waste any water, because somebody had to carry it up a steep hill to the house.

In five years, the McCances had "proved up" on their homestead. They had lived on it long enough and put enough work into it so that the land was legally theirs. They then sold it, bought a quarter section (160

acres), and started all over on a new farm. The new farm's soddy had a bedroom, a sitting room, and a big kitchen.

Toward a Better Life

When Grace was nine, she attended school again, but only part of each day. She was needed to herd cattle mornings and afternoons.

That year, the McCance family got something wonderful. They bought a new kitchen stove with an attached tank for heating water. Later they got something else that delighted them—a washing machine. It wasn't electric. That kind of washing machine was yet to be invented. But it certainly beat the old washboard. A three-legged "dolly" under the lid was attached to a handle on top and was turned back and forth by means of "child power." Fifteen minutes of sloshing could clean a whole tubful of laundry.

At the same time that the McCances got their "child-powered" washing machine, another fine improvement was

then added. Grace's mother had always done her canning in tin cans. She sealed the lids on with hot sealing wax. Now she had glass jars for the first time, with lids that screwed on. They were easier to use, they looked very pretty lined up on the shelves, and they didn't have to be labeled.

Bad Times, Good Times

Prosperity wasn't always with the McCances, however. In 1894, there was a drought. The cattle became thin. There was no corn for the pigs. Two younger sisters now herded the cattle, while Grace kept moving the pigs to fields where they could find enough shoots and stems to keep them alive.

One day a terrible windstorm sent the family flying to the cellar for safety. The barn was ruined, and the corn crib was damaged. Most of the chickens were killed. When harvest time came, there was nothing to harvest. Mr. McCance tried to sell his cattle because there was no feed for them. But he couldn't even give them away, because nobody else had feed either.

In 1895, things were better. The family moved again. Their new home was a tall house made of real lumber. It was big enough so that, for the first time, they didn't have to keep a bed in the parlor.

Within the next few years, Grace's younger sisters took over much of the farm work. Grace was now able to study to become a teacher. After the turn of the century, Grace married and started to raise her own family. More than sixty years later, when Grace was in her eighties, she wrote a book about her family's life as sod-shanty pioneers.

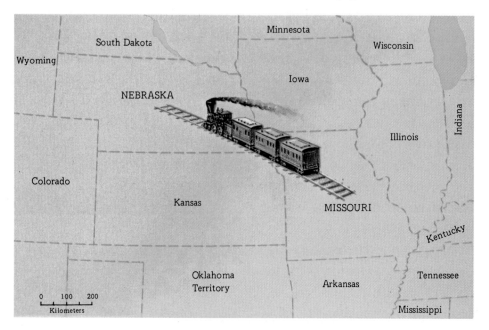

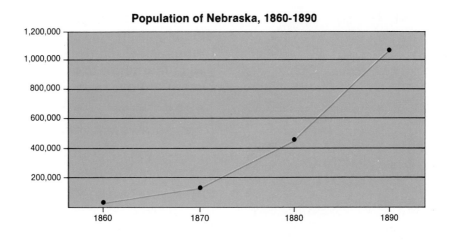

Population of Nebraska, 1860-1890

Understanding What You've Read

1. How could a person get land under the Homestead Act?
2. What was a soddy and how was it made?
3. Describe the weather of the Nebraska prairie.
4. Why do you think Grace McCance wrote a book about her family's life as sod-shanty pioneers?

Applying the Skills Lesson

1. Look at the graph above. Is this a bar graph, a line graph, or a pictograph?
2. During which ten-year period did the population of Nebraska increase most?
3. When did the McCance family move to Nebraska? Did they move during the ten-year period of the greatest or least growth of Nebraska?
4. Estimate the number of kilometers distance the McCance family traveled when they moved from Missouri to Nebraska. Use the center of each state as end points to figure the distance.

In this selection, you'll find many details in the graphic aids. The graphic aids and the text may help you to learn how to learn about the history of your town or city.

Does your town or city have a Main Street? If it does, you can learn a lot about your local history if you find the answer to the question . . .

Whatever Happened to Main Street?

by David Weitzman

Does your town or city have a Main Street, a Center Street, a First Avenue, or an A Street? If it does, it may be the oldest-looking street around. If you were to look closely for dates on the cornerstones and arches along that street, you'd probably find that it has some of the first buildings built in your town or city.

Chances are this street is not the main street, center street, or first avenue anymore. But it once was. So let's take a walk down Main Street, into the past.

Here on Main Street you can close your eyes and imagine the sounds of the past: old cars, horses, trolley cars, and carts.

Here you can begin to understand something of your town's or city's history if you watch carefully for the small bits of the past. Sometimes there are cobblestones showing through the pavement. Sometimes there are old trolley tracks. There may be an iron drinking trough for horses.

Lots of cities began as railroad stations. Today they may still have railroad tracks running right through them. Let your imagination carry you back into the past. Imagine that just off Main Street of Anywhere, U.S.A., is the old yellow and brown station. Take a look inside its

windows. Seventy or a hundred years ago that station may have stood alone. Perhaps there was nothing for miles around until the cattle drive began. Thousands of head of cattle arrived for shipment by train to the big city. Then, over the years, things changed. Bigger cattle pens were built. Hotels sprang up, as did general stores. There were banks and firms that bought and sold cattle. Of course, there had to be houses for all the people running these businesses.

Soon manufacturers arrived so that they could be near railroads. The town then became a large transportation and manufacturing center. It had more houses and stores. Soon the town became a city, which grew out and away from its reason for being—the railroad tracks.

Other cities began as transportation towns, too. They were for ships and shipping. These towns grew around the docks along rivers or around natural harbors on the seacoast. Even today, you can see the pattern of growth of river and seaport towns as you walk away from the docks. You may notice how the city becomes newer the farther out you get.

Still another kind of city started at a crossroad. It began with a gas station, then a restaurant and bus stop, then a general store. Then there were some houses, schools, and other buildings.

There are still other kinds of beginnings for cities. Some begin as university towns, county seats, state capitals, and mining towns. Whole cities have grown around recreation areas.

Now, does that give you any ideas on how your town or city began and why? It may be a little hard to tell just what the first purpose of your town or city was— things have changed so much. For example, many railroad towns may have become manufacturing towns. If you don't come up with an answer right away, there are some ways that you can find out more about the history of your community.

One way is to spend some time in the old part of your community. There you can "collect" some bits and pieces of the past that interest you.

The first thing you can do is to

make an Old Town map. It doesn't have to be a fancy map. It should be one you can write all over and keep notes on. Before you leave home, make sure you've got a pencil and either a note pad or a clipboard with some paper. If you have a camera, take it with you.

If you've made a guess about how your town or city began, start investigating. Begin at the railroad tracks or at the dock. Or you can begin at a large meat-packing plant. Don't worry if your guess turns out to be wrong. You'll have fun anyway.

When you get to what you think is the oldest part of your community, try to make a rough map as you go along. Your first notes might look like this.

OLD CABOOSE. DATE ON SIDE, 1936

FIRST ST.

RAILROAD STATION 1888

ABANDONED WAREHOUSE (NO DATE.) LOOKS OLD. ALL WOOD

CHURCH. ARCH OVER FRONT DOOR HAS DATE 1875

SECOND ST.

All the time you're walking, keep on the lookout for some of the following clues.

Watch for dates. They are cut into cornerstones, in the stones around doors, or on the sides of buildings. They may also be on metal plaques.

Watch for old sidewalks. Often you'll find that the name of the company that put down the sidewalk is stamped into the wet cement. The stamps are often dated. Metal plates are sometimes set into the sidewalk.

Watch for cast-iron building fronts. Watch for lampposts and fire hydrants. Watch for railings and fences with dates on them.

Watch for old signs on the sides of buildings. What kinds of businesses are here? Is there more of one kind of business than another? Write down some of the names you see on the old

signs. Were the townspeople once mostly of one nationality?

Watch for clues at the railroad station. Are there maps painted on the sides of the old freight cars or the station's walls that show the old routes? Is there something around that shows what the trains carried in and out of your community? For example, do you see grain silos or sawmills?

Do you suppose you've really found the oldest part of your community all by yourself? Most likely you have. If you want to check up on how you're doing, there are several ways of finding out how well you have guessed.

Go to the town, city, or county clerk's office. Ask to see the oldest map of your community that they have. Ask how you can get a copy of the map.

Visit your main library. Ask the librarian where the local history section is. Ask if there are any histories of the community in a special collection.

Tell people what you're doing. They'll get interested, too. They may be able to give you information and ideas for many history projects.

Find groups of people who, like you, are interested in the history of their community and are trying to save it.

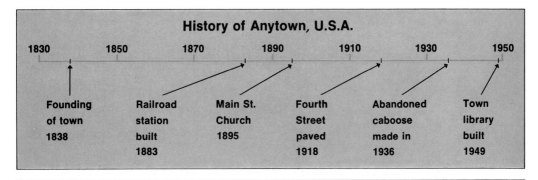

History of Anytown, U.S.A.

| 1830 | 1850 | 1870 | 1890 | 1910 | 1930 | 1950 |

Founding of town 1838

Railroad station built 1883

Main St. Church 1895

Fourth Street paved 1918

Abandoned caboose made in 1936

Town library built 1949

Understanding What You've Read

1. What are some clues to the past that the author suggests you might find in your community?
2. Name at least three ways in which cities have begun.
3. How does the author suggest you find out about the history of your community?
4. The author tells you to look for dates as you walk the older streets of your community. Where does he suggest these dates might be found?

Applying the Skills Lesson

1. Look at the rough map on page 365. Which of the following details does the map show?

   a. location of railroad station and date
   b. the first building in the town
   c. information about the location of some buildings that are still standing

2. Look at the time line above. Which is older, the railroad station or the church? Which is older, the church or the library?

Maps and Graphs

In many of your textbooks you'll find maps and graphs. These special kinds of graphic aids give important information. They give details that explain the text or details that you will not find in the text. As you read each selection and study the graphic aid that goes with it, refer to the sidenotes. They will help you understand some of the information.

Maps in Science

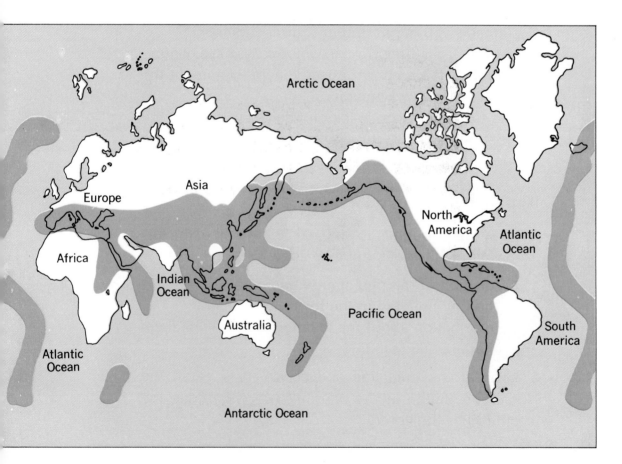

You might well think that there is nothing people can do about earthquakes. It turns out, however, as scientists investigate, that something can be done. Scientists have made maps showing where earthquakes happen. The areas colored orange on the map are called earthquake belts. Notice that earthquake belts are along some seacoasts. Some belts are along chains of islands. These belts show where earthquakes are likely to happen. A building put up in an earthquake belt can be built to resist earthquake shocks.

Refer to the map as you read the text. Then study the map to see what else it shows that the text does not mention.

—*Concepts in Science:* Purple
Harcourt Brace Jovanovich

Building Skills

Below are some details from the science textbook. Which ones are in the text only? Which are in the map only? Which are in both the text and the map?

1. Earthquake belts are along some seacoasts.
2. A building put up in an earthquake belt can be built to resist earthquake shocks.
3. Some belts are along chains of islands.
4. All along the west coast of North and South America there is an earthquake belt.
5. Part of the Indian Ocean is an earthquake belt.

Graphs in Mathematics

Notice that some of the pictures are not complete. Each incomplete picture stands for fewer than one million farms.

NUMBER OF FARMS

Each 🏭 stands for

one million farms.

1920	🏭	🏭	🏭	🏭	🏭	🏭	◢
1930	🏭	🏭	🏭	🏭	🏭	🏭	◢
1940	🏭	🏭	🏭	🏭	🏭	🏭	▮
1950	🏭	🏭	🏭	🏭	🏭	🏠	
1960	🏭	🏭	🏭	🏭			
1970	🏭	🏭	🏭				
1980	🏭	🏭	🏭				

1. Compare 1920 with 1930. In 1930, were there more farms, fewer farms, or about the same number?

2. Compare 1960 with 1970. About how many fewer farms were there in 1970?

Graphs often give information that will help you make a prediction. What is your answer to question 3?

3. Use the graph to predict the future. Would you say the number of farms will increase, decrease, or stay about the same?

370

AVERAGE SIZE OF FARMS

Each ■ stands for 10 hectares.

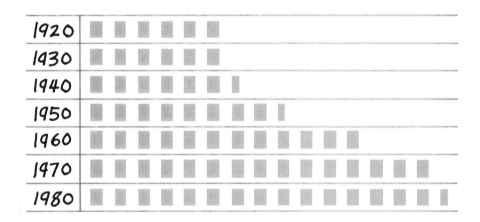

1920	■ ■ ■ ■ ■ ■
1930	■ ■ ■ ■ ■ ■
1940	■ ■ ■ ■ ■ ■ ▌
1950	■ ■ ■ ■ ■ ■ ■ ■ ▌
1960	■ ■ ■ ■ ■ ■ ■ ■ ■ ■ ■
1970	■ ■ ■ ■ ■ ■ ■ ■ ■ ■ ■ ■ ■
1980	■ ■ ■ ■ ■ ■ ■ ■ ■ ■ ■ ■ ■ ■ ▌

4. Is the average size of a farm increasing or decreasing?

5. The average size of a farm in the 1920's was about 60 hectares. By what year did the average size double?

6. The number of farms is decreasing. The average size of a farm is increasing. Do you think farms today are producing more food, less food, or about the same amount as in 1920?

— Growth in Mathematics: Purple
Harcourt Brace Jovanovich

Building Skills

Answer questions 4, 5, and 6 above.

Books About America's Past

Totems, Decoys and Covered Wagons: Cardboard Constructions from Early American Life by Jeremy Comins. Lothrop, 1976.   The author tells how to make copies of toys, houses, furniture, and other important objects from early Native American and colonial life.

Lady for the Defense by Mary V. Fox. Harcourt Brace Jovanovich, 1975.   You'll learn about Belva Lockwood, a lawyer who took many interesting cases and ran for President of the United States in 1884.

Immigrant Kids by Russell Freedman. Photos by Jacob Riis and others. Dutton, 1980.   The lives of children who arrived in America during the late 1800's and early 1900's are illustrated in this book.

Why Don't You Get a Horse, Sam Adams? by Jean Fritz. Coward, 1974.   Take a funny but fact-filled look at one of the founders of the United States.

How the Settlers Lived by George Laycock, Illustrated by Alexander Farquharson. McKay, 1980.   This book shows how the pioneers carved their lives out of the American wilderness.

New England Village: Everyday Life in 1810 by Robert H. Loeb, Jr. Doubleday, 1976.   This lively book recreates life in New England nearly 200 years ago.

What Ever Happened to the Baxter Place? by Pat Ross. Pantheon, 1976.   You'll find out how a quiet farm gradually changed as a nearby town grew.

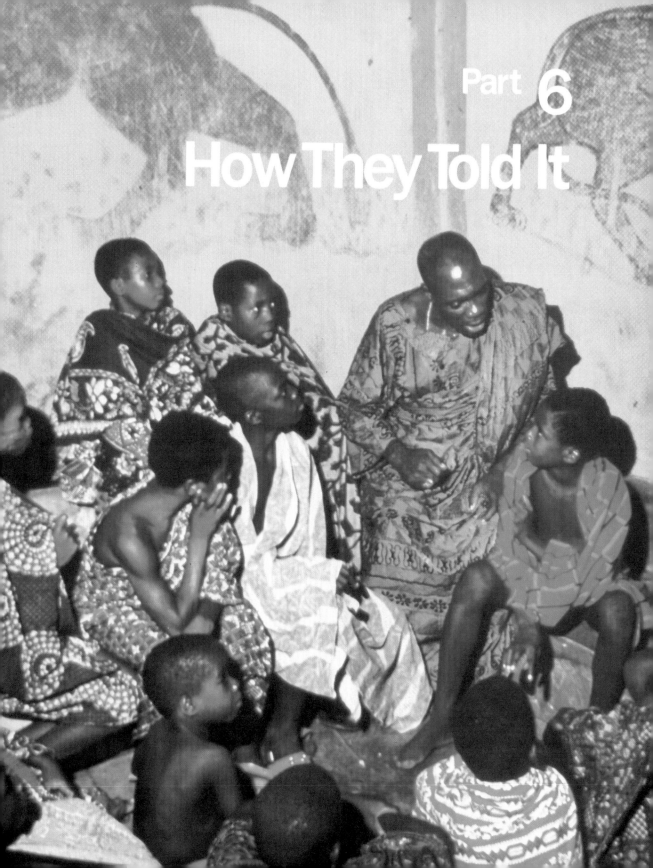

Part **6**

How They Told It

UNDERSTANDING AND APPRECIATING LITERATURE

Theme

Prince Royal in the cartoon above seems to have ignored some good advice. Read the cartoon. Does Prince Royal turn back when the people warn him? Does he pay attention when he sees the warning signs? No, he doesn't. What is the important idea in this cartoon story? The author has a dragon tell you—"Listen to good advice if you want to keep out of trouble." This is the theme of the cartoon story.

Understanding Theme

The **theme** of a story is an important idea that the author wishes to share with you. The events in the story and the things the characters do and say work together to illustrate the theme.

Most authors do not state the theme of a story in one sentence. You must think about what happens in the story and what the characters do and say. Then you must decide for yourself what important idea the author wants to share with you. This is the theme.

Read the following story. What is the theme?

Once there were three poor sisters. Their names were Tam, Cam, and Maria. One day the sisters came to a wide river. They met a little boy carrying a dog.

"Please," he said. "My home is across the river. Will you help me build a raft and take my poor dog home?"

Tam and Cam shook their heads. "It would take too much time and trouble. We will swim across."

Maria's answer was different. She immediately began to bind tree branches together to make a raft.

When Tam and Cam tried to swim across the river, the waves forced them back to shore. They became frightened and ran home.

Maria was not afraid. When the raft was ready, Maria, the boy, and his dog got aboard. The waves carried the raft across the river.

When the travelers reached the other shore, the boy and his dog suddenly turned into a king and his brother. The king explained that Maria had broken an evil spell.

Maria stayed in the king's country and became a great and famous woman. As for Tam and Cam, they stayed at home and never did much of anything.

What is the theme of this story? To decide, look for the important idea that the author wants to share with you. Look for the events in the story and what the characters do and say. What happened to Maria, who was kind? She became a great and famous woman. What happened to Tam and Cam? They stayed home and did nothing. What is the theme of the story? The author seems to be saying, "If you are kind, you will do well."

Remember, the theme of the story is an important message that the author wishes to share with you. You can take the theme with you and think about it long after you have finished a story.

Try This

Read the following story. Then answer the questions.

Midas was king, but he had no gold. This made him unhappy. He thought that a king needed gold to be great.

One day a stranger appeared in Midas's court. The stranger told Midas, "Wish for whatever you want most and your wish will come true." Then the stranger disappeared.

"I wish that all I touch would become gold!" he cried.

Midas went from room to room. Whatever he touched turned to gold. Soon the palace was full of golden rugs, tables, and chairs. Suddenly Midas saw his daughter, Marygold. He ran to tell her the good news. When he touched her, she turned to gold.

"Stranger," he called, "come take anything I have, but save my child!"

The stranger reappeared. He clapped his hands and changed everything back. King Midas was a wiser and happier man.

1. Why did Midas wish to turn things to gold?
2. What did he expect to happen after his wish came true? What really happened?
3. Which of the following is the theme of this story?

   a. Gold is the best color for furniture.
   b. Kings are greedy people.
   c. People are more important than riches.

Writing

1. Write one or more sentences to complete the story below. The theme of the story is: "If you are kind, you will be rewarded."

   One rainy day Nancy found a dog outside. She took the dog in and fed it. She knew that the dog's owners would want to find their pet. Nancy worked all afternoon making posters to tell about the lost dog. She put the posters up all over the neighborhood.

2. Rewrite the cartoon on page 374 as a paragraph. What is the theme? Who are the characters? How do they illustrate the story's theme?

   As you read "How They Told It," look for the theme—the most important idea—in each folktale.

The Oba Asks for a Mountain

a Nigerian tale

by HAROLD COURLANDER
and EZEKIEL ADEROGBA ESHUGBAYI

It was long ago. There was an Oba, or powerful chief, in the land of the Yoruba. He was not known for any virtues but for his love of war. It came to his ears that the kingdom of Ilesha was rich and prosperous. He decided he would loot Ilesha of its wealth, but he had no excuse to make war. So he sent messengers to Ilesha with a demand for tribute. The messengers arrived. They said, "The great Oba has sent us. He demands that a certain thing be done. If it is not done, his soldiers will come. They will make war. That is all. What is your answer?"

The people said, "What is the thing that is to be done? We will do it. We do not want war."

The messengers said, "The Oba has heard of the fine vegetables that are grown here. He wants a great quantity of these vegetables brought to him by the next festival day. But there is one thing. They must not be wrinkled and dried. They must be as fresh as when they are just taken from the earth."

The people said, "We shall bring them." But when the messengers had departed, the people said, "How can the vegetables be fresh when it takes a person fifteen days to go from here to there? They will be wrinkled and dried, and the Oba will make war upon us."

378

There was a man among them named Agiri-Asasa. He listened thoughtfully to what they said. "There is a way this thing can be done," Agiri-Asasa said. "Bring many pots and bowls. Dig up the vegetables with the earth around them and transplant them into these vessels. In this fashion they can be carried to the Oba."

As he described it, so it was done. They dug up the vegetables, earth and all, and carried them in pots and bowls to the distant town where the Oba lived. There they took the vegetables from the earth and brought them to the Oba's house. He was perplexed, for the vegetables were fresh and sweet. He said nothing. He wondered what task he could give to the people of Ilesha that they could not perform, so that he would have an excuse for war.

The next morning as the people of Ilesha were preparing to leave, the Oba sent for them. He presented them with a thigh of beef, saying, "One thing more must be done if there is to be no war. This thigh of beef I entrust to you to keep for me. Return it to me on the third day before the yam harvest festival. But take care that it is returned to me as fresh as it is now. Do not allow it to become spoiled and moldy. Otherwise I shall send my soldiers to make war against Ilesha."

The people took the thigh of beef. They went out of the town. They talked. One said, "How can we do it? This meat will be spoiled before we reach home. It will soon be nothing but carrion." Another said, "Yes, it is so. The Oba means to destroy us."

Then Agiri-Asasa spoke, saying, "No, there is a way to deal with this matter. Let us take it with us a little way." So they took the thigh of beef and continued their journey. Even before the sun went down, they came to a place where a man was preparing to slaughter a bull. Agiri-Asasa said to him, "Do not hurry to slaughter the bull. Take this thigh of beef instead. We entrust it to your keeping. Three days before the yam festival we will come again. Slaughter your bull on that day and give us the thigh. Thus nothing will be lost, and it will save us from carrying this meat on the road." It was arranged.

On the third day before the festival, the people of Ilesha returned and received the thigh of the newly slaughtered bull. They carried it to the Oba, saying, "See, as you have directed, we return the beef thigh to you. It is as fresh as the day it was given to us." The Oba examined the meat. He was puzzled. He sent the people away.

He was angry. He determined to give Ilesha a task it could not perform. He sent messengers again to Ilesha. They stood in the marketplace and delivered the words of the Oba. "The great Oba has this to say. The people of Ilesha must bring him the mountain called Oke-Umo. Otherwise, he will be compelled to bring war to Ilesha." The people listened. They were worried. But they showed the messengers great respect. They gave them food and drink.

When the messengers slept, the people discussed the matter. Agiri-Asasa had a plan. He said, "When morning comes, let us go to the mountain called Oke-Umo." When day arrived, ten thousand men of Ilesha escorted the messengers to the mountain. Every man had a carrying pad on his head. They surrounded the mountain in a circle. Agiri-Asasa called out, "Now lift the mountain and rest it on your carrying pads!" The ten thousand men tugged at trees and rocks, but they could not lift the mountain. At last Agiri-Asasa addressed the messengers this way: "Messengers of the great Oba, you see that we are willing to bring the mountain as the Oba has demanded. You see that we have ten thousand men ready to carry it. However, we cannot lift it. If the Oba will send his strongest men here to lift it onto our carrying pads, we will bring it to him without delay."

The messengers went home. They told the Oba. He listened. He said no more about the matter. He put Ilesha out of his mind.

Since that day, there has been a saying in Ilesha:

"There are people to carry the mountain,
But there is nobody to lift it."

Understanding What You've Read

1. Why did the Oba ask the people of Ilesha to do things that seemed impossible?
2. What was the first thing the Oba asked the people of Ilesha to do? How did they do it?
3. What was the last thing the Oba asked the people to do? What was their reason for not doing it?
4. Which of the following sentences best explains the theme of this story?

   a. It takes many people to lift a mountain.
   b. Fresh vegetables taste better than dried ones.
   c. Don't ask someone to do the impossible unless you are ready to do it yourself.

Writing

1. Write one or more sentences to complete the story below. The theme of this story is: "Cleverness can be more valuable than power." Make sure that the story ending you write fits the theme.

   > One day a hungry lion trapped the Oba, ten of his men, and Agiri-Asasa in a hut. Although the Oba and his men had weapons, none of them wanted to go out the door and face the lion. Agiri-Asasa knew that they would all be safe if they could somehow get out. Quickly, he snatched the Oba's sword and cut an opening in the back of the hut.

2. Write a sentence in which you explain in your own words the theme of "The Oba Asks for a Mountain."

The Seeing Stick

by JANE YOLEN

Once, in the ancient walled citadel of Peking, there lived an emperor who had only one daughter, and her name was Hwei Ming.

Hwei Ming had long black hair smoothed back with ivory combs. She had tiny feet encased in embroidered slippers. And she had small slim fingers covered with jade rings.

But rather than making her happy, such possessions made her sad. For Hwei Ming was blind, and all the beautiful handcrafted things in the kingdom brought her no pleasure at all.

Her father was also sad that his only daughter was blind, but he could not cry for her. He had given up weeping when he ascended the throne. Yet still he had hope that one day Hwei Ming might see. So he resolved that anyone who could help her would be rewarded with a fortune in jewels, and he sent word of his offer to the Inner and Outer Cities of Peking and to all the towns and villages for hundreds of miles around.

Monks came with their prayers and prayer wheels, for they thought in this way to help Hwei Ming see. Magician-priests came with their incantations and spells, for they thought in this way to help Hwei Ming see. Physicians came with their potions and pins, for they thought in this way to help Hwei Ming see.

But nothing helped. Hwei Ming had been blind from the day of her birth, and no one could cure her.

Now one day an old man, his clothes tattered from his travel, stopped by the gates of the Outer City. Far away in the south country where he lived, he had heard tales of the blind princess and of the emperor's offer. And so he had taken his few possessions—a long walking stick, made from a single shoot of golden wood, and his whittling knife—and started down the road.

The sun rose hot on his right side, and the sun set cool on his left as he made his way north to Peking to help the princess see.

The guards at the gate of the Outer City did not want to let in such a ragged old man. "Grandfather, go home. There is nothing here for such as you," they said.

The old man touched each of their faces in turn with his rough fingers. "So young," he said, "and already so old." He turned as if to go.

Ashamed that they had been unkind to an old man, the guards stared at the ground and shifted their feet uneasily.

The old man smiled to himself at their distress and turned back. Then he propped his walking stick against his side and reached into his shirt for his whittling knife.

"What are you doing, Grandfather?" called out one of the guards.

"I am going to show you my stick," said the old man. "For it is a stick that sees."

"Grandfather, that is nonsense," said the second guard. "That stick can see no more than the emperor's daughter. And she, poor child, has been blind from birth."

"Just so, just so," said the old man, nodding his head. "Still, it is a stick that sees."

"Indeed, Grandfather," said the second guard, "to repeat nonsense does not turn it into sense. You might as well say that the princess has eyes in her fingers."

"Just so, just so," said the old man. "But stranger things have happened." And so saying, he picked up the stick and told the guards how he had walked the many miles through villages and towns till he came with his seeing stick to the walls of Peking. As he told his tale, he carved pictures into the stick: an old man, the two guards, the walls of Peking.

The two guards watched in amazement. They were flattered by their likenesses in the golden wood of the old

man's stick. Indeed, they had never witnessed such skill. "Surely this is something the guards at the wall of the Inner City should see," they said. So, taking the old man by the arm, they guided him through the streets of the Outer City, past flower peddlers and rice sellers, past silk weavers and jewel merchants, up to the great stone walls.

When the guards of the Inner City saw the story stick, they were surprised and delighted. "Carve our faces, too," they begged like children. Laughing and touching their faces as any fond grandfather would, the old man did as they bid.

In no time at all, the guards of the Inner City took the old man by the arm and led him to the wall of the Imperial City and through the gate to the great wooden doors of the emperor's palace.

Now when the guards and the old man entered the throne room of the palace, it happened that the emperor's blind daughter, Hwei Ming, was sitting by his side — silent, sightless, and still. She listened as the guards told of the wonderful pictures carved on the golden shoot. When they finished, the princess clapped her hands. "Oh, I wish I could see that wondrous shoot," she said.

"Just so, just so," said the old man. "I will show it to you. For it is no ordinary stick, but a stick that sees."

"What nonsense," said her father in a voice so low it was almost a growl.

But the princess did not hear him. She had already bent toward the sound of the old man's voice. "A seeing stick?"

The old man did not say anything for a moment. Then he leaned forward and touched Hwei Ming's head and cheek. For though she was a princess, she was still a child. The old man smiled, reached into his shirt, and pulled out his knife.

Then, with the stick in one hand and his knife in the other, he began again to tell the story of his long journey to Peking. As he introduced each character and object, he carved a face and figure into the shoot. And as he finished each one, the old man took Hwei Ming's small fingers in his and placed them on the shoot. Finger on finger he helped her trace the likenesses.

"Feel the long flowing hair of the princess," the old man said. "Grown as she herself has grown, straight and true."

And Hwei Ming touched the carved shoot.

"Now feel your own long hair," he said.

And she did.

"Feel the lines in the old man's face," he said. "Years of worry and years of joy." He put the stick into her hands again.

And Hwei Ming's slim fingers felt the carved shoot.

Then he put her fingers onto his face and traced the same lines there. It was the first time the princess had touched another person's face since she was a very small girl.

The princess jumped up from her throne and thrust her hands before her. "Guards, guards," she cried out. "Come here to me."

And the guards lifted their faces to the princess Hwei Ming's hands. Her fingers, like little breezes, brushed their eyes and noses and mouths, and then found each face on the seeing stick.

Hwei Ming turned to her father, the emperor, who sat straight and tall and unmoving on his great throne. She reached out, and her fingers ran eagerly through his hair, down his nose and cheek, and rested curiously on a tear they found there. And that was strange, indeed, for had not the emperor given up crying when he ascended the throne?

They brought her through the streets of the city, then, the emperor himself leading the procession. And Princess Hwei Ming touched men and women and children as they passed. Till at last she stood before the walls of Peking and felt the great stones themselves.

Then she turned to the old man, her voice bright and full of laughter. "Tell me another tale," she said.

"Tomorrow, if you wish," he replied,

For each tomorrow as long as he lived, the old man dwelt in the Innermost City. The emperor rewarded him with a fortune in jewels, but the old man gave them all away. Every day he told the princess a story. Some were as ancient as the city itself. Some were as new as the events of the day. And each time he carved wonderful images onto a shoot of golden wood.

As the princess listened, she grew eyes on the tips of her fingers—at least that is what she told the other blind children whom she taught to see as she saw, with her hands. Certainly it was as true as saying she had a seeing stick.

But the blind princess Hwei Ming believed that both things were true.

And so did all the blind children in her city of Peking.

And so did the blind old man.

Understanding What You've Read

1. Why was Hwei Ming unhappy?
2. What did the emperor do to help his daughter?
3. Which of the following sentences best fits the theme of this story?

    a. Sticks and stones may break your bones, but names will never hurt you.
    b. You see and understand the world around you, *not* with your eyes, but with your heart.
    c. Princesses and emperors lived in Peking.

4. Why do you think the old man succeeded in helping the princess when so many others had failed?

Writing

1. Pretend that you are the princess or the old man. Write a sentence or two that explains how the seeing stick helps you see.
2. Write a paragraph or two that explains this theme: "You see and understand the world around you, *not* with your eyes, but with your heart." Use one of the following real people as a character in your paragraphs:

    a. Louis Braille, a blind man who invented an alphabet people read with their fingertips
    b. Helen Keller, a blind and deaf young woman who learned how to read using the braille alphabet and became a famous author
    c. José Feliciano, a blind musician discussed earlier on pages 175–178 in this book

Petronella

by JAY WILLIAMS

In the kingdom of Skyclear Mountain, three princes were always born to the king and queen. The oldest prince was always called Michael, the middle prince was always called George, and the youngest was always called Peter. When they were grown up, they always went to seek their fortunes. What happened to the oldest prince and the middle prince no one ever knew. But the youngest prince always rescued a princess, brought her home and, in time, ruled over the kingdom. That was the way it had always been. And so far as anyone knew, that was the way it would always be.

Until now.

"Now" was the time of King Peter the Twenty-ninth and Queen Blossom. An oldest prince was born and a middle prince. But the youngest prince turned out to be a girl.

"Well," said the king gloomily, "we can't call her Peter. We'll have to call her Petronella. And what's to be done about it, I'm sure I don't know."

There was nothing to be done. The years passed, and the time came for the princes to go out and seek their fortunes. Michael and George said good-by to the king and queen and mounted their horses. Then out came Petronella. She was dressed in traveling clothes, with a sword by her side and her bag packed.

"If you think," she said, "that I'm going to sit at home, you are mistaken. I'm going to seek my fortune, too."

"Impossible!" said the king.

393

"What will people say?" cried the queen.

"Look here," said Prince Michael, "be reasonable, Pet. Stay home and wait. Sooner or later a prince will turn up."

Petronella smiled. She was a tall, handsome girl with flaming red hair, and when she smiled in that particular way, it meant she was trying to keep her temper.

"I'm going with you," she said. "I'll find a prince if I have to rescue one from something myself. And that's that."

The grooms brought out her horse, and she said goodby to her parents. Up she sprang to the saddle, and away she went behind her two brothers.

They traveled into the flat lands below Skyclear Mountain. After many days, they entered a great, dark forest. They came to a place where the road divided into three, and there at the fork sat a little, wrinkled old man covered with dust and spider webs.

Prince Michael said, haughtily, "Where do these roads go, old man?"

"The road on the right goes to the city of Gratz," said the old man. "The road in the center goes to the castle of Blitz. The road on the left goes to the house of Albion the enchanter. And that's one."

"What do you mean by 'And that's one'?" asked Prince George.

"I mean," said the old man, "that I am forced to sit on this spot without stirring, and that I must answer one question from each person who passes by. And that's two."

Petronella's kind heart was touched. "Is there anything I can do to help you?" she asked.

The old man sprang to his feet. The dust fell from him in clouds.

"You have already done so," he said. "For that question is the one which releases me. I have sat here for sixty-two years waiting for someone to ask me that." He snapped his fingers with joy. "In return, I will tell you anything you wish to know."

"Where can I find a prince?" Petronella said promptly.

"There is one in the house of Albion the enchanter," the old man answered.

"Ah," said Petronella, "then that is where I am going."

"In that case I will leave you," said her oldest brother, Michael. "For I am going to the castle of Blitz to see if I can find my fortune there."

"Good luck," said Prince George. "For I am going to the city of Gratz. I have a feeling my fortune is there."

They embraced her and rode away.

Petronella looked thoughtfully at the old man, who was combing spider webs and dust out of his beard. "May I ask you something else?" she said.

"Of course. Anything."

"Suppose I wanted to rescue that prince from the enchanter. How would I go about it? I haven't any experience in such things, you see."

The old man chewed a piece of his beard. "I do not know everything," he said, after a moment. "I know that there are three magical secrets that, if you can get them from Albion, will help you."

"How can I get them?" asked Petronella.

"You must offer to work for him. He will set you three tasks, and if you do them you may ask for a reward. You must ask him for a comb for your hair, a mirror to look into, and a ring for your finger."

"And then?"

"I do not know. I only know that when you rescue the prince, you can use these things to escape from the enchanter."

"It doesn't sound easy," Petronella sighed.

"Nothing we really want is easy," said the old man. "Look at me — I have wanted my freedom, and I've had to wait sixty-two years for it."

Petronella said good-by to him. She mounted her horse and galloped along the third road.

It ended at a low, rambling house with a red roof. It was a comfortable-looking house, surrounded by gardens and stables and trees heavy with fruit. On the lawn, in an armchair, sat a handsome young man with his face turned to the sky and his eyes closed.

Petronella tied her horse to the gate and walked across the lawn.

"Is this the house of Albion the enchanter?" she said.

The young man blinked up at her in surprise.

"I think so," he said. "Yes, I'm sure it is."

"And who are you?"

The young man yawned and stretched. "I am Prince Ferdinand of Firebright," he replied. "Would you mind stepping aside? I'm trying to get a sunburn, and you're standing in the way."

Petronella snorted. "You don't sound like much of a prince."

"That's funny," said the young man, closing his eyes. "That's what my father always says."

At that moment, the door of the house opened and out came a man dressed all in black and silver. He was tall and thin and as sinister as a cloud full of thunder. His face was stern but full of wisdom. Petronella knew at once that he must be the enchanter.

He bowed to her, politely. "What can I do for you?"

"I wish to work for you," said Petronella, boldly.

Albion nodded. "I cannot refuse you," he said. "But I must warn you it will be dangerous. Tonight I will give you a task. If you do it, I will reward you. But if you fail, you must die."

Petronella glanced at the prince and sighed. "If I must, I must," she said. "Very well."

That evening, they all had dinner together in the enchanter's cozy kitchen. Then Albion took Petronella out to a stone building and unbolted its door. Inside were seven huge black dogs.

"You must watch my hounds all night," said he.

Petronella went inside, and Albion closed and locked the door.

At once, the hounds began to snarl and bark. They showed their teeth at her. But Petronella was a real princess. She plucked up her courage. Instead of backing away, she went toward the dogs. She began to speak to them in a quiet voice. The dogs stopped snarling and sniffed at her. She patted their heads.

"I see what it is," she said. "You are lonely here. I will keep you company."

And so all night long she sat on the floor and talked to the hounds and stroked them. They lay close to her, panting.

In the morning, Albion came to let her out. "Ah," said he, "I see that you are brave. If you had run from the dogs, they would have torn you to pieces. Now you may ask for what you want."

"I want a comb for my hair," said Petronella.

The enchanter gave her a comb carved from a piece of black wood.

Prince Ferdinand was sunning himself and working at a crossword puzzle. Petronella said, in a low voice, "I am doing this for you."

"That's nice," said the prince. "What's 'selfish' in nine letters?"

"You are," snapped Petronella. She went to the enchanter. "I will work for you once more," she said.

That night, Albion led her to a stable. Inside were seven huge white horses.

"Tonight," he said, "you must watch my steeds."

He went out and locked the door. At once, the horses began to rear and neigh. They pawed at her with their iron hooves.

But Petronella was a real princess. She looked closely at them and saw that their ribs stuck out. Their coats were rough and their manes and tails full of burrs.

"I see what it is," she said. "You are hungry and dirty."

She brought them as much hay as they could eat and began to brush them. All night long, she fed them and groomed them, and they stood quietly in their stalls.

In the morning, Albion let her out. "You are as kind as you are brave," said he. "If you had run from them, they would have trampled you under their hooves. What will you have as a reward?"

"I want a mirror to look into," answered Petronella. The enchanter gave her a mirror made of gray silver.

She looked across the lawn at Prince Ferdinand, who was doing sitting-up exercises. He was certainly very handsome. She said to the enchanter, "I will work for you once more."

That night, Albion led her to a loft above the stables. There, on perches, were seven great red hawks.

"Tonight," said he, "you must watch my falcons."

As soon as Petronella was locked in, the hawks began to beat their wings and scream at her.

Petronella laughed. "That is not how birds sing," she said. "Listen."

She began to sing in a sweet voice. The hawks fell silent. All night long she sang to them, and they sat like feathered statues on their perches, listening.

In the morning, Albion said, "You are as talented as you are kind and brave. If you had run from them, they would have pecked and clawed you without mercy. What do you want now?"

"I want a ring for my finger," said Petronella.

The enchanter gave her a ring made from a single diamond.

All that day and all that night, Petronella slept, for she was very tired. But early the next morning she crept into Prince Ferdinand's room. He was sound asleep, wearing purple pajamas.

"Wake up," whispered Petronella. "I am going to rescue you."

Ferdinand awoke and stared sleepily at her. "What time is it?"

"Never mind that," said Petronella. "Come on!"

"But I'm still sleepy," Ferdinand objected. "And it's so pleasant here."

Petronella shook her head. "You're not much of a prince," she said, grimly. "But you're the best I can do. Come along."

She grabbed him by the wrist and dragged him out of bed. She hauled him down the stairs. His horse and hers were in another stable, and she saddled them quickly. She gave the prince a shove, and he mounted. She jumped on her own horse, seized the prince's reins, and away they went like the wind.

They had not gone far when they heard a tremendous thumping. Petronella looked back. A dark cloud rose behind them, and beneath it she saw the enchanter. He was running with great strides, faster than her horse could go.

"What shall we do?" she cried.

"Don't ask me," said Prince Ferdinand, grumpily. "I'm all shaken to bits by this fast riding."

Petronella desperately pulled out the comb. "The old man said that this would help me," she said. And because she didn't know what else to do with it, she threw it on the ground. At once, a forest rose up between her and the enchanter. The trees were so thick that no one could get between them.

Away went Petronella and the prince. But the enchanter turned himself into an ax and began to chop. Right and left he chopped, flashing, and the trees fell before him. Soon he was through the wood, and once again Petronella heard his footsteps thumping behind.

She reined in her horse. She took out the mirror and threw it on the ground. At once, a wide lake spread out behind her, gray and glittering.

Off they went again. But the enchanter sprang into the water, turning himself into a salmon as he did so. He swam across the lake and leaped out of the water onto the other bank. Petronella heard him coming thump! thump! behind them again.

This time, she threw down the ring. It didn't turn into anything, but lay shining on the ground.

The enchanter came running up. He jumped over the ring. And as he jumped, the ring opened wide and then snapped up around him, holding his arms tight to his body in a magical grip from which he could not escape.

"Well," said Prince Ferdinand, "that's the end of him."

Petronella looked at him in annoyance. Then she looked at the enchanter, held fast in the ring.

"Brother!" she said. "I can't just leave him here. He'll starve to death."

She got off her horse and went up to him. "If I release you," she said, "will you promise to let the prince go free?"

Albion stared at her in astonishment. "Let him go free?" he said. "What are you talking about? I'm glad to get rid of him."

It was Petronella's turn to look surprised. "I don't understand," she said. "Weren't you holding him prisoner?"

"Certainly not," said Albion. "He came to visit me for a weekend. At the end of it, he said, 'It's so pleasant here, do you mind if I stay on for another day or two?' I'm very polite, and I said, 'Of course.' He stayed on and on and on. I didn't like to be rude to a guest, and I couldn't just kick him out. I don't know what I'd have done if you hadn't dragged him away."

"But then—" said Petronella. "But then—why did you come running after him this way?"

"I wasn't chasing him," said the enchanter. "I was chasing you. You are just the woman I've been looking for. You are brave and kind and talented—and beautiful as well."

"Oh," said Petronella.

"I see," she said.

"Hm," said she. "How do I get this ring off you?"

"Give me a kiss."

She did so. The ring vanished from around Albion and reappeared on Petronella's finger.

"I don't know what my parents will say when I come home with you instead of a prince," she said.

"Let's go and find out, shall we?" said the enchanter, cheerfully.

He mounted one horse and Petronella the other. And off they trotted, side by side, leaving Ferdinand of Firebright to walk home as best he could.

Understanding What You've Read

1. Why did Petronella go to the house of Albion the enchanter?
2. Which of the following themes best fits this story?

   a. Horses need to be brushed and combed every night.
   b. All princes are selfish.
   c. If you are kind and brave, you will do well.

3. Find at least three details on pages 398–401 that illustrate the story's theme.
4. Before Petronella got to know Albion and Ferdinand, what did she think of them? What details on pages 397–398 tell you this? What did she think of them at the end of the story? What details on pages 403–404 tell you this?

Writing

1. Pretend that you are the old man who met Petronella. (See pages 394–396.) Write two or more sentences about the meeting. Explain how she was kind to you, and tell what you did in return to help her do well.
2. Write a paragraph that tells what happens after Petronella returns home. The theme for your paragraph is: "A kind heart can be better than a royal name." Include in your paragraph, along with Petronella and Albion, the characters Prince Ferdinand and the king and queen.

More Folktales to Read

The Golden Lynx and Other Tales selected by Augusta Baker. Lippincott, 1960. A well-known storyteller retells tales of spells and enchantment from sixteen countries.

And It Is Still That Way edited by Byrd Baylor. Scribner, 1976. In this book, Papago, Navajo, Hopi, Pima, Apache, Quechei, and Cocepah legends of how and why are retold by today's children of these cultures.

The Enchanted Orchard and Other Folktales of Central America edited by Dorothy Sharp Carter. Harcourt Brace Jovanovich, 1973. These tales of magic and adventure reflect the many cultures that make up Central America.

The Piece of Fire and Other Haitian Tales by Harold Courlander. Harcourt Brace Jovanovich, 1964. Here are twenty-six tales that reflect Haiti's European and African heritages.

Clever Gretchen and Other Forgotten Folktales retold by Alison Lurie. T. Y. Crowell, 1980. These folktales tell of clever and brave women from all over the world.

The Toad Is the Emperor's Uncle and Other Stories by Vo-Dinh. Doubleday, 1970. These folktales from Vietnam are full of animals, surprises, and humor.

The Moon Ribbon and Other Tales by Jane Yolen. T. Y. Crowell, 1976. These six stories are traditional in feeling, yet all are new and original.

Part 7

Discoveries, Ideas, and Inventions

Separating Facts from Fictional Details

1

KNOBBY

2

What is the main difference between the two pictures above? Picture 1 is a photograph of a real computer. Picture 2 also shows a computer. Like a real computer, "Knobby" has dials and buttons and gives answers. But the big difference between the two pictures is that the computer in picture 1 is real. Knobby, however, is made up. An artist **imagined** what a computer with a personality would be like.

Is It a Fact?

We say that stories that are made up or imagined are **fiction.** Many books are a mixture of fact and fiction. Some details are facts. A **fact** is something that can be proved. Some details are fiction—that is, the author made up these details.

Which of the sentences below state facts?

1. Marie and Pierre Curie discovered radium in 1898.
2. Benjamin Franklin invented the lightning rod.
3. Covered in bearskin blankets, the Stone Age family shivered in their cave.

In an article about Marie and Pierre Curie in an encyclopedia, you would find that statement 1 is a fact. Marie and Pierre Curie did discover radium in 1898. You could also find the fact in sentence 2 in an encyclopedia.

Is sentence 3 a statement of fact or of fiction? Since no one living today was alive during the Stone Age, and since Stone Age people left no written records, the writer must have imagined this scene.

Imagination is an important tool for authors who want to tell about the past. In order to make books about the past seem real and interesting, authors often imagine conversations and actions that may have happened. They do this after learning everything they can about the person or time they are writing about.

Fictional Details Based on Facts

When you read about something that happened in the past, do you ever wonder where the author got his or her information? As you read the following paragraphs about Betty Zane, think about which details might be facts. Which details do you think the author may have made up?

1. In September 1782, the settlement of Fort Henry, in what is now Wheeling, West Virginia, was attacked. Thirteen-year-old Betty, her uncle Ebenezer Zane, and the other settlers were in the fort when the fighting began. When the settlers' supply of gunpowder was almost gone, Betty's uncle realized that their only hope was a keg of gunpowder that had been forgotten in the Zane cabin. The cabin was outside the fort. But who would make that dangerous run? Many were wounded and too weak to make the run. Colonel Shepard finally agreed to allow Betty to go.

2. "Please let me run for the gunpowder, Colonel Shepard," Betty pleaded. "You can't spare a sharpshooter. Many are too weak from wounds to go. I am young and I am a fast runner."

There are no records to prove that Betty said these words to Colonel Shepard. However, the facts in paragraph 1 show that Betty *might* have said such words.

Here are some other facts about Betty Zane and this event:

a. Betty brought the gunpowder back to the fort.
b. The settlers were able to fight off the attackers and save Fort Henry.
c. It was the last frontier battle of the American Revolution.

411

Now read paragraphs 3 and 4. Notice how the author presents some of the facts through Betty's and Colonel Shepard's words.

3. "You are a brave young woman, Betty," Colonel Shepard said. "You made it possible for us to withstand the fight and save Fort Henry."
4. "Thank you, Colonel Shepard," Betty answered. "I'm glad I was able to make the run. I can tell you now that no trip of one hundred miles could have seemed longer than the hundred yards back to the fort."

There are no records that show that Betty and Colonel Shepard said these words. But is it *possible* that they said these words?

How to Recognize the Difference Between Facts and Fictional Details

It is not always easy—or even possible—to recognize the difference between facts and fictional details. Authors generally try to make imagined events seem like facts. Nevertheless, as a critical reader, you should be aware that an author may be using fictional details along with facts. You should try to understand where the author got the facts on which to base his or her writing. Was a conversation written down at the time it was held? Did the famous person in history keep a diary or write a book about his or her experiences? Did an event take place long before anyone kept records? Is an event taking place in the future? If you ask yourself such questions, you will understand how the writer has made fact and fiction work together to make a more interesting story.

Try This

Read the paragraphs below. Which one states only facts? Which one seems to mix facts and fictional details? What are the fictional details?

1. Sacajawea saw Clark's compass fall from his hand into the rushing waters. Sacajawea knew how much the red-haired man needed the compass. She dived. Immediately she felt the shock of the cold and the current's force.

2. Sacajawea, a Shoshone woman, led the Lewis and Clark expedition over the Rocky Mountains in 1804. Sacajawea knew how to get food in the wilderness. She was able to judge the best ways over the mountains and across the rivers. Lewis and Clark's journals make it clear that she was the most important member of the expedition.

Antonyms

The almost kind Professor Crum sat in the flickering light of a candle and wrote in his diary.

Dear Diary,

Oh horror of horrors! My **evil** plan has failed! Instead of a **victory**, I'm afraid I must record my defeat. You see, I had the nasty idea of not removing the grapefruit seeds from the freshly squeezed grapefruit juice (hee, hee, hee). I expected everybody to develop a great dislike toward me. You know how much I love to be hated. But guess what happened? They showered me with **affection**! They thought the grapefruit seeds were a good gift! How was I supposed to know they grow into nice plants?

Gosh! Being rotten used to be **fascinating**. Now it's dull. I'm afraid the evil Professor Crum is all washed up.

Word Play

Read each sentence below and choose an antonym (word with an opposite meaning) for the word in boldface. Then make a sentence using each word in boldface.

1. They showered me with **affection**!
   a. perfume   b. love   c. dislike

2. Instead of a **victory**, I'm afraid I must record my defeat.
   a. success   b. defeat   c. win

3. Being rotten used to be **fascinating**.
   a. frightening   b. interesting   c. dull

4. My **evil** plan has failed!
   a. good   b. nasty   c. stupid

The events in the following selection took place a few years ago. The author made up some of the conversation. Look for facts on which the conversations were based.

Why did a school in California need 501 balloons? It was so that the students could be . . .

THE WIND WATCHERS

by Edith Battles

Mr. Boone, the principal, looked surprised. "Five hundred balloons! Whatever would you do with five hundred balloons?"

"Oh, not just for us," said Scott. "For the whole school. Everybody."

"We need balloons," Lori said, "to let them float away. Then we will know in which direction the wind blows."

"Wouldn't one balloon do?" asked Mr. Boone.

Scott frowned. "One might get lost and we'd never know where it went. Besides, there are 500 kids at 230th Street School. All the kids will want to launch their own balloons. And, out of 500, some of them have got to be found."

"Well," said the principal slowly, "I really don't see how we can do it with 500 balloons. I'm sure that is the wrong number."

The children's hopes fell.

"So I'll order 501," said Mr. Boone. "You see," he went on, "each child will want to launch a balloon. They add up to 500. I want to launch one, too! That's one more."

Making Plans

Scott and Lori's class began to make plans right away. They knew that for a balloon to stay up, it must be filled with a gas that is lighter than air. Hydrogen or helium will keep a balloon up. But the class decided to use only helium. It is a safe gas because it will not burn or explode.

Ms. Green, Lori and Scott's teacher, sent for books and movies about wind and weather. The children searched through the books and the encyclopedia. They made instruments to measure the wind's speed. They made wind vanes to show the direction of the wind. Each morning and afternoon for a week, they checked how fast the wind blew and where

it blew from. They wrote down what they learned.

"What did you find out?" asked Ms. Green a week later.

"The wind has more speed in the afternoon," said Lori. "And it usually blows from the west."

Joan waved her hand wildly. "They call our California winds the 'prevailing westerlies.' I read it in the encyclopedia."

Jerry raised his hand. "Well, we *think* the balloons will all blow to the east. But how can we know for sure? We won't see any of them land."

"Why will the balloons land at all? Why don't they just stay up?" asked Mary.

"They lose some of the gas," said John. "Then they are too heavy to float in air."

"Jerry's question wasn't answered," said Ms. Green. "How can we check to find where the balloons land?"

The children all had ideas, but Scott had the best one. He suggested that they tie a post card to each balloon. The school's address would be on one side. A message on the other side would ask the finders to write to the school about when and where they found the balloons.

Then Scott had a question. "We are near an airport. Will our balloons bother the pilots?"

To find out, one of the children called the airport. "Your balloons are not large enough to cause us any problem," said the man at Airport Tower Control. "But we must be told the time you plan to release them so that our pilots will not be surprised."

Scott and Lori made a note on their long list of things to do.

Getting Started

Scott and Lori thought that only a few people would want to send messages, but nearly every child in the school brought nickels and pennies to buy a post card. Then Scott and Lori went to the post office and bought enough post cards for everyone. The children all signed their names on the cards.

Scott and Lori decided to sign the same card. Each of them made a secret wish about whom they wanted to find their balloon.

One morning Mr. Boone came to the classroom. "The Weather Service says that no storm will come until the end of the week. So let's set the day for Wednesday. I ordered balloons to be here by then."

As Wednesday drew near, Ms. Green's class was very busy. Scott checked off the things that needed to be done. When each job was finished, he drew a line through it on the list.

"The balloons are here," Mr. Boone told them. There were more than 500 of them, just in case some balloons burst. Scott drew a line through the words ORDER BALLOONS.

"The helium is here," said the science teacher. Scott drew a line through the words ORDER HELIUM.

"Your cards are finally stamped with the school's address," said the school secretary. Scott drew a line through ADDRESS POST CARDS.

The children brought large plastic bags. Scott drew a line through the words GET BAGS TO HOLD FILLED BALLOONS.

On the last day, the younger children tied the post cards on strings. In the science room, the teacher and older children took turns filling the many balloons with helium.

Sometimes a balloon burst. Sometimes a balloon got away and went straight to the ceiling.

Up, Up, and Away

A few minutes before two o'clock, the teachers led their classes to the playground. When everyone was gathered—all 500 children and many, many balloons—Mr. Boone gave the go signal.

The children released their balloons. Everyone began to shout. The big balloon clusters lifted smoothly. In a few seconds they were colorful shapes in the sky. Post cards fluttered in the sunlight.

"They're going east! They're going east!" Ms. Green's children called out.

"I see mine!" "There it goes!" "I lost it!" "It's gone."

Mr. Boone let his own balloon go free. It rose in the sunlight. It, too, went east with the others. The balloons were like marbles now, and then stars, and then—nothing.

"We may never know where most of them go," said Ms. Green. "Away from the cities, America has much empty land. Many balloons will be lost. But some will be found and their cards returned. We'll mark each place on our map."

The Answers Come

Two days later, two post cards arrived in the mail. On the same day as the launching, three small boys had found a balloon near the freeway. A workman had found some balloons in a half-built building twenty miles east.

Each day during the next two weeks, cards arrived from farther away. Every balloon had gone eastward. A few had fallen fifty miles east of the city.

Joan's card was signed by a motel owner in Arizona, over 400 air miles away. "It *did* go over the mountains!" she said.

Each time a post card arrived, a colored pin was placed on the

map showing where it came from. Most of the pins were clustered near the city. But more and more began to scatter farther east.

As the days followed, fifty-four children learned where their balloons had gone.

"But not me," said Lori. "I wished on my balloon, but I never got an answer."

Scott was very quiet. He had wished on the same balloon as Lori.

Some Surprises

One day, nearly a week after the last post card had straggled back, Mr. Boone came to the classroom.

"Boys and girls, my card came in the mail today."

"From where?" asked the children.

"Guess," said the principal.

All the children raised their hands and made guesses. No one was right. "We give up."

"Hawaii!" said Mr. Boone.

They all laughed and hooted. "It couldn't go to Hawaii," John said. "That is west. The winds carried your balloon east. I saw it go. Even if it rose as high as the jet stream, it just couldn't get all the way around the world and back to Hawaii."

"Well," admitted Mr. Boone, "it needed a little help. It landed on an ocean liner in Long Beach

harbor, and the finder mailed the card to me from Hawaii.

"But that isn't the main reason I came. I have a letter for Scott and Lori. It's postmarked Colorado. Do you know anybody in Colorado?"

Scott and Lori raced to the front of the room. They read the letter together:

Dear Lori and Scott,

I was feeling very lonely today when our dog, Alfred, found your balloon in my yard. It was like having a visit with grandchildren to have your message drop in that way. I live a thousand miles from California on an old-fashioned sheep ranch in Colorado. My husband and I take care of the ranch ourselves. When we take the sheep to the high mountains to graze each summer, Alfred helps us watch the sheep.

My husband and I think it would be very nice to have a letter from California telling us all about your school. If you know any children out there who would like to write to two faraway grandparents, tell them about us.

Your balloon friends,
Jennie and George Johnson
and Alfred

Lori read each word with delight.

"The wish did it! Wishes really *can* be made on balloons!"

Scott said, "Well, I wished that our balloon would be found by someone who has lots of room to run and play and a dog and other pets to play with. I want to visit them someday."

"I wished my balloon would find me a grandmother," Lori told Scott. "And it did."

"We both got our wish then!"

Understanding What You've Read

1. What did the children wish to show through their balloon launching?
2. What materials did the children need in order to do their study?
3. In which direction did the children *expect* the balloons to go? In which direction did the balloons go? What did this show about the winds in California?

Applying the Skills Lesson

1. Find at least three examples of quotations the author might have made up. Explain why you think these words are made up.
2. Read again the sixth and seventh paragraphs on page 420. Who is saying the words in quotation marks? Do you think the speakers actually said these exact words—or did they say something *like* this?

TEXTBOOK STUDY

Separating Facts from Fictional Details

Textbooks are mostly factual. Sometimes, however, the facts are not known for certain. When you read about people and events from the past, be aware that only some statements may be based on facts. The author may also have used fictional details.

As you read the following selections, think about which statements may be based on facts. Try to answer the questions in the sidenotes that go with the first selection.

Separating Facts from Fictional Details in Social Studies

The Canoe

Black Moon stepped out of his wigwam with a tingle of excitement. It flowed through him as he stood there in his moccasins and leather trousers. Today, after long weeks of labor, his canoe would be finished.

This story is set about 500 years ago. Black Moon is a *fictional character.* That is, the author made him up. What facts might the author have based this story on?

Long ago he had found a birch tree of the size and type he needed. Carefully, using his stone knife, he cut great sheets of bark from the birch. He had then chopped down a giant cedar tree. It gave him strong, clean wood for the ribs and framework of his boat. Finally, he dug up long tough roots from a black spruce tree. With these he sewed together the sheets of bark.

Now all around him lay his tools. There were his axe, hammer, wedge, scraper, and his knife with its leather handle. All of these he had made himself from stone. There were also pointed sticks of hard wood, and the bow of bone with which he drilled holes for the framework of his canoe. Finally there was his measuring stick with its carefully placed notches. With it he made sure that the sides of his boat were even and the ribs properly placed.

How would the author know that Black Moon's tools were made of stone? How would the author know what kinds of tools Black Moon made?

— *The United States*
Houghton Mifflin

Building Skills

Below are some facts that the author might have used when writing about Black Moon. In the selection above, find sentences based on the following facts:

1. Archaeologists have found 500-year-old stone tools in North America.
2. Scientists have been able to make a canoe using stone tools like those described in the selection.
3. Some Native Americans today make canoes from cedar, birch, and spruce trees.
4. For hundreds of years, some Native Americans have worn leather moccasins and trousers.
5. Archaeologists have found 500-year-old "drills," fashioned out of animal bone, that could be used to bore holes.

Separating Facts from Fictional Details
   in Language Arts

There are no sidenotes for this selection. Read it and then answer the questions that follow it.

Study the following notes. They are based on an encyclopedia article about Christopher Columbus.

Oct. 10, 1492

Unhappy crew agreed to sail three more days before going back home

Oct. 12, 1492

Island of San Salvador sighted
Columbus thought he was near Japan or an island of the Indies

Oct. 28, 1492

Reached Cuba, thinking he was in China
Saw people smoking cigars

Jan. 16, 1493

Began return trip to Spain

Mar. 15, 1493

Reached Palos, Spain. Went to Barcelona and received grand reception
Named *Admiral of the Ocean Sea* and *Viceroy of the Indies*
Began getting ready for second voyage

Now pretend for a moment that you are a Spanish newspaper reporter in 1493. Read this example of a news story you might have written for your newspaper.

Explorer Returns Safely

Barcelona, March 30, 1493. Christopher Columbus was the guest of honor at a large party given by the King and Queen last week. Columbus was given the title of *Admiral of the Ocean Sea* for his great courage in sailing west to China. Besides the weather, he had to worry about a possible mutiny among his crew members.

Columbus was named *Viceroy of the Indies* for discovering a new route to that part of the world. He reached an island of the Indies on October 12, 1492, and he named the island San Salvador. He was very interested in meeting the Chinese emperor, but he couldn't find anyone who knew where the emperor lived.

Columbus has many stories to tell about the people of the islands he visited. One such story has to do with their custom of smoking a leaf that they grow. Columbus said it smells awful.

He is now preparing for his second voyage to the Indies. This time he hopes to meet the emperor of China and the rulers of Japan.

— Discovery in English
Laidlaw Brothers

Building Skills

Read the following sentences from the newspaper story. On which facts from the encyclopedia article is each sentence based?

1. Christopher Columbus was the guest of honor at a large party given by the King and Queen last week.
2. Besides the weather, he had to worry about a possible mutiny among his crew members.
3. One such story has to do with their custom of smoking a leaf that they grow.
4. Columbus said it smells awful.
5. He is now preparing for his second voyage to the Indies.

Drawing Conclusions

What's happening in the picture? What are the children doing? How are they feeling?

If you said that the children are watching a funny movie, you **drew a conclusion.** How did you draw this conclusion? If you've ever been to a movie theater, you know it is dark and has rows of seats like those in the picture. What made you draw the conclusion that the movie is *funny*?

You have been drawing conclusions most of your life. For instance, suppose you see smoke. You draw a conclusion that there's a fire. Suppose you hear a horn honking outside your window. You draw the conclusion that the driver of a car or truck is trying to get someone's attention.

Using the Facts

When you read, you draw conclusions, too. You think about the facts that the author presents. You use these facts to draw a conclusion. Read the paragraph below. What conclusions can you draw from the facts given?

Supposedly, around the year 2,000 B.C., some Phoenician sailors moored their ship off a beach in the Mediterranean Sea. The ship had been carrying blocks of soda. The sailors built a fire on the beach to cook their dinner. They needed something to hold their cooking pot over the fire. So they used a block of soda. The soda and the sand, heated by the fire, turned into a bubbly liquid. How surprised the sailors must have been when the liquid cooled and turned into a smooth sheet of glass!

Which of the following conclusions can you draw from the facts given in the paragraph?

1. Glass can be made by heating sand and soda.
2. Glass can *only* be made by heating sand and soda.
3. The Phoenician sailors discovered glass by accident.

Sentence 1 is a good conclusion. The paragraph tells you that the soda and sand, heated by the fire, turned into a liquid. The end result was a smooth sheet of glass.

The paragraph does not give you enough information to draw the conclusion in sentence 2.

Why is sentence 3 a good conclusion? Did the Phoenician sailors set out to make glass? What words in the paragraph help you to know that their discovery was an accident?

Using Facts Plus Your Own Experience

Sometimes, to draw a conclusion, you need more than the facts that the author gives. You may also need to use your own experience or knowledge. What conclusion can you draw from the following sentence?

When the woman heard the news, her face turned pale, her eyes filled with tears, and her smile turned to a frown.

The author did not actually say that the news was bad. But you can draw the conclusion that it was. In the sentence, there are three clues to help you: (1) the woman's face turned pale; (2) her eyes filled with tears; and (3) her smile turned to a frown. You know that people who behave in this way are usually upset. So you can *conclude* that the woman was upset because the news was bad.

432

Authors depend on the reader to draw conclusions. They expect the reader to use knowledge and reasoning to understand ideas that are not actually stated. In this way, authors expect the reader to "read between the lines."

Try This

Read the following paragraphs. Study the conclusions that follow each. Choose the one conclusion that can be drawn from each paragraph.

Pluto

Neptune

1. The farther a planet is from the sun, the colder it is. Pluto is the ninth planet from the sun. Neptune is the eighth planet from the sun.

    a. Neptune is colder than Pluto.
    b. Pluto is colder than Neptune.
    c. Neptune and Pluto are the same temperature.

2. An island is a body of land surrounded by water. Hawaii is made up of 8 major islands and 124 small islands. The largest of the 8 islands is called Hawaii.

    a. Hawaii is a state.
    b. Each of the Hawaiian Islands is surrounded by water.
    c. There is no map large enough to show all 132 of Hawaii's islands.

3. Jane sat between Rob and Carl. Carl sat between Jane and Leslie. Rob was on the end of the row, but Leslie was the next-to-the-last person in the row.

    a. Leslie sat between Carl and Rob.
    b. Only four people are in the row.
    c. Jane and Carl sat between Rob and Leslie.

VOCABULARY STUDY

Homophones

"As a joke we want to give Doc Mirth a **skull** for her birthday."

"That's pretty funny, giving her *the bony part or skeleton of the head.* But for a minute there, I thought you meant **scull**, *a long oar worked from side to side over the rear of a boat.* Actually, we should give her a skull and a scull. Then she'd be able to bone up on her rowing!"

"I like that idea. She certainly deserves it. Good old Doc Mirth. She has *good moral standards.* Everyone agrees she has the best **principles**."

"You're telling me! Not only were her school **principals** the best, but so were her teachers. That's why she's such a good doctor today."

"I agree. Doc Mirth has very few *equals* in her field. She's a doc with no **peers**."

"Hmmm. No **piers**, eh? No *landing places jutting out into the water*? Maybe we shouldn't get her that scull after all. She won't have any place to keep it."

"Sure she will! Why do you think we call her *Doc*?"

Word Play

Homophones are two words that sound the same but have different meanings. Match the homophone in the column on the left with its definition in the column on the right. Then make a sentence using each homophone.

skull	good moral standards
scull	persons of equal standing
principals	the skeleton of the head
principles	landing places jutting out into the water
piers	a long oar
peers	people who are heads of schools

Think about the details in Mary Ann Anning's life. What conclusions can you draw from these details?

In the 1800's, Mary Ann Anning became famous for her . . .

Curiosities from the Cliffs

by Ruth Van Ness Blair

The cliffs near Lyme Regis in England were once part of the sea bottom. Millions of years ago, the ancestors of mollusks—soft creatures without backbones— died and drifted down to the ocean floor. Many of the ancient mollusks were much like the snails and clams of today. They had outer shells. Others, with inner shells, looked like squid.

After a long time, the mollusks were covered with mud that slowly hardened. In most cases, the minerals in their shells slowly became petrified—that is, they turned to stone.

These shells were the "curiosities" Mary Ann Anning and her father collected. Scientists called them *fossils*. Mr. Anning sold them in his carpentry shop in Lyme Regis.

A Good Hunting Day

One day in the early 1800's when Mary was about nine years old, she and her father set out for the cliffs to look for more curiosities. A storm the day before had broken great chunks of earth from the cliffs, exposing the rock underneath. The Annings began their search in this rock and in the mud at the cliffs' base.

Almost at once, Mary found a curiosity that pleased her. She began to tap at it.

"Be patient, lass," her father said. "Use your hammer and chisel with great care. Curiosities are easily broken."

As the Annings worked their way along the cliffs, Mary asked, "What are curiosities, Father? Where did they come from?"

"About three hundred years ago," Mary's father explained, "there was an artist named Leonardo da Vinci. He thought curiosities might be the remains of living creatures."

"Was he right, Father?"

"I do not know, lass. But it does seem it might be true."

"If this were a living creature," said Mary, "it must have died a long time ago."

Mr. Anning turned the shell over and over in his hand. This one, like most of the other curiosities they found, was a curled shell. The Annings called such shells "horns of ammon." They looked like rams with curled horns.

Mary smiled at her father. "Today was a good hunting day!"

Mary's Monster

Within a few years of that day, Mary's father died. Mary took over his business of selling curiosities. Her collection grew larger and more interesting. In it was a strange skull over two feet long. It had a long mouth, full of sharp teeth. Mary's brother, Joseph, found it, quite by accident, and gave it to her.

"I think the rest of it is somewhere in the cliff near Charmouth," he said.

Mary thought the skull was that of a crocodile. She put it away on a shelf with some other strange bones she had found.

One night after Mary went to bed, there was a terrible storm. The next morning, Mary got up early and, with her dog, Tray, set out for the cliffs.

It was a beautiful day in the year 1811. Mary was almost twelve years old. The sun shone as if there had been no storm. But the beach was littered with overturned fishing boats.

Mary noticed that the cliffs had lost great chunks of soil and rock which now lay in piles at their base. Very carefully, she began to search for curiosities.

As Mary peered at the cliffs, something unusual caught her eye. She saw what seemed to be bones lying in the rock in front of her.

She tapped the crumbling rock with her hammer. Chunks of it fell away. Mary tapped again. More bones appeared. She backed away for a better look. "What is it?" she thought.

With her chisel, Mary carefully lifted away pieces of the splintered rock. Underneath lay other bones. Finally, a huge backbone, with large curving ribs, stood out as the rock fell away.

She walked along the cliff face a few feet, tapping as she went. At every tap, more bones appeared. Soon the skeleton of a strange, large animal began to take shape.

"But what can it be?" cried Mary. "Where is its head?" Then she remembered. The skull that Joseph gave her—could that be it? She would find out as soon as she could remove this huge curiosity from the cliff.

As Mary stood there wondering how she could get it safely out of the cliff, her friend Henry ran down the beach toward her.

"What is that?" he yelled.

"I don't know."

"What are you going to do with it?"

Mary thought a bit. "I'll hire

the quarry workers," she said. "They can cut it out of the cliff."

"I'll fetch them," Henry cried as he darted away.

"Wait," said Mary. "Tell Joseph to bring the head."

"The head! What head?"

"Just tell him to bring it. He'll know."

It was almost an hour before Henry and Joseph came running back with the quarrymen. As soon as Joseph saw the bones in the cliff, he shouted, "You found it, Mary. You found the rest of it!" He ran to the skeleton and held the skull where the head should have been.

What a fearsome thing the creature became when its head was added. Now it was a monster! It was twice as long as Joseph was tall. It had short flippers or feet. Its sharp teeth looked ready to bite. And its enormous eye socket seemed to glare at those who looked at it.

It took most of the afternoon for the quarrymen, with the help of Joseph and Henry, to remove the monster from its resting place. Tray stood guard. Mary gave directions as the skeleton was carefully cut into pieces small enough to lift.

Mary would rather have kept her monster. It was the biggest

curiosity she had ever seen. But where could she put it? No shelf in her house would hold such a large skeleton. So when someone in the town offered her twenty-three pounds (then about $50.00) for it, she accepted.

A Very Old Monster, Indeed!

As soon as scientists heard of Mary's fantastic discovery, they flocked to Lyme Regis. Some had seen petrified bones of such a creature before, but no one had seen such bones assembled in an almost perfect skeleton.

One of the scientists who came to Lyme Regis was William Buckland.

"Miss Anning," he said, "would you care to show me where you found your mysterious creature?"

Mary was delighted to have such an important person interested in her discovery. So the two of them, with Tray in the lead, went tramping off to the Charmouth cliffs.

As they neared the cliffs, Tray raced ahead with excited yelps. He stopped suddenly at a pile of rocks.

"That's the place," said Mary. "Tray remembers it. I found the skeleton there—in the blue Lias [lī′əs] layer of the cliff."

Mary and her scientist friends could tell that the earth was in

layers. But at that time no one knew that the Lias layer was about 180 million years old. It was formed in an age when great dinosaurs roamed the earth. Flying reptiles and birdlike creatures had just begun to appear.

Other strange bones had been found in England. But no one knew for certain that they were dinosaur bones. Many people still thought they were the remains of dragons, elephants, or giants. So Mary and her friends had no way of knowing that her monster was a dinosaur.

Naming the Curiosities

When Mary was fourteen years old, a friend gave her a geology book. This book was a great help. Now Mary could study the layers of the earth with greater knowledge. She learned to call horns of ammon "ammonites." She began to recognize other forms of fossils, such as footprints in rocks.

Seven years passed and Mary's monster still had no name.

Finally, in 1818, George Koenig, of the British Museum, said: "Everyone agrees the creature is a seagoing reptile. It has a fishlike shape. So why not call it ichthyosaurus? The Greek word *ichthyo* means 'fish.' *Sauros* means 'lizard.' "

It must have been a good name, for it hasn't changed to this day.

More Monsters

In 1821, Mary discovered another monster. It, too, was a sea reptile. It had a short, wide body with four large paddles and a long, long neck. It looked like a turtle shell with a snake threaded through it. This monster was later called plesiosaurus—meaning "nearly like a lizard."

In 1828 Mary discovered the bones of a very different creature. It was a flying reptile. Because of the long finger that edged the wing, it was called pterodactyl—meaning "winged finger."

Mary kept on hunting for monsters. The creatures she discovered were remarkable. And so was Mary. No other woman of her day made the study and selling of fossils her full-time profession.

Many of Mary's monsters can now be seen at the British Museum of Natural History in London. There is also a picture of Mary with her old dog, Tray.

Today, scientists remember Mary with affection and great pride. For they knew that, in 1811, Mary and her monster had helped open the door to the far-distant and fascinating past of all living things.

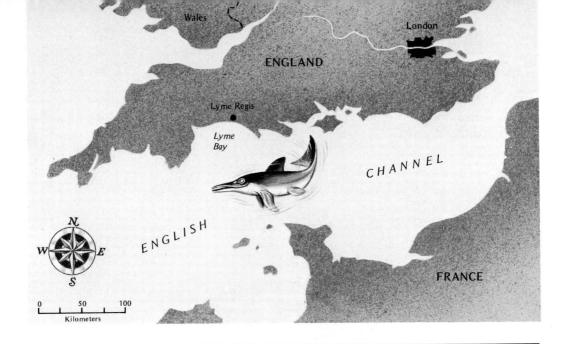

Understanding What You've Read

1. What "curiosities" did Mary and her father collect? What is the scientific name for these "curiosities"?
2. Why were scientists so interested in Mary's discovery of the monster skeleton?
3. How old was the ichthyosaurus that Mary found?
4. Why is the discovery of fossils important?

Applying the Skills Lesson

Answer the following questions *yes* or *no*. Explain how you drew your conclusions.

1. Did Mary and the scientists of her time know that the ichthyosaurus was 180 million years old?
2. Could the scientists tell what color skin "Mary's Monster" had?
3. Have all the fossil bones from 180 million years ago been found by scientists?
4. In 1811, did scientists know everything there is about the distant past of living things?

The selection will give you information from which you can draw a conclusion about Ben Franklin and his lightning rod.

It's 1753. Through his simple idea for "catching" lightning bolts . . .

Ben Franklin Changes the World

by Isaac Asimov

Modern science began about the year 1600, but for nearly one hundred fifty years, it didn't have much effect on the lives of ordinary people. Scientists, for example, found out that the earth went around the sun instead of the sun circling the earth, but that didn't make the crops grow better or keep people healthy.

Then, in 1752, for the first time, a scientific discovery was made that affected everyday life. It saved people from a natural disaster. And it changed the world. From then on, many people turned to science rather than superstition to keep harm away.

You might have thought this would have happened in Europe, where, in those days, science was most advanced. It didn't. It happened in Philadelphia, in the American colonies.

In the early 1700's, many scientists in Europe were interested in electricity. They had found that if they rubbed rods of glass or sealing wax, the rods attracted lightweight objects such as feathers and small bits of wood. The rubbed objects were said to be "charged" with electricity.

Some devices could be charged with a great deal of electricity. One such device was studied at the University of Leyden in the Netherlands. It was called a "Leyden jar." If a Leyden jar is filled with a particularly large charge of electricity, that electricity might suddenly pour out the way air pours out of a punctured balloon. When electricity pours out, or "discharges," it heats the air, causing a little spark. The air expands with the heat. Then the air cools and contracts, all in a split second, making a crackling sound.

In the American colonies, a scientist named Benjamin Franklin was interested in electricity and experimented with Leyden jars, too. He discovered that if he attached a small metal rod to the Leyden jar, the discharge came off the end of the rod. If the Leyden jar was charged highly enough, and if something was brought near the rod, a spark would shoot off the rod. There would be a crackle.

The thinner the rod, the quicker the discharge would come. If a very thin rod with a sharp end was used, a charge couldn't be built up in the Leyden jar at all. As fast as an electric charge was transferred into the jar, it leaked out of the sharp end of the rod. And it leaked out so quietly that there was no spark or crackle.

Some people said the spark and crackle were like tiny lightning and thunder. Franklin thought of it the other way. Could real lightning and thunder be a huge electric discharge from a cloud or from the ground?

This was an important new thought. Everyone was afraid of lightning. It struck without warning. It could set a house or a barn on fire. It could kill an animal or a human being. The ancients believed that lightning was a weapon used by the gods. The Greeks thought that Zeus hurled lightning bolts. And the Norse thought that Thor threw his fiery hammer. Now, if Franklin could find out that lightning was an electric discharge, it might be possible to understand lightning better—and fear it less.

In June, 1752, Franklin made a kite and tied a metal rod to it. He ran a large twine from the kite and placed a metal key at the bottom end. Then, during a thunderstorm, he went out to fly the kite. He hoped to see if electricity would flow from the clouds down to the key. He didn't hold the twine with his hand for fear the electricity would flow into him and kill him. Instead, he tied a silk thread to the twine and held that, because electricity doesn't travel through silk.

When the kite vanished into a storm cloud, he carefully brought one knuckle near the key. The key discharged, producing a spark and a crackle, just as a Leyden jar would. And the spark felt the same on his knuckle as a spark from a Leyden jar.

Franklin had an uncharged Leyden jar with him. He brought it near the key. Electricity flowed from the clouds into the key and from the key into the Leyden jar. The Leyden jar was charged with electricity from the sky, but it behaved just as though the charge had been produced on Earth. Franklin thought this meant that lightning in the sky would follow the same rules that electricity on Earth would.

During a thunderstorm, the ground could become filled with a charge of electricity. If it did, there might eventually be a huge discharge—a lightning bolt. If the discharge worked its way through a building, the heat could set the building on fire.

But Franklin had found that if a thin rod was attached to a Leyden jar, it wouldn't build up a charge. The electrical charge would leak out of the sharp end of the rod as quickly as it was built up. There would be no spark. Suppose the same thing was done to a building? Suppose a thin metal rod was placed on top of a building and connected to the ground? In a thunderstorm, the ground under the building would not build up a charge because the charge would leak quietly away through the thin rod. The building would therefore not be hit by lightning.

Franklin called such a device a "lightning rod." Every year, he published an almanac in which he printed information about all

447

sorts of things. In the 1753 edition, he described how to put a lightning rod on a house or a barn to keep it from being hit by lightning.

It was such a simple thing to do, and people were so afraid of lightning, that soon after the almanac came out, lightning rods began to be placed on houses all over the colonies. They were used in Europe, too.

And it wasn't a superstition. It worked! For the first time in history, one of the terrors of the world could be controlled — and it was science that did it. Never

mind spells and magic. Simply by understanding what lightning was and how electricity worked, people could take advantage of that knowledge and protect themselves.

Gradually people began to understand that science worked and superstition didn't. In 1767, for instance, the citizens of the Italian city of Brescia [bre'shä] stored a great deal of gunpowder in the cellar of a tall building that did not have a lightning rod. They thought the gunpowder was safe there because the building was a church. But the church was

struck by lightning during a storm and all the gunpowder exploded, destroying much of the city and killing three thousand people. This great tragedy ended any doubts about lightning rods.

From that time on, in many, many ways, science helped people where superstition had just fooled and confused them. In 1798, an English doctor learned how to inoculate against smallpox. That was the beginning of the victory of science over sickness. In the 1840's, doctors learned how to use certain chemicals to put patients to sleep during operations. That was the beginning of the victory of science over pain.

And these beginnings, which enabled science to help ordinary people in a practical way, owed much to a remarkable American colonial named Benjamin Franklin, who flew a kite in a thunderstorm and changed the world.

Understanding What You've Read

1. Why does Isaac Asimov say that the discovery of the lightning rod "changed the world"?
2. Why was it more likely in the 1700's that great scientific discoveries would be made in Europe rather than in America?
3. What is the difference between superstition and science?

Applying the Skills Lesson

Below are two conclusions you can draw using facts from the selection, plus your own knowledge. What facts from the selection support each conclusion?
1. In the early 1700's there were many more universities in Europe than there were in America.
2. Benjamin Franklin was interested in a great many things.

Drawing Conclusions

Textbook authors often give you information and then draw a conclusion from it. You have to ask: Is the conclusion supported by the information given? Sometimes an author gives information and allows the reader to draw a conclusion from it. You have to think about the evidence and weigh the ideas carefully in your mind.

As you read the following selections, refer to the side-notes. They point out information that will help you draw conclusions.

Drawing Conclusions in Science

Protecting the Young

In early spring, robins build their nests. A male robin and female robin collect twigs and mud and build a nest shaped like a bowl. (Other birds build other kinds of nests. The robin always builds a robin's nest, not an oriole's or an eagle's nest.) In the nest, the female robin lays from 4 to 6 blue eggs.

While a robin's egg is developing, it is kept warm and protected by the parents. How different this is from what happens to a frog's eggs! Frogs do not protect their eggs. Their egg cells divide and develop in the water. Most of the eggs, and most of the young, are eaten by other animals.

Can you draw the conclusion that some scientists can tell what kinds of birds live in an area from the kinds of empty nests the scientists find?

Which egg has a better chance of hatching—a robin's egg or a frog's egg? Which facts support your conclusion?

—*Concepts in Science:* Purple
Harcourt Brace Jovanovich

Building Skills

Which of the following conclusions is a good one? Which are *not* supported by the facts from the selection?

1. Robins' eggs are white.
2. It is not unusual for a robin to lay five eggs during one spring.
3. It takes longer for a robin's egg to hatch than it does for a frog's egg to hatch.

Drawing Conclusions in Health

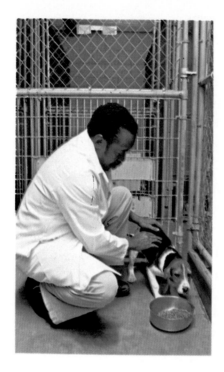 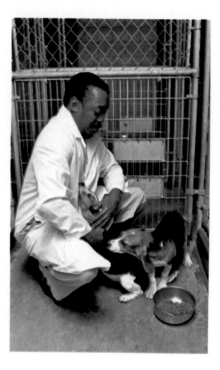

What Else Is Important?

This puppy lives in a safe, roomy cage. It has plenty of food and water. All its physical needs are taken care of.

The other puppies are cared for in just the same way. But there is one difference between their lives and the first puppy's life. What is it? What need does the first puppy have that is not being satisfied?

In one investigation some researchers studied puppies like these.

The author asks you to draw two conclusions using information from the pictures.

They found that puppies that were kept by themselves grew up differently from others. The lonely puppies stayed away from other puppies. They didn't seem able to get along with them. And they didn't get along with people. What might be the reason for this?

First the author gives facts. Then the author asks you to draw a conclusion from the facts.

—Balance in Your Life: Purple
Harcourt Brace Jovanovich

Building Skills

Find the three sentences that ask you to draw conclusions. State the three conclusions you can draw.

Generalizing

"We raccoons will eat almost anything."

The raccoon in the cartoon is **generalizing.** Raccoons are known to eat many different kinds of foods. But there are some things that even a raccoon won't eat!

A **generalization** is a special kind of conclusion. It is a broad statement based on several facts. Read the following paragraph. From the facts given, you can draw two conclusions.

Below the soil of the earth is a layer of hard rock called the *crust.* When the crust shifts quickly, it causes an *earthquake.* The 1976 earthquake in China destroyed many buildings in Peking. Thousands of people were hurt by the falling buildings.

From the facts given in the paragraph, you can draw these conclusions:

1. The crust under Peking shifted quickly in 1976.
2. Earthquakes can cause damage to property and people.

Notice that sentence 2 is more than a conclusion. It is a generalization. It is a broad, or general, statement about earthquakes.

Using the Facts

Generalizing is "making a broad statement *based on several facts.*" A valid generalization should cover more than one or two specific cases.

Read the following paragraph. What's wrong with the generalization in the last sentence?

My first grade teacher, Mrs. Zimmerman, had gray hair. My cousin's first grade teacher, Mrs. Carr, also had gray hair. All first grade teachers have gray hair.

The generalization in the last sentence is not valid. It is based on only two cases. Is it possible that some first grade teachers do not have gray hair?

Using Qualifying Words

Read the following paragraph.

Three First Ladies of the United States—Elizabeth Kartwright Monroe, Eleanor Roosevelt, and Jacqueline Kennedy Onassis—were born in New York State. The famous opera singers Beverly Sills and Roberta Peters were also born in New York State. Some famous actors born in New York State are Kirk Douglas, Lauren Bacall, Peter Falk, and Lucille Ball.

Which of the following generalizations can you make based on the facts from the paragraph?

1. All famous people are born in New York State.
2. Some famous people are born in New York State.
3. Most famous people are born in New York State.

Sentences 1 and 3 are not valid generalizations based on facts from the paragraph. The paragraph does not tell you about *all* famous people. It doesn't even tell you about *most* famous people. It tells you about only *some* famous people. So only sentence 2 in the list on page 456 is a *valid* generalization based on facts from the paragraph.

Words like *all, some, many, most, several, none,* and *a few* are **qualifying words** that are often used in generalizations. When you make a generalization, be careful to think about the qualifying words you use. If the facts deal with *all* cases, you may use words such as *all, every, none,* or *always.* If the facts do *not* deal with all cases, use *most, many, some, several,* or another qualifying word.

Try This

Read the following paragraph and the generalizations that follow it. Choose the one generalization that can be made based on the facts from the paragraph.

Albert Einstein was a poor student when he was young. He grew up to be an important scientist. Wilma Rudolph was crippled as a child. She exercised and later became a champion athlete. Helen Keller became blind, deaf, and mute when she was about nineteen months old. She grew up to be an author and educator.

1. Everyone who has a problem as a child grows up to be successful.
2. Some people who have problems in their childhoods can grow up to be successful.
3. No one who has problems as a child can grow up to be successful.

Suffixes

"Stop the cooking contest!"

"Who are you?"

"I am the famous Luigi Macaroni, author of the book, *How to Cook Spaghetti and Play Tennis at the Same Time.*"

"Are you a tennis pro?"

"No! I'm a chef. I also wrote the screenplay for the movie, *2001 Tricks with Spaghetti.* Tell me, what is that awful **pastelike** mess you're making?"

"You mean this white stuff that 'looks like paste'? It's a spaghetti patty."

"Leaping linguini! Spaghetti is **threadlike**. It's supposed to 'look like threads,' not a big round blob. How do you expect to wind that around a fork?"

"I don't, and that's the beauty of it. You see, the tomato sauce is inside. It's an all-in-one dish. It's a real **improvement** on the original design, don't you think?"

"You call that the 'result of being improved'? Bah! It's the dumbest thing I've ever seen! You never got that stupid recipe from my book!"

"No. That's true. I didn't. I saw the movie."

Word Play

1. Give the meaning of each word in boldface below.

    a. The spaghetti patty looked very **balloonlike**.
    b. This land is a good spot for a housing **development**.
    c. My goodness! Those plastic figures look so **lifelike**.
    d. Sal took a **measurement** of the room.

2. In the story, find other words with suffixes. Make up sentences using the words you find.

The sentence that leads into the title states a generalization. What other generalizations can you make, based on the facts given in the selection?

There's a simple idea behind each of the . . .

460

Little Things You Use Every Day

by Kathryn Hitte

One day more than a hundred years ago, Mr. Walter Hunt sat down to think. He needed fifteen dollars badly. If he could come up with a good idea for a new invention, he was sure he could sell it. He often did. Well, then! What kind of invention would people find useful, really useful, and want to buy? How about— how about a pin with a guard to cover the point?

Hunt made a drawing and then a sample. It worked. It was safer to use than the common straight pin. Users would not be so likely to pin *themselves!* So the safety pin was born, and Hunt sold his idea for $400.

Walter Hunt got a bright idea when he needed one. Once another man had a bright idea when a neighbor needed one. And as a result he gave us the ice-cream cone.

461

It happened in 1904, at The World's Fair in St. Louis, Missouri. An ice-cream salesman was doing a big business—so big that he kept running out of dishes. A neighboring dealer had a helpful thought. Why not make a dish that could be eaten? Why not roll a waffle into a cone shape? We've had ice-cream cones ever since.

They're "little" inventions, the cone and the safety pin. They haven't really changed the world, as the greatest inventions have. But we're used to them and we like them. We wouldn't want to do without them—or without a lot of other "little things," either.

We don't know much, as a rule, about the invention of everyday things. Often we have only a jumble of facts about their history. Some of these are odd facts, and rather useless. But they can be fun. Like these:

The first alarm clock in America would ring only at four o'clock. It couldn't be set for any other time. The inventor, Levi Hutchins, made it that way because he needed to wake up each morning at four. He wasn't inventing a clock for the world— just for himself. It took many improvements by other inventors to give us the alarm clocks we have today.

The first zippers were called "hookless fastenings." They were used only for shoes. Whitcomb L. Judson had invented the zipper in 1893 when people wore high shoes with many buttons. The new fastener saved a lot of time and trouble. Later the zipper was used on many things.

Imagine going into a field of grain to get a hollow stem to use as a drinking straw: For hundreds of years, the only straws people had were grain straws. Paper straws were invented about 1885. Cleaner and stronger than grain straws, they were a big success. Today, of course, most drinking straws are made of plastic.

The history of many other "little things" can only be guessed at. What brought the inventions about? Accidents? Bright ideas at the right time? Certain needs? Take the first pencil with its own eraser, for instance. It was invented in 1858 by Hyman L. Lipman. What pushed him to do it? Was he always losing erasers?

man in the United States Patent Office. That's a place that deals every day with new inventions. A long time ago, the Director of the Patent Office wanted to give up his job. "Everything seems to have been done," he said. He knew of about 10,000 inventions. What would he think of the millions we know of today?

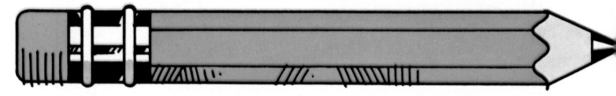

It's fun to imagine the stories behind many of these little inventions. But it would take a lot of hunting to find out all the facts. And even a lifetime of hunting might not give us facts about who invented many common things we use each day.

We do know one amazing fact, though. More than three million inventions have been created in the United States alone. Probably at least half of these are everyday things. Surely thousands more must have been invented elsewhere.

Figures like these are hard for some people to believe. An amusing story is told about a

"If you can build a better mousetrap," a wise person once said, "the world will make a beaten path to your door." It's

generally true. People do want new things, better things, more useful things. But somehow the maker of the "mousetrap" is often forgotten. The work doesn't get praised in the history books. And that seems a shame.

So how about a little praise right now? Three cheers for the paper clip! Three cheers for thumbtacks, and zippers, and snaps! And for easy-open bottle caps! Shoelaces, and the helpful little tips on the ends. Those tiny gummed circles for mending notebook-paper holes. Potato peelers. Bobby pins. Safety matches, envelopes, pocket knives . . . and more, more, more! For all the "better mousetraps" of the world—hurrah! Three cheers for our *wonderful* little ordinary, everyday things!

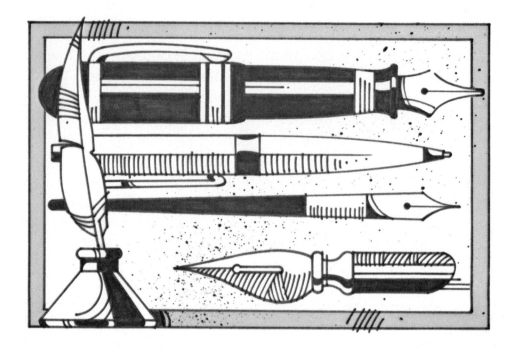

Understanding What You've Read

1. Why did Walter Hunt invent the safety pin?
2. The selection gives examples of two reasons why things are invented. Find these reasons.
3. What is the Patent Office?
4. What was the author's purpose in writing this selection—to inform, entertain, or both?

Applying the Skills Lesson

Which of the following generalizations are valid?

1. Some inventions are the results of "lucky accidents."
2. Inventions always need improvements.
3. All inventors become rich.
4. Many inventions are born from need.

As you read, look for generalizations that the author makes. Use the facts given to make your own generalizations.

How different our lives would be without our two precious . . .

GIFTS FROM CHINA

by Albert Barker

467

Suppose you woke up one morning and discovered that there were no newspapers and not a single book or magazine. Suppose there were no shopping bags, no tickets, no labels, no cardboard boxes, no paper money—nothing made of paper!

If you had lived two thousand years ago in China, the lack of paper wouldn't have bothered you. You would have written your lessons on strips of bamboo or on blocks of wood. Sometimes, you might write a letter on silk. But silk was expensive and wood was heavy.

One day in A.D. 105, a Chinese man named Ts'ai Lun got tired of carrying his master's heavy wooden blocks. He thought, "If I could make something that is light, strong and cheap, my master could write on it, and it would make my burden easier."

Ts'ai Lun noticed that old rags and fishnets were made out of tiny fibers—thousands of fine threadlike strings. Looking closely at the bark of mulberry trees and hemp plants, he

could see more fibers. These tiny fibers gave him an idea.

Taking the rags, nets, bark, and hemp, he dumped them into a kettle of boiling water. As they boiled, he pounded them to separate the fibers. When nothing remained but a thick soupy liquid, he poured it onto a flat screen. The thousands of fibers spread out across the top of the screen. When the fibers had dried, they formed a thick, rough sheet that could be written on.

At last, Ts'ai Lun had found a way to make his burden lighter! This was the first step in China's papermaking process. For many years, the Chinese were able to keep papermaking a secret.

The Chinese, however, were not satisfied just to write on their paper. They wanted to find a way to print on it.

The need for printing arose because hand-lettering was a slow, tiresome, and costly process. Printing would be faster and cheaper. Mainly, it would be a way to make many copies from one original piece of writing.

The Chinese carved designs on one side of small wooden blocks. In order for the blocks to print, only the raised surface of the designs were inked. The cut-away areas were not inked. A black pastelike ink was used.

Then the block was pressed down on the paper.

Printing with blocks was clumsy and slow, so the Chinese looked for a faster way to print. They took soft clay and carved a symbol on it. Then they baked the clay until it was hard. They made hundreds of these clay symbols, which could be arranged to form sentences.

After the clay symbols were inked, paper was pressed down on them. These symbols are called *type,* a word meaning "impression." Because this type could be rearranged and used over and over again, it is called *movable type.* However, the Chinese language is made up of over forty thousand different symbols. Even though the clay type could be moved, the work of printing a single book often took many months to complete.

Of course, these two secrets —papermaking and movable type—could not remain hidden forever. By the sixth century A.D., traders from the West were able to smuggle samples of paper and type into other

Asian countries. Eventually, in the year 1150, these Chinese secrets reached Europe.

In Europe, only scholars, royal families, and a few rich merchants could read or write. Now, with the two Chinese inventions at hand, it was possible to print books that would teach many people to read.

Understanding What You've Read

1. What did people write on before the invention of paper?
2. How were copies of books made before the invention of wooden printing blocks?
3. Why was movable type an improvement over printing with wooden blocks?
4. How many years passed between the time that Ts'ai Lun invented paper and the time that Europeans learned how to make paper?

Applying the Skills Lesson

Which of the following generalizations are valid? Which of the valid generalizations are supported by facts from the selection? Which are supported only by something you already know?

1. The world's most important inventions came from China.
2. Most writing today is done on paper.
3. All writing today is done on paper.
4. All people today know how paper is made.
5. The secrets of papermaking and movable type could not remain hidden forever.
6. It is harder to learn the Chinese writing symbols than it is to learn the alphabet.

Recognizing Generalizations

Remember that a generalization is different from a conclusion in that it is a broad statement. When you read textbooks, look for generalizations and the facts that support them. Often you will be asked to make a generalization based on facts that are given in the textbook. The sidenotes in the first selection will help you see some generalizations.

Recognizing Generalizations in Science

Cells

This part of the sentence is a generalization. What word *qualifies* the generalization?

Though living things are different in many ways, most living things are alike in one special way. That is, most living things are made up of *cells.*

472

Cells are tiny units of living matter. Do you think all living things are made up of the same number of cells? Why or why not?

In general, cells are so small that they can be seen only with the aid of a microscope. For this reason, it takes many cells to make up the bodies of most living things. Your body, for example, is made up of billions of cells.

What words in this sentence are a clue that the statement is a generalization?

—*Exploring Science:* Green Book
Laidlaw Brothers

Building Skills

Here is a generalization from the selection you just read: *Living things are different in many ways.* What facts can you think of that would support this generalization?

Recognizing Generalizations in Social Studies

There are no sidenotes for this selection. Read it and then answer the questions that follow.

Another Invention
Helps Cities Grow Tall

While many inventions allowed the city to grow outward, there was one that allowed it to grow upward. That was the elevator. For some time, engineers had known how to build tall

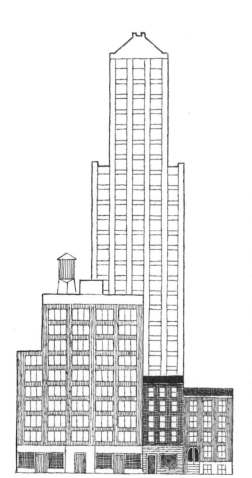

buildings. But why build them if the only way to get to the top was to climb hundreds of stairs?

In 1857, people began to experiment with elevators. Finally, in 1889, a manufacturer made an electric elevator that was safe for passengers.

Safe, but not too comfortable. One of the speedy new elevators was in a Chicago office building. Here is how one person described a trip in one of the new elevators in the 1890's:

"The slow-going stranger . . . feels himself loaded into one of those frail-looking baskets of steel netting, and then the next instant the elevator-boy touches the trigger, and up goes the whole load as a feather is caught up by a gale. The descent is more simple. Something lets go, and you fall from ten to twenty stories as it happens. There is sometimes a jolt, which makes the passenger seem to feel his stomach pass into his shoes. . . ."

But with all the bumps and jolts, the elevator did its job. Beginning in the 1880's, tall buildings appeared in New York, Chicago, and a few other large cities.

—People in the Americas
Silver Burdett

Building Skills

1. Which of the following generalizations can you make based on the facts in the selection?

   a. All tall buildings built in the 1880's had elevators.
   b. Some tall buildings built in the 1880's had elevators.
   c. All passengers thought that the first elevators were uncomfortable.
   d. Most passengers thought that the first elevators were uncomfortable.

2. What is the qualifying word in each of the sentences above?

SKILLS LESSON

Understanding Comparison and Contrast

"I'm a bird, too. I have feathers, I have wings—sort of!"

What is the little penguin doing? It is thinking about how it is like the eagle. The penguin is **comparing** itself to the eagle.

Authors often make comparisons, too. What is being compared in each of the following sentences?

1. The plesiosaurus looked like a turtle shell with a snake threaded through it.
2. Many ancient mollusks were like the snails and clams of today.

Authors make comparisons in order to help readers understand a new idea. You may not know what a plesiosaurus looked like. But you can imagine a turtle shell with a snake threaded through it. Do you know what snails and clams look like? If so, then you know what ancient mollusks were like. Sometimes an author uses words such as *like, as, too, also,* or *in comparison* to signal a comparison.

Study the cartoon below. The penguin is *not* thinking about how it is like the eagle. What is the penguin thinking?

"I can't fly like an eagle. However, I'm kind of cute. Eagles are not cute!"

Now the penguin is thinking about how it is *different* from the eagle. It is **contrasting** itself with the eagle.

Authors sometimes use contrasts to help you understand a new idea. Words such as *but, however, nevertheless,* and *although* are often clues that two things are being contrasted. What two things are being contrasted in each of the following pairs of sentences?

1. In the northern half of the world, July is a summer month. But in the southern half of the world, July is a winter month.
2. The "covered wagon pioneers" crossed America by foot or in wagons. However, the "sod-shanty pioneers" traveled west by railroad.

In the first pair of sentences the word *but* is a clue to a contrast. July in the northern half of the world is contrasted with July in the southern half of the world. In the second sentence pair, "covered wagon pioneers'" and "sod-shanty pioneers'" choices of travel are contrasted. What word is a clue to this contrast?

Time words can also be clues to contrasts. In the following paragraph, two different times are contrasted.

Long ago, most sports equipment was made from natural materials like wood and leather. Today fiberglass or plastic is often used instead of wood or leather.

In the paragraph above, the materials used long ago to make sports equipment are being contrasted with what is often used today. Time words, such as *today, now,* and *used to,* are often clues that two different times are being contrasted.

478

Try This

1. What is being compared in the following sentences?

   a. The modern Olympics are very much like the ancient Greek Olympics.

   b. Then, as now, contestants had to train for a long time.

2. What is being contrasted in the following sentences?

   a. People came from all over Greece to take part in the ancient contests. Today's Olympic contestants come from most of the countries throughout the world.

   b. The first Olympics were held to honor the Greek gods and goddesses. However, the reason for today's Olympics is to build a spirit of world friendship.

3. Give the clue words that signal a comparison or contrast in the following sentences. Then make up a sentence using a clue word that signals a comparison or contrast.

   a. Maria's dress is like mine, but it's a different color.

   b. Although my car is smaller than yours, it uses more gas.

VOCABULARY STUDY

Getting Meaning from Context Clues

The kind Professor Crum excused himself from the party in his honor to scribble something quickly in his diary.

Dear Diary,

I have to make this fast because my **loyal** friends are waiting for me in the next room. The people who have been faithful to me while I worked in the health food store are giving me a party. They **insisted** we celebrate my new job. They felt so strongly about it that I had to give in.

You see, I'm a full-time juice squeezer! Everyone says I'm **competent**. And I guess I am capable of making good juice. They think I should make squeezing juice my **career**. I can't imagine selling cherry juice as my life's work, but it's a start.

Eventually—not right away, of course—I'd like to buy an orchard. That would take a **considerable** amount of work, but that's OK. The rather large effort would be **worth** it. To me, the value of the orchard would be that my beautiful peaches and apples would make people happy.

By the way, I told Leo the Rat about how I earned **extra** money in the health food store. He wants me to set him up with a part-time job so he can also earn additional money. I think I'll **recommend** him for the sandwich bar (hee, hee, hee). After all, if I can't praise him, who can? Besides, he makes a mean omelette. And who knows? Maybe we can turn him into a good egg!

Word Play

1. Look back over the diary page. The meaning of each word in boldface is suggested by other nearby words or phrases. These words or phrases are called context clues. Find the context clues to the meaning of each word in boldface.
2. Look up *orchard, effort,* and *omelette* in a dictionary. Use each word in a sentence. Try to include context clues for the word.
3. Write a short page to go into a make-believe diary. Use as many of the words in boldface as you can.

W. VA.

How was Benjamin Banneker's life like his neighbors' lives? How was it different? Look for examples of comparison and contrast as you read this selection.

Learn what happened to Benjamin Banneker when . . .

He Reached for the Stars

by Lavinia Dobler *and* Edgar A. Toppin

When Benjamin Banneker was growing up, Maryland was a colony belonging to England. Benjamin was born on November 9, 1731, three and one-half months before George Washington. His birthplace was his grandparents' farm about ten miles from Baltimore. He had three sisters.

Benjamin's grandmother had taught him to read. She had also taught him many wonderful things about nature. He knew where to find roots, grasses, fruits, nuts, and berries that were good to eat. He knew when the howling wind changed its course. He knew when a

THE FARM

N.J.

BALTIMORE

MARYLAND

DEL.

WASHINGTON
D.C.

VA.

CHESAPEAKE
BAY

deer or fox had been in the fields or orchards. He knew how to tell the age of a tree.

One spring morning in 1737, five-year-old Benjamin woke up and quickly dressed. All he could think of was "This is the day!" Today his parents and his grandparents were going to buy land.

Buying the land proved to be a good investment. People often talked about the fine crops that the Banneker family produced, even when there was no rain and other farmers had poor crops.

Benjamin's father had grown crops in Africa. So he knew a lot about the soil. He dug ditches. Then when the soil was dry, the water from the deep springs on the hill irrigated the land. He and his wife Mary also built gates and locks to control the flow of the spring water.

Benjamin started school in 1737. Every school day was a new adventure for him. He listened carefully to every word the teacher said. But it was arithmetic that he liked best of all. He quickly learned how to add and subtract. And he liked multiplication and division.

In 1746, when he was fifteen, his nine years of schooling were over. Benjamin missed going to school, especially because there were so few books at home. He continued to be a careful observer of nature. He listened to anyone who could give him information.

Benjamin was twenty-eight when his father died. Benjamin continued to live on the farm. He plowed and hoed the fields, planted crops and cared for the bees. He also found time to study mathematics.

People who knew Benjamin Banneker were impressed with his ability. When, in 1761, he built a wooden clock, his fame spread far beyond Baltimore County.

Banneker had never seen a clock before. But he had seen a pocket watch which served as his model. The clock he made was many times larger than the watch.

A century later, an article in *The Atlantic Monthly* described the wooden clock: ". . . this was the first clock of which every part was made in America. It is certain that it was purely his own invention. It was as if none had ever been made before."

When word got around that he had made a clock with wooden parts that worked, visitors came from miles around to the Banneker farm.

As time went by, people became more aware of Banneker's remarkable abilities. He was now known as one of the best mathematicians in the Baltimore area. Scholars from other sections of the thirteen colonies sent him puzzles to test him. As soon as he received them, he would sit down at his table and start figuring them out. With his quick mind, he would have the correct answers in no time at all.

Even though Banneker was becoming well known, he was really very lonely. There was no one in his neighborhood who could talk about mathematical and scientific problems with him.

Then, in 1772, something wonderful happened. That year the three Ellicott brothers—George, Joseph, and Andrew—moved nearby. They were millers. Joseph, like Banneker, had made a clock that had received considerable attention.

The Ellicotts became lifelong friends of Banneker and helped him in many ways. Indeed, their arrival marked the turning point in Banneker's career.

One day, in 1787, George Ellicott offered to lend Banneker some books on astronomy. From that time on, astronomy became almost an obsession with Benjamin Banneker. As a boy, he had been fascinated with the stars that shone so brightly. But up to now he had never had the good fortune to see books on the subject.

Every night as soon as it was dark, Banneker would leave his log cabin so that he could watch the stars. In the early dawn, he was still outside, his eyes fixed on the heavens.

Banneker's scientific observations brought results. Through his study of astronomy, Banneker predicted a solar eclipse in 1789. Through watching nature he was able to observe that locusts seem to come in seventeen-year cycles. He was able to explain how they lay eggs. Banneker also observed that a strong hive of bees often takes the honey of a weaker hive.

Until the 1790's, Banneker was still known only locally. Then in the next ten years he became known around the world in two ways. In July 1790, Congress passed a law to make a United States capital on the Potomac River. President George Washington was to

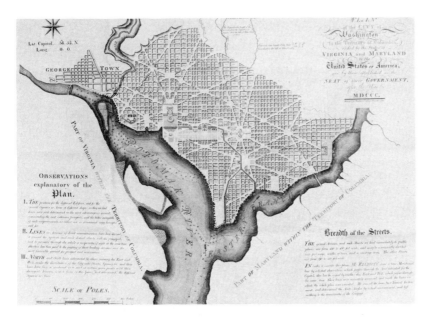

Map of the city of Washington by Andrew Ellicott, 1792.

name three commissioners to survey and plan the location of the buildings.

In February 1791, President Washington sent Andrew Ellicott to survey the general site, under the direction of the three commissioners.

At the request of Mr. Ellicott and Thomas Jefferson, then Secretary of State, Benjamin Banneker was given the job of helping Ellicott survey the land. This was the first national recognition of Banneker's abilities.

Banneker worked ably on the survey, impressing his colleagues. He served from 1791 to 1793.

During that time, Banneker put some of his mathematical and astronomical findings into an almanac. This was to be his second well-known accomplishment. Almanacs then were one of the highest examples of scientific achievement. They served as a needed source of weather and tide news and of entertainment.

Banneker was sixty years old when his first *Almanac* was published in 1791. He continued to publish almanacs regularly until 1802.

In his *Almanac* for 1793, Banneker proposed a remarkable Plan for Peace. He suggested that a Secretary of Peace be appointed to the President's cabinet. This plan contained farsighted ideas about making the world better. The plan, too, was a great tribute to Banneker's independent thinking.

Understanding What You've Read

1. What kinds of things did Banneker learn from his grandmother?
2. Why did Banneker miss going to school?
3. Several things that Banneker did brought him fame. Name three of these things.

Applying the Skills Lesson

Read each of the following sentences. Which states comparison? Which show contrast? What is being compared or contrasted in each sentence?

1. Joseph, like Banneker, had made a clock that had received considerable attention.
2. Even though Banneker was becoming well known, he was really very lonely.
3. The clock he made was many times larger than the watch.

Look for comparisons and contrasts as you read this selection. Notice that Daniel Villanueva's way of making a dream come true is contrasted with other people's ways.

How can one person's idea and hard work affect millions of people?

Daniel Villanueva: The Idea Is to Care

by
Al Martínez

Not very long ago, Daniel Villanueva answered several questions in a questionnaire. One of the questions was, "What was the most memorable experience of your life?" He answered, "It is yet to come."

Such an experience will truly have to be memorable. For Daniel Villanueva has already experienced a lot. He has played professional football. He has also helped create the first Spanish-language TV network in the United States. He is a respected TV news reporter and executive, business leader, and leader in the Mexican-American community.

Daniel Villanueva was born in Tucumcari [tōō′kəm·kâ′rē], New Mexico, in 1937. He was one of eleven children. When he was a young child in school in New Mexico, some people thought Daniel was a "slow learner." However, he made it through school just fine.

After graduating from New Mexico State College, he played professional football. He began with the Los Angeles Rams and then played with the Dallas Cowboys. But while he loved sports, Villanueva felt that he could not serve the needs of his people by playing football. He left the sport in 1968 and joined KMEX-TV, a Spanish-language station in Los Angeles. He started as news director and director of community relations. In 1969 he became station manager. By 1971 he was vice-president and general manager. He is now president and general manager.

Some people sit back and just hope that their dreams will come true. But this wasn't the way for Daniel Villanueva. He worked hard to make his dream become real. For years he had wanted to see a Spanish-language TV network stretching beyond Los

Angeles. By 1972, he had helped create SIN-West, the first Spanish TV network in the United States. (SIN is for *Spanish International Network*.)

Daniel Villanueva is president and general manager of SIN-West. This network reaches millions of people in California and Mexico. The network also owns stations in cities such as Miami, New York, and San Antonio.

During his free time, Daniel Villanueva works hard helping people. He spends much of that time working for the Mexican-American community. He works with scholarship programs and youth programs. He is chairman of the board of a savings-and-loan company. He has also served as chairman of the California State Park and Recreation Commission.

For his work helping Spanish-speaking people, Daniel Villanueva has been given many honors. One of these was the Aztec Award. This award honored him for developing opportunities for Mexican-American workers. Villanueva received this award in

1971 from the Mexican-American Opportunity Foundation.

Remember the questionnaire that was mentioned earlier? Well, another question asked Daniel Villanueva who had been the most important influence in his life. He answered, "My father. Because of his total dedication to serving others, his total commitment to his mission."

Like father, like son.

Understanding What You've Read

1. What did Daniel Villanueva mean when he said his most memorable experience "is yet to come"?
2. Why did Daniel Villanueva leave professional football in 1968?
3. What is SIN-West? Why was its creation important?

Applying the Skills Lesson

The following sentences show comparisons and contrasts. What is being compared or contrasted in each group?

1. Some people sit back and just hope that their dreams will come true. But this wasn't the way for Daniel Villanueva. He worked hard to make his dream become real.
2. Another question asked Daniel Villanueva who had been the most important influence in his life. He answered, "My father. Because of his total dedication to serving others, his total commitment to his mission."

    Like father, like son.

TEXTBOOK STUDY

Recognizing Comparison and Contrast

In order to help you understand something new, textbook authors may *compare* it to something you most likely already understand. Or they may *contrast* something new with something you already know about. When authors contrast ideas about different times, they often use words such as *today, now, then,* and *used to.* Look for these words as clues.

As you read the following selections, refer to the sidenotes. Try to answer the questions in them.

Recognizing Comparison and Contrast in Language Arts

Read the following conversation. Then answer the questions that follow the conversation.

What is being contrasted in this selection? How is the American's language like the Englishman's? How is it different?

ENGLISHMAN: I'm going to the ironmonger's to buy a spanner.

AMERICAN: You're going where for what?

ENGLISHMAN: To the ironmonger's. That's a shop where they sell tools.

AMERICAN: Oh, you mean a hardware store. But what is a spanner?

ENGLISHMAN: That's a tool that you use for tightening nuts and bolts.

AMERICAN: A wrench? Well, I'll go with you. I need a flashlight.

ENGLISHMAN: What's a flashlight?

AMERICAN: It's a small light that operates on batteries.

ENGLISHMAN: That's what we call a torch.

- What country does each person come from?
- What language is each person speaking?
- Why are the two people having trouble understanding each other?

Notice that the distances between the countries are being compared.

English is spoken in many countries around the world—countries as far apart as America and England, Canada and India, Scotland and Australia. In most ways the English spoken is the same in all countries where it is used. But there are some differences.

—Discoveries in English
Laidlaw Brothers

Building Skills

The selection beginning on page 494 showed you likenesses and differences by example. The sentences below state the likenesses and differences. Which of the sentences is a comparison? Which is a contrast?

1. The British, like the Americans, speak English.
2. The British and the Americans use different names for some things.

496

Recognizing Comparison and Contrast in Health

This selection compares and contrasts the effects of transportation on people's lives. Notice that both the good effects and the harmful effects are described.

Going from Place to Place

The man in the first picture has just been flown 2,000 kilometers (1,240 miles) for special medical treatment. He will probably live a long and healthy life because of this treatment.

The first two paragraphs of the selection show how people's health (and lives) are *different* because of the airplane.

Why couldn't this picture have been taken 100 years ago? What might have happened to the man if he had lived then?

This airplane is bringing a doctor to a village in Alaska. There are no roads into the village. It used to take a doctor two weeks to get here from the city. Today this doctor can visit five villages in one day. How has this airplane helped to keep the people in the villages healthy?

Other kinds of transportation also affect people's health. The truck in the third picture carries vegetables to people's houses. What else do trucks carry that is important to you? How do the clothes you wear get from factories to stores? How is meat carried long distances without spoiling?

Suppose there were no trucks and cars. List five ways this would make a difference in your life.

What things is the writer asking you to contrast here?

For most of us, cars are necessary. Yet they can be dangerous, too. Car accidents kill thousands of people and injure millions every year.

Cars can be harmful in other ways, too. The smog in the air is partly caused by car waste products. A few years ago, a law was passed to help keep the air cleaner. Car owners must now make sure their cars are not adding to the pollution.

—Balance in Your Life: Purple
Harcourt Brace Jovanovich

Building Skills

1. Read again the second paragraph of the selection. What two things are being contrasted?
2. Both the good effects and the harmful effects of transportation are presented in the selection you just read.

   a. Which paragraphs describe the good effects? What are those effects?
   b. Which paragraphs describe the harmful effects? What are those effects?

Books About Discoveries, Ideas, and Inventions

Gigi: A Baby Whale Borrowed for Science and Returned to the Sea by Eleanor Coerr and Dr. William Evans. Putnam, 1980. A baby gray whale is captured so that scientists can study the behavior of a whale first-hand.

Why Didn't I Think of That: From Alarm Clocks to Zippers by Webb Garrison. Prentice-Hall, 1977. You'll meet the woman who invented windshield wipers, the man who invented blue jeans, and several other little-known inventors.

Eight Black American Inventors by Robert C. Hayden. Addison-Wesley, 1972. This is the story of eight inventors and their contributions to American life.

Marie Curie by Robin McKown. Putnam, 1971. You'll read about the life of a great scientist, her research with radium, and the uses of radium.

The Polynesians Knew by Tillie S. Pine and Joseph Levine. McGraw, 1974. The authors tell about the inventions and customs of the people of Polynesia, and how these inventions and customs compare with ours.

Nature's Weather Forecasters by Helen Sattler. Nelson, 1978. Here is information about some of the many ways people—and animals—use nature to predict the weather.

How Sports Began by Don Smith. Watts, 1977. This book is full of facts and legends about the beginnings of baseball, tennis, basketball, gymnastics, and so on.

Part 8

The Way It Was

UNDERSTANDING AND APPRECIATING LITERATURE

Historical Fiction

A realistic story that contains made-up characters and events is called realistic fiction. Realistic fiction that contains facts about important real people or events from history and fictional details is called **historical fiction**. Historical fiction combines historical facts with fiction.

Understanding Historical Fiction

Read box 1. Who are the important people from history in the cartoon? They are Thomas Jefferson, John Adams, and

Benjamin Franklin. What is made-up, or fictional, in the cartoon? The meeting for a meal and the conversation of these important people are fictional.

Read box 2. The people in this cartoon are not important historically. What important historical event is shown? The California gold rush of 1849 is an actual historical event. The characters, conversation, and details such as the sign on the wagon are fictional.

Read the following paragraph. Look for real historical characters and events and fictional details.

Ben Franklin's Trip to France

My name is Benjamin Franklin Bache. I came to France with Benjamin Franklin, my grandfather, to get help for the United States. Grandfather wants to make a treaty saying that France and the United States are friends. But he can't do much about that treaty now, because he can't get to see the king of France. The king of France doesn't want to meet Grandfather yet. He's waiting to see how General Washington makes out with the war.

Which characters were real people? Benjamin Franklin, the king of France, and George Washington were important historically. Benjamin Franklin really had a grandson named Benjamin Franklin Bache. What events are important historically? The treaty between the United States and France during the Revolutionary War is a real historical event. What is fictional? Benjamin Franklin Bache's words and his grandfather's words are fictional. The combination of historical people and events with fictional details makes this paragraph historical fiction.

Read the following story. Look again for the historical facts and the fictional details.

The Big Race

Amanda had heard about a strange race in Baltimore between two horses, an "iron horse" and a real one. Amanda hurried to see the iron horse.

It didn't look like a horse. It was a wagon with a big round tank on top and four iron wheels. A fire was in a stove under the tank. Steam was spitting from the pipes. Amanda learned that a man named Peter Cooper had made it and named it the *Tom Thumb* because it was small. It ran on two iron strips called a track.

The race started and Amanda followed in her wagon. The *Tom Thumb* pulled ahead. Everybody clapped and whistled. Then there was a bang, and the *Tom Thumb* came to a stop. The real horse sailed by. Cooper and his "iron horse" lost the race.

Was there really a race? Yes, there was. Peter Cooper, an iron-maker, built the *Tom Thumb*, a train engine. In August 1830, the *Tom Thumb* lost a race to a horse in Baltimore. The race was important historically because the *Tom Thumb* was one of the first steam-powered train engines. Amanda and her words are fictional.

Historical fiction contains important historical people or events, and sometimes both. It also has fictional parts. In historical fiction, fact is combined with fiction to make history come alive.

Try This

Read the following story, then answer the questions.

In 1776, thirteen-year-old Phoebe Fraunces took an important job. Posing as a servant, she went to General George Washington's headquarters to try to save his life. Phoebe knew that a person known as "T" was planning to harm Washington.

"But who is T?" Phoebe wondered.

Phoebe served dinner. Everyone looked friendly. Who wished to harm General Washington?

"Where is my bodyguard, Thomas Hickey?" Washington asked, as Phoebe gave him his dinner.

Could *T* be for "Thomas"? Phoebe remembered that Mr. Hickey was in the kitchen when she prepared dinner. Phoebe grabbed the plate of food.

General Washington was astonished. Phoebe had saved his life. Thomas Hickey had tried to poison the general.

1. Which characters were probably real people? Which events might really have taken place?
2. Which parts of the story are fictional, or made-up?

Writing

1. Choose one of the historical people and events below. Write a sentence telling something fictional about that person.

   a. telegraph invented by Samuel F. B. Morse
   b. Lewis and Clark Expedition, guided by Sacajawea
   c. phonograph invented by Thomas A. Edison

2. Choose some facts from a selection listed below and write a paragraph of historical fiction.

   a. "Lady Moody's Dream" (page 292)
   b. "The Peddler's Pack" (page 306)
   c. "The Journey of the Tejas Woman" (page 286)

The stories in "The Way It Was" are historical fiction. As you read, look for the real people and events from history.

Hamilton Hill
September 18, 1784

by JEAN FRITZ

All day long as Ann went about her chores, she felt out-of-sorts and out of courage. She didn't know what was bothering her, but everything she did went wrong. She cut her finger when she was chopping pumpkin for her mother to make a pumpkin pie. She spilled half a pail of milk. She caught her dress on a prickly bush and tore it. And every time she picked up the baby, he cried.

"This isn't your day," her mother said toward the middle of the afternoon. "Why don't you go on down the road and try to find some grapes? You'll like that. But mind you don't go too far."

It certainly wasn't her day, Ann thought crossly as she took the empty pail and went out the cabin door. But when she reached the road, she wondered. Maybe, after all, something might yet turn the day her way. The road seemed to have more magic to it than she had ever known. The sun's rays slanted down on it as though they were lighting up a stage where something important was going to happen. There was a difference in the mood of the road. It wasn't a happy, dancing mood, or a mysterious, moonlight mood. Today there was a grandness to the road, as though it were a carpet unfurling over the hill before some glorious secret. As Ann stood in the middle of the road, holding her pail in front of her, two golden leaves drifted down, turning slowly over and over in the air, and settled in the bottom of her pail. A wild goose dipped low, honking, from the sky, like a herald sent ahead with news.

Ann walked down the hill, captured by the spell of the road. As she rounded each bend, she found herself half expecting something wonderful to be waiting on the other side. She didn't know what, but something. From time to time she stopped to pick grapes. On all the hill, the only sounds were the plopping of grapes in her pail and the occasional long honk of a passing goose. Ann followed the road as it wound its way down the hill, turning corner after corner, looking for grapes, but secretly hoping for something she couldn't even put into words.

Her pail was almost full when she suddenly noticed where she was. She was almost to the bottom of the hill. She had let the road lead her farther than she had ever gone alone.

And then Ann heard hoofbeats. They were coming from the east—not just one horse but three or four, and they were not far away.

Ann ducked down behind some tall grass by the side of the road and made herself into the smallest ball she could possibly squeeze into, wrapping her arms tightly around her knees. She held her breath as the first horse rounded the bend of the road. She must not move—not even a finger. She kept her eyes on the road, counting the legs of the horses as they came into sight. Now there were two horses . . . three

. . . four. If four men were traveling together from the East to the West at this time of year, they were probably not settlers. They were likely up to no good. They must be the Doane gang that her brother David had warned her about.

All at once Ann began to tremble all over. The first horse had stopped on the road in front of her. Then the other horses came to a stop. As Ann peeped out between the tall grasses, all she could see was a forest of horse legs. From some place way up high above the legs of the first horse came a deep voice. "Little girl," it said, "I wonder if you could tell me what your family is having for dinner tonight."

The voice didn't sound like the voice of a horse thief. Slowly Ann lifted her eyes from the legs of the horse to the boots of the rider. Slowly she lifted them to the place where the voice had come from. Then she found herself looking into the most wonderful face she had ever seen.

It was a strong face, kind and good, and there was something strangely familiar about it. It was as if Ann ought to know this man, as if she almost knew him. No matter what David had said about strangers, somehow Ann knew deep inside that he hadn't been talking about this one. She stopped feeling afraid. She stood up.

"We are having peas and potatoes and corn bread for our evening meal," she said, "and my mother is baking pumpkin pie."

The man smiled. He leaned toward Ann. "Would you tell her," he said, "that General George Washington would like to take supper with her?"

For a moment Ann could not believe her ears. General Washington on Hamilton Hill! Then all at

once she knew it was true. This was the way she had pictured George Washington. This must have been just how Washington looked, riding among the men at Valley Forge.

Ann swallowed hard. She tried to drop a curtsy but it turned out to be just a stiff little bob. She tried to find her voice, but it didn't turn out any better than the curtsy. It was more like a squeak. "My mother will be pleased," she said. "I'll tell her."

Afterward Ann could never remember just how she introduced General Washington and his friends to her mother. When she caught her breath again, they had started on a tour of the farm with David. Ann and her mother were alone in the cabin with supper to prepare.

Mrs. Hamilton's eyes were shining as she stepped away from the door. "Now is the time to use the linen tablecloth, Ann," she said, "and the lavender flowered plates."

Ann spread out the white linen cloth on the table. She smoothed it gently over the rough boards. She pulled it to hang even on all sides. She unwrapped nine flowered plates and placed them around the table. She put knives, forks, and spoons at each place and set new tall candles in the center of the table.

Then Ann stepped back to look at what she'd done. Somehow the whole room seemed changed; it seemed larger and more dignified. The clothes hanging awkwardly on hooks along the wall drew back into the shadows. All the light from the fire and from the open doorway fell on the gleaming white party table, waiting for General Washington.

Later the table looked even more wonderful, piled high with steaming food—hot yellow corn bread, round bowls of green peas, roasted brown potatoes, a platter of cold venison, golden pumpkin pies. It was the same meal they had had nearly every evening all summer on Hamilton Hill, but tonight with the lavender flowered plates, it managed to look different.

"I hope I look different too," Ann thought as she fingered her two blue hair ribbons and hastily tied the sash of a fresh apron.

She felt different. General Washington and Mr. Hamilton led the others into the cabin, and suddenly Ann found herself feeling strangely shy. All the time they were taking their places at the table, she kept her eyes down. It was not until her father was asking the blessing that she stole her first look up from under half-closed eyelashes. When she saw George Washington's head bowed over the white tablecloth and lavender plate, the peas and potatoes, Ann thought she could hardly bear her happiness.

During the meal, Ann followed the conversation in a kind of daze. She didn't seem to hear anything that anyone said, except General Washington. Everything he said rang out clear, with a special meaning, it almost seemed, just for her.

"If I were a young man," General Washington said, "preparing to begin the world, I know of no country where I should rather live."

"I am determined to find a way," he said again, "that we can join the waters of the West with those of the East so that the two countries may be close together."

Ann held onto every word, turned them over in her mind, locked them away in her heart. It was after the evening meal, after all the thank-you's had been said and General Washington and his party were preparing to leave that he said what Ann was to treasure forever afterward. He stood at the doorway, looking toward the west, his eyes resting on Hamilton Hill, yet somehow going beyond.

General Washington turned to Ann. "Through the courage of young girls as much as anyone's, our country will grow. You will live to see this whole country a rolling farmland, bright with houses and barns. Some day. I envy you, Miss Hamilton."

Ann felt her heart turning over within her. Even after General Washington had gone, she went on standing in the doorway. She looked out on Hamilton Hill. It seemed to her she had never seen it so beautiful.

That night, in the home of a Colonel Cannon several miles west of Hamilton Hill, before he blew out his candle, General George Washington sat down at a table and wrote this in his diary:

"September 18, 1784. Set out with Doctr. Craik for my Land on Miller's Run, crossed the Monongahela at Devore's Ferry . . . bated at one Hamilton's about 4 miles from it, in Washington County, and lodged at Colo. Cannon's."

That night in the cabin on Hamilton Hill, Ann took down from her shelf her deerskin-covered diary. Her heart was too full to write all she wanted. Instead she wrote in big letters across a whole page:

September 18, 1784
George Washington was here.

Tomorrow she would write more.

A Note from the Author

If you look in George Washington's diary, you will find that his words are written there exactly as they are in the diary in this story. On September 18, 1784, he "bated," or took supper, with the Hamiltons.

I don't know if Ann really kept a diary or not. Most of what happened to her in this story is just a story, but some of it is true. There really was an Ann Hamilton; she was my great-great-grandmother. As long as she lived, she told the story to her children and her children's children, about the wonderful evening when George Washington rode up Hamilton Hill.

Understanding What You've Read

1. Which characters and events in the story were probably real, not made up by the author?
2. Which parts of the story were probably made-up? Find five examples on pages 509–510.
3. Why was Ann excited when General Washington stopped at her house for dinner?
4. Why did Ann treasure Washington's words to her about her future as a young woman in the United States?
5. What do you learn in the Author's Note, page 512, about sources of the facts used in this story?

Writing

1. Suppose you wanted to write a historical fiction story about a boy or girl in the year 1930. Write some questions you could ask people to find out about that time in history. You might ask how they dressed, what they studied in school, and what games they played.
2. Pretend that you are George Washington writing in your diary on April 30, 1789, the day you became President of the United States. Tell what happened and how you felt. Use these historical facts to help you:

   a. George Washington rode to Federal Hall in his carriage as part of a big parade.
   b. He was sworn in on the steps of Federal Hall in New York City.
   c. The army gave him a thirteen-cannon salute at the conclusion of the ceremony.

Tempe Wick was a real person who lived in Jockey Hollow, New Jersey. Ten thousand soldiers spent the winter of 1780–1781 at Jockey Hollow. Tempe Wick was glad to help feed and clothe these Revolutionary War soldiers, but when some soldiers mutinied, things changed.

The Temper of Tempe Wick

by PATRICIA LEE GAUCH

It was the camp blacksmith who ran by and told Tempe the news.

"It's a mutiny, ma'am. Take cover," said the blacksmith.

"From our own soldiers, sir?" said she.

"Aye. They're agin their own captains. They're agin their own general. They may be agin you! You've food to fill their stomachs and a horse to get them away. That's reason enough!"

And off he ran.

He didn't even see Tempe get mad. But she did.

"Agin me!" she said to herself, pushing up the sleeves of her nightgown. "Agin me, indeed! I've shared the

wheat from my fields, sir, and the cows from my herd.
And I do not see how it will serve their war to make a war
on me. But if any soldier takes from my home or steals
from my barn or tries to take my horse, he'll have to battle
me first!''

Tempe loaded her rifle, then poked it through a small
crack in the kitchen window. She vowed not to move
from the spot until every soldier was off her farm.

And she kept her word. Until just after midnight.
Then a thousand soldiers, followed by one general,
marched off to Philadelphia. They wanted to tell the
leaders of all America how they were hungry and cold
and poor. As they passed, the men shouted. The fifers
fifed. The drummers drummed. But when the cannoneer

fired off his cannon three times, the very windows in the Wick house rattled. Mrs. Wick woke up and started to cough.

Nor was it an ordinary cough. Mrs. Wick coughed until her ears flushed pink. She coughed until the bed shook. She coughed and coughed and coughed.

And Tempe knew she wouldn't stay put. Her mother needed medicine, and only Dr. William had it. At daybreak, soldiers or no soldiers, she would have to leave the house. She would have to get to the barn. Then she would ride Bonny down the trail to the doctor's farm.

It was then she learned that all the soldiers had not gone to Philadelphia. Soldiers were everywhere. Some were still celebrating in the cornfield. Some were sleeping against the smoke-shed. Others were at the well.

But Tempe went anyway. She didn't go shouting, and she didn't go shooting. Not this time. After hiding her mother in the cellar, she bundled up in her Sunday coat and fine hat. She walked . . . slowly . . . to the barn, just as if she were alone in the world. She pretended not to see the soldier peeking through the fence at her. She pretended not to see the soldier duck up into the loft.

She whistled a little tune and went right to Bonny's stall. Coolly and calmly and casually she put on her bridle and saddle and rode, coolly and calmly and casually, right past them all. It was as if she were the white-horse lead in a military parade.

The soldiers just watched.

Not until she got to the road did she hurry. Then she touched her Bon with a stick and raced down the road to Dr. William's. It had all been so easy. Probably, she thought, those soldiers didn't want anything from the Wicks at all. Probably the blacksmith had been just the smallest bit nervous.

But when she left Dr. William's with a full bottle of medicine, she learned differently. Out of the thicket, right in front of the doctor's house, jumped two soldiers.

Even Tempe's stomach took a flip.

"Pretty young lady," said the one, "that's a fine horse you have."

"Thank you, sir." She smiled and started by.

But the other, a thin man with sideburns that curled like an S around his ears, stopped her.

"I imagine a fine mare like that could carry me and my friend, say, all the way to Philadelphia," he said.

"I imagine," Tempe said. She tried to get by again.

"Then we'll try her now!" he said. Quickly, he grabbed the reins from Tempe. "Get down!"

Tempe didn't even blink. Not this time. She turned her head, coyly, so sweetly, so perfectly, and said, "But, sir, 'tis my best horse Bon."

"Then she'll do her best for us. Get down I say." He was terribly gruff.

But Tempe was not. She said, still coyly and sweetly and perfectly, "Then perhaps you will help me down, sir."

And, frowning, he reached to help. But as he did, Tempe snatched the reins back. Then she put a stick to Bon's hide, and raced off down the lane toward the Wick farm.

"Come on, speeder," she whispered as she hung on Bon's neck.

Both of the soldiers started running after them. The one fired a shot. BAM! But it merely sent Bonny flying faster and faster down the road. Her nostrils steamed. Her hooves pounded so fast, they barely touched the ground. The clickety-clackety sounded more like a gentle rain on the frozen road.

All of the other soldiers were gone when Tempe rode up under the willow that guarded the back door. But she didn't try to squeeze Bonny in the smoke-shed. She'd quickly be found. Nor did Tempe even hide Bon in the woods. The soldiers knew the woods well.

No, Tempe did a most surprising thing. She led Bonny right in the back door and into the kitchen of the Wick house!

Of course, Tempe didn't tie her there. Everyone visited the kitchen first, particularly when the blizzards whipped around the Wick house in January. Tempe led Bon straight through the sitting room, too. Old Bon might not treat kindly her Grandmother Wick's fine desk from England or her mother's favorite fiddleback chair. And Tempe's mother's cough was not apt to improve with a horse sharing her bedroom!

So Tempe took the mare into her own room, the tiny dark room with the two tiny windows in the back of the house. She left her, happily nibbling at the flax-woven spread on Tempe's bed.

And just in time. Tempe had just brought her mother up from the cellar when there came a terrible thumping on the back door.

It was the man with the curled sideburns. He bellowed through the crack in the door, "I want that gray mare!"

But Tempe answered lazily, as if she had been spinning wool all afternoon, "A gray mare, sir? Have you lost one?"

Well, the man and his friend didn't even reply. They stalked off across the kitchen garden. Tempe scratched a peekhole in the frosted window. It was just big enough

for her to see them stomp into the barn. They sent the cow out mooing. They sent chickens out flying. And hay tumbled out of the loft like a dust storm in January when they searched there. Nor had they any better luck in the smoke-shed or the woods.

The soldiers by now were terribly red in the face. They returned to the Wick house just long enough to promise, "We know she's here . . . somewhere, pretty lady. And we intend to wait until we find her!"

Wait?

Even Tempe was surprised at that! How long could she hide a horse in her bedroom?

But Tempe didn't worry long. Not this time. For now, her house was her fort. For later, perhaps the general and his men would come back from Philadelphia and capture the runaway soldiers. Perhaps Dr. William would drop by to see how her mother was faring and run the soldiers off. Perhaps with a healthy dose of medicine her mother could help. Two against two were happier odds. Or perhaps the two soldiers would just go away by themselves.

Satisfied with all the possibilities, Tempe stayed at her window post until dark. Then she curled up on the kitchen settee (having a guest in her bedroom) and went to sleep.

But the next morning the general and his men were not back from Philadelphia. There was no sight of Dr. William. The medicine had stopped Mrs. Wick's cough, but it had also made her sleep and sleep and sleep. And the two soldiers were still there. They were pacing the barnyard.

To make things worse, Bonny was hungry.

First she just walked angry circles around Tempe's bed. Then she started thumping her hoof at the door.

Finally she let out a "Whiiiiiiinnnnnnnnyyyyy" that Tempe was sure could be heard all the way to the barn.

Tempe knew Bonny had to be fed.

She bundled herself up and headed into the north wind toward the barn.

She quickly fed the other animals, then stacked both arms full of hay and was about to return when a voice boomed at her from the loft.

"Ah-ha!" It was the soldier with the curled sideburns. "Where are you going with the hay, miss?" he asked.

"To the house, sir," Tempe answered lightly. "My mother is ill, and last night the wind blew through the cracks in our roof like a gale of ice. The hay will stop up the cracks."

The soldier grumbled something quietly to himself. But he let her pass.

All day the two soldiers hovered around the barnyard. There was nothing for Tempe to do but wait. Yet little happened. Her mother slept on and on. The general did not come, nor did Dr. William. And while the hay promised to last another day, Tempe saw the little water she had for Bonny was quickly disappearing.

In the morning it was gone. Bonny grew so thirsty she licked the frost off the window. She licked Tempe's washbowl dry. Finally she whinnied, this time so loudly Tempe was sure, had the soldiers been anywhere in Jockey Hollow, they would have heard her!

Bonny had to be watered.

When Tempe had drawn three buckets at the well, both soldiers stepped up behind her.

"May we help, pretty lady," said the one.

"No thank you, sir," said she. "I go only to the house, and I am quite able." She balanced one bucket under her arm and gripped the two in her hands.

"You must be very thirsty," said the other. "Why, there is enough water there for a horse!"

Tempe smiled. "Perhaps," she said, "but these bucketfuls are to wash my floors. It is said a fierce winter is followed by an early spring, and I am but preparing for that. But I thank you."

She curtsied slightly and started toward the door.

Again the soldiers grumbled, but let her pass.

On the third day, Tempe had stopped looking for anyone to come to help. The soldiers had moved closer to the house, and she worried about Bonny.

Bon didn't circle the bed or thump the door, and she let loose only the tiniest whinny. Tempe barely heard it in the kitchen. But that is what worried Tempe.

"Bonny's spirits are low," Tempe said to her mother, who was still half asleep. "She must need oats."

That morning Tempe fed the hog and the cows and the sheep as usual. Then she began to gather her oats. She put some in her pockets. She stuffed more in her bag. She filled her bucket to the brimful, then started back. The soldiers were waiting by the gate when she passed.

"Surely," said the one, looking in the bucket, "you don't eat unground oats, my dear."

"Oh yes," said Tempe, walking on. "Boiled, they make a fine porridge."

"But," said the one, following her, "so many oats for two ladies, and one so ill?"

"It is barely enough," said Tempe. "Some days, after chores, I eat three bowls at one sitting."

Still he followed.

"Some days," Tempe went on, "I eat four!"

He was at the door in front of her.

"Next to applesauce with brown sugar, I like oats most!" she said, looking directly into his eyes. "These will last only a day."

"Just the same," said the soldier, "I begin to think there is a third lady in the house. A gray mare that can race like the wind. And I wish to see for myself."

With that, the one soldier pushed right past Tempe into the house. He stomped into the kitchen, knocking the pots off the table and the wood across the floor. He stomped into the pantry, shaking the jars from the shelf.

Then he heard the slightest whinny — or was it a cough? He stomped through the sitting room toward the bedroom, brushing the ink from Grandmother's desk and finally tipping over Mrs. Wick's favorite fiddleback chair.

But that was one push too many. And this time Tempe didn't get mad, she got storming, had-quite-enough mad. She began to look a good bit like the Wicks' bull Joshua.

"That," she said — neither coyly, nor sweetly, nor perfectly — "was my mother coughing. But if it were a herd of gray horses feeding on my bed, I would not let you through that door, smashing and breaking."

The soldier scoffed. He went for the cellar door.

Tempe was there first. "Not into the cellar, sir."

He darted for the attic door.

Tempe beat him there, too. "Not into the attic."

He eyed the bedroom door again.

"Not anywhere," she said.

And before the soldier had time to doubt it, Tempe kicked open the door with one foot, kicked his musket out of his hand with the other — and pushed him right out the doorway.

For a moment — was it two? — the soldier lay sprawled on the path. He glared at Tempe, his face reddening around his curled sideburns. But Tempe stood firm in the doorway with *his* musket in *her* hand and glared back.

Finally, he picked up his hat and paced to his friend at the fence. They huddled, then started — on foot — down the road to Pennsylvania. At last they disappeared.

Understanding What You've Read

1. What parts of this story are probably based on facts? What parts are probably made-up, or fictional?
2. What details tell you that this story takes place during the American Revolution?
3. What did Tempe do to be able to leave her farm without making the soldiers suspicious?
4. Why did Tempe's room make a good hiding place for her horse?
5. How does the author's sense of humor increase your enjoyment of the story?
6. Why is "The Temper of Tempe Wick" a good title for this story? How did Tempe Wick's temper help her?

Writing

1. Think of a historical incident, such as the Boston Tea Party, the landing of the Pilgrims at Plymouth Rock, or the battle between the *Monitor* and the *Merrimack*. Write one or more sentences in which you tell what happened in the incident as though you were involved in what happened. Or, write one or more sentences in which you tell what happened from the point of view of an outsider. Use an encyclopedia to help you find important facts.
2. Pretend that General George Washington, leader of the American Army in the Revolution, visited Tempe Wick after the soldiers left her farm. Write a paragraph in which Tempe tells George Washington about the incidents that occurred on her farm. Tell what you think Washington might have said to Tempe about the incidents.

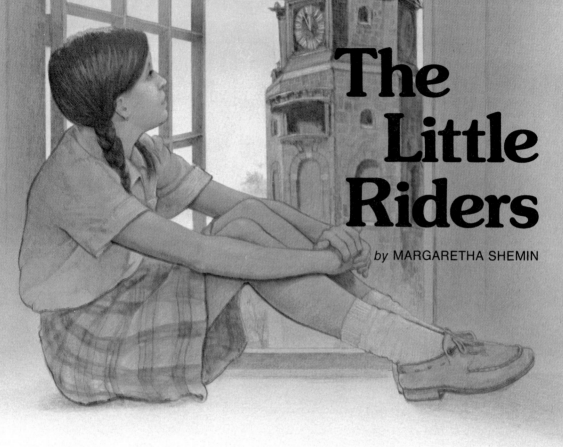

The Little Riders

by MARGARETHA SHEMIN

In 1939, World War II began and the German Army invaded Holland. This story is about a fictional character named Johanna. In the story, Johanna could not return to her mother and father in America because of the war. She had to stay in Holland with her grandparents.

From the window of her room in Holland, Johanna could see the special clock under the church steeple. In the old clock were twelve statues of people on horseback. For hundreds of years, these little riders had ridden around the clock every hour when it chimed. Johanna's grandfather took care of the clock and the little riders. But then German soldiers came, and the little riders and the entire town were in danger.

One day at dinner, Grandfather looked straight at Johanna, and his eyes were filled with pride and love. "There is bad news today, but nothing so bad that we can't bear it. A German soldier came to requisition a room in our house for a German officer, a certain Captain Braun. I explained to him that we used all the rooms and didn't have one room to spare. He never listened to me. He took your room," Grandfather continued. "There was nothing I could do about it, although I tried very hard for you."

It would be extremely dangerous, Johanna realized, to have a German soldier in the house. Johanna knew about the radio hidden in Grandfather's den and the weekly meetings Grandfather held upstairs. She knew there were many other dangerous secrets that Grandfather and Grandmother had never told her. All these secrets the house had kept within its walls, and the house had been the only safe place in a world full of enemies and danger. Now the house had been invaded too.

All afternoon, Johanna helped Grandmother. She took all her clothes out of the attic closet. Now that the closet was empty she could almost see the cubbyhole hiding all the way at the back of the closet. It had always been Johanna's secret hiding place. She opened the small door that was only big enough for her to crawl through. In the cubbyhole were some of her old toys, her teddy bear, which had traveled with her all the way from America to Holland, and some seashells her father had once brought back for her from a far country. She never played with them anymore, but she didn't want to leave them with Captain Braun.

When Captain Braun arrived, he clicked his heels and made a little bow in the direction of Grandmother and Johanna. Johanna turned her head away.

"I apologize to you," he said in broken Dutch. "I will try to cause no trouble to you. I wish you a good evening." Then he turned directly to Grandfather. "Would you be kind, sir, and show me the room?"

Grandfather didn't speak but led Captain Braun to the stairs and mounted them quickly. Captain Braun picked up his heavy sack and followed slowly. Johanna could hear the sack bump heavily on every step till it was carried all the way high up to her attic room. Then she heard the door close and Grandfather's footsteps coming downstairs.

Johanna went to bed early that night. She had felt tired, but now she couldn't fall asleep. She kept tossing in her new bed. There were strange, unfamiliar shadows on the wall. The big gray wall of the church seemed so near, ready to fall on top of the room. Faintly she heard the clock strike ten times. Then the door was opened very softly, and Grandfather came into the room. He sat down in the chair next to Johanna's bed and took her hand in his own.

"Why don't you sleep, Johanna?" he asked. "You should try to sleep now. We have all had a hard day and so much has happened."

"I hate him," Johanna said, "and I hate this room too. From here I can see only the gray wall of the church. I can't see the riders, I can't even hear the carillon very clearly. How can I ever fall asleep without the little riders? I have always watched them just before I went to sleep. In the morning the carillon woke me up. Now a German soldier has my room that once was Father's room. He has no right to sit there and watch the riders and listen to the carillon."

Grandfather got up from the chair and walked over to the window. He looked up at the gray wall of the church.

"Captain Braun," he said, "will never see the little riders ride out on their horses and he will never hear the carillon. Today an ordinance came from the town commander. The riders are not allowed to ride anymore and the carillon may not play again. I just went to the church tower."

Grandfather turned away from the window and paced up and down the small room.

"All these years I have taken care of the riders so that they could ride when the clock struck the hour. But tonight I closed the little doors."

Johanna sat up in her bed, her arms around her thin knees. Her face looked small and white, her eyes big and dark.

"Why?" she asked Grandfather. "Why may the little riders not ride out anymore?"

"They didn't give us any reasons," Grandfather answered, "but we have seen this coming for a long time. This ordinance is only the beginning. The little riders are made of lead. The Germans need metal, and they may throw them into a melting pot to make munitions out of them for their armies. Everywhere the occupied countries are being plundered, their treasures taken away, and the bells of their churches melted down to be made into weapons. Grandmother and I have often talked of what to do if this ever threatened to happen to the little riders."

Grandfather patted Johanna's hand gently. "We will have to hide the riders, Johanna, if we want to keep them for the town. Go to sleep now, there is much to be done tomorrow."

Grandfather tucked the blanket around Johanna and left the room, but Johanna didn't want to sleep. She wanted to think about everything Grandfather had told her. The night was cool and quiet. From somewhere she heard the sound of a flute. She walked across the room and opened the door to the hall. The sound came from the top of the house. Barefoot, Johanna climbed silently up the attic stairs. Halfway up she could see her room.

Captain Braun had left the door open so that the cool night wind could blow through the warm room. He was sitting on Johanna's windowsill. His back was turned to the door, his long legs dangling out of the window. And he played his flute over the silent marketplace.

Johanna didn't watch him for long. She went downstairs without making a noise. She didn't close her door with a bang, but she closed it very firmly. When she was back in bed, she pulled the cover over her ears so that she couldn't hear a sound that could keep her awake. But it was a long time before she fell asleep.

The next day, everybody looked up at the church steeple, wondering what had happened. It was the first time in many hundreds of years that the little riders had not ridden out and the carillon had not played. Soon the town buzzed with the news of the ordinance from the town commander.

After a few days something happened—something of such tremendous importance that the Germans had suddenly much more urgent and grave matters on their minds than the twelve little riders high up on the church tower. Grandfather didn't think anymore about hiding them.

Johanna was sitting with Grandfather and Grand-mother in the den, listening to the radio hidden behind the books in the bookcase. Then the big news came

crackling and almost inaudible, and none of them dared to believe it was true. Allied armies had landed in France. All morning long, Johanna and her grandparents kept the radio on. They had to hear over and over again the crackling voice that kept repeating the same bulletin.

Grandfather and Grandmother and Johanna spent much time upstairs in the den, listening to the radio. At first the liberating armies advanced fast. The south of Holland was free. Then the days became weeks and the weeks became months. The liberation of the north still seemed sure, but not so near anymore. Johanna still dreamed about her father, but she was afraid he would not come soon.

Life went on as it had in the four years before. Grandfather started to think again about a safe hiding place for the little riders, because now more than ever the Germans needed every scrap of metal for ammunition.

Now Johanna was almost used to the presence of Captain Braun in the house, but still she had never seen his face. In the morning she met him on the stairs, she going down for breakfast, he going up to his room after morning drill. In the evening she met him again, she going up to the den, he going down on his way out for dinner. He always said "Good morning" and "Good evening." Johanna always turned her head away from him and never answered. He walked softly in his heavy boots except when he had to ask Grandfather or Grandmother something. Then he stamped noisily with his boots so that they could hear him long before he knocked on the door. There was always time to hide the radio behind the books in the bookcase.

At night now Johanna sometimes forgot to close the door of her room, and she could hear the music of the flute. When the summer nights were quiet, Captain Braun always played. But often now the air outside was filled with the droning sounds of heavy airplanes flying over. On such nights Johanna climbed out of her bed and leaned far out the window to see their lights high against the dark sky. She knew that many of them were American planes, and she imagined that her father might be in one of them. They were airplanes flying over Germany. On those nights Captain Braun did not play his flute.

One day when Captain Braun had gone out, Johanna went upstairs and looked at her old room. Her closet was full of coats and army caps with the German eagle on them.

On the wall, where once her pictures had hung, were now the pictures of Captain Braun's family. In one, an older lady and an older man were standing arm in arm in a garden full of flowers. In another, a young woman and a laughing boy were standing on skis in dazzling white snow. It was strange to see real Germans in a garden full of flowers and with skis on a sunny mountain slope.

Before Johanna left the room she sat down on her windowsill and looked at the church steeple. The little doors were closed now and the steeple looked old and gray, like any other church steeple.

"Don't worry, little riders," Johanna whispered to the closed doors. "It will be all right, the Germans will not get you." Tonight, Grandfather had told her, they would hide the little riders.

The night was loud with the sounds of the wind and the rain, but there were no overflying airplanes. Grandfather crossed the street first to open the door. Then came Grandmother and last Johanna.

Inside the tower it was completely dark. Grandfather had climbed the steps so often that he led the way. No one talked, and Johanna could not remember when the steps had ever seemed so long and steep. As they climbed higher, the sound of the wind and rain came louder and louder. Grandfather had already reached the top of the stairs, and now he handed the riders and the horses to Grandmother and Johanna.

The staircase was so narrow and steep they could take only one rider at a time. It was too dark for Johanna to see the little rider that she carried. She could only feel the cool metal against her hands. The rider was bigger than she had expected, reaching up almost to her waist. She started to carry him down. The rider, although made of lead, was hollow inside and not too heavy, but was clumsy to carry on the narrow, steep staircase. Each trip across the street and back up the church tower was harder than the one before. The last little rider seemed heaviest of all. Grandfather made one more trip to lock the door of the church tower.

In their own house they must be careful to make no noise that could waken Captain Braun, but here the stairs were wider and Grandfather and Grandmother could carry two riders at a time. Johanna felt weak and shaky when the last rider with his horse was finally carried safely into Grandfather's den.

The next morning after breakfast, Grandfather went to a nearby village where he had a friend who was a farmer. Dirk was one of the few farmers who had been allowed to keep his horse and wagon. Because he delivered eggs and fresh milk several times a week at the house of the German town commander, the German sentries who stood guard at the entrances of the town

536

never searched his wagon. Many times young men who
were hiding from the Germans had left town in Dirk's
wagon, hidden underneath the tarpaulin between the
empty egg boxes and the rattling milk containers.
Grandfather and Dirk had often worked together to take
such young men to safer places in the country, and

Grandfather was sure Dirk would help hide the little riders. He knew they would stay hidden on Dirk's farm until they could return to the church steeple.

When Grandfather returned, it was still a few hours before dark. He and Johanna went upstairs to put the riders and their horses in the burlap sacks so that they could be taken away without delay when Dirk came. Johanna looked for the last time at the riders' faces. With her hands she covered their small hands that so many times had lifted the swords in proud salute to each other. The Germans will not get them, she thought. They will always ride over the town. Even a hundred years from now.

It was still light when Johanna and Grandfather finished and went downstairs. Except for the bark of a dog and the cooing of the doves that nested under the eaves of the church tower, it was quiet outside. Then, from the side street that led to the marketplace, came the sound of marching soldiers. It was unusual for a group of soldiers to be exercising at this late hour.

The doorbell rang loudly and insistently, and Grandfather went to open the door. Grandmother and Johanna

followed him into the hall. Nine soldiers were standing on the doorstep, and one of them was the spokesman.

"We are sent by the town commander to requisition from you the key to the church tower." As he spoke he looked around with his shiny little eyes. "We will take the statues of the riders with us tonight, and you can get the key back afterward at Headquarters. Hurry, we don't have all night," he concluded.

Grandfather reached up slowly for the big iron key that always hung on a peg near the stairs. He handed the key to the soldier. When they had gone, he closed the door and for a moment leaned heavily against it. Johanna saw small drops of perspiration under his nose and on his forehead.

"They will be back as soon as they have seen the riders are gone," Grandmother said. "We will have to hide them better."

"There is no time," Grandfather said. "They will be back in a few minutes, and where can we hide the riders? No, our only chance is somehow to keep them from going upstairs. If we can tell them something that will make them go away, even if it's only for a short time . . ."

Grandmother looked doubtful, Johanna thought, but Grandfather couldn't talk about it further. The soldiers were back. This time they didn't ring the doorbell. Instead they pounded the stocks of their rifles on the door. The spokesman was hot and red and angry.

"The old man and the old woman will come with us to Headquarters. The town commander can conduct the hearing himself. If he orders so, we will search the house later. We will not leave a thing unturned, and if those riders are hidden here," he said, shrugging his shoulders in disgust, "we will find them. And these people will learn what happens to those who dare defy an order given by a German officer." He looked at Johanna. "The child can stay," he said.

When the last soldier slammed the door behind him, Johanna found that her knees were shaking. She had to sit down on the bottom step of the staircase. The clock in the hall ticked, and the minutes passed by.

"If those riders are hidden here, these people will learn what happens to those who dare defy an order given by a German officer," the soldier had said.

They must be hidden more safely, Johanna knew, and she would have to do it. Dirk would certainly not come now. The neighbors must have seen what happened and they would have warned Dirk to stay far away from the house. Johanna looked out of the peephole in the door. One soldier was left standing on guard.

"We will not leave a thing unturned, and if those riders are hidden here, we will find them," the German had said.

The riders were big and there were twelve of them and the horses, too. What hiding place would be big enough? Sitting on the bottom step of the stairs, Johanna's mind wandered through the whole house, thinking of all the different closets, but not one was big enough to hide the riders safely. At last she thought of her attic room. Of course, her own secret hiding place was there. It was certainly big enough, but it was right in Captain Braun's room. But the more she thought about it now, the more she became convinced that it would also be the safest place to hide the riders. The Germans would certainly not think that the riders might be hidden in the room of a German officer, and they would probably not search his room. Captain Braun probably had not discovered the cubbyhole. Anyhow, it was the only place in the house where she could hide the riders. She would leave them in the burlap sacks and push them all the way deep in.

Tonight was Friday night and Captain Braun was not home. If she worked fast, the riders would be hidden before he came back. Johanna ran upstairs and started to carry the sacks to the attic room. She didn't put on the light for fear the soldier on guard would see it and come to investigate; instead, she took Grandfather's flashlight. She decided to do the heavy work fast and carry everything upstairs. Putting the riders in the cubbyhole would be easier. She decided also to take the radio from behind the books and put it in the cubbyhole, too.

It wasn't easy. By the time the last horse and rider were in the attic room, Johanna was out of breath. Her hair was mussed and her skirt was torn in several places. It had also taken her much longer than she had expected, but if she worked fast there was still time enough before Captain Braun came home. In the closet, she pushed Captain Braun's uniforms aside and reached to open the bolt of the little door, but it had become stiff and rusty. She got down on her knees and tried again. The bolt didn't yield. Johanna felt warm and her hands started to tremble. Surely she would be able to open the bolt, it had never given her trouble before. But no matter how hard she tried, she could not open the bolt on the little door. She forgot everything around her, even the riders and Grandfather and Grandmother and the danger they were in at this moment. She thought only of one thing. The door must open. It must.

She was so busy she didn't hear the footsteps on the stairs nor the door of the attic room opening. She first saw Captain Braun when he was standing in the door of the big closet. He had to bend down a little not to hit his head against the low ceiling.

"What are you doing in the dark in my closet?" he asked.

He switched the light on so that Johanna's eyes were blinded by it, and she turned her head away. Around her on the floor were the sacks with the riders. The radio was right beside her and Johanna pushed it behind her back, but she couldn't hide the riders. Captain Braun kneeled down and opened one of the bags. There was nothing Johanna could do or say. He took out a white

horse with gentle black eyes and a fierce curly mane. Then he opened the other bags. The little riders and their horses were laying helpless on their backs on the floor of the closet. The legs of the horses were bent as if they wanted to get up and gallop away. The riders looked more brave and proud than ever, but Johanna knew that no matter how brave and proud they looked, they were forever lost and she could not save them anymore. Everything she had ever felt against the Germans welled up suddenly in her.

"I hate and I despise you," she burst out, "and so does every decent person and you'll never win the war. Grandfather says that you have already lost it." She talked so fast that she had to take a deep breath.

Then Johanna raised her eyes and looked at Captain Braun's face for the first time. He did not have a soldier's face. He had the face of a flute player.

"So these are the famous little riders," he said quietly. "I would like to look at them much longer, but it would be safer for them and for you to put them back in the sacks and hide them where they will not be found."

"But I can't," Johanna said. She wasn't feeling angry anymore, only very frightened. "The bolt of the door is rusty. I can't open it." She was surprised to hear that she was crying. "And they took Grandfather and Grandmother. They said, 'If we find the riders in this house, you will see what happens to people who disobey an order given by a German officer.'"

Captain Braun kneeled beside Johanna. His hands were strong and quick as he slipped aside the stiff bolt. He took the sacks and started to put the riders back in.

"What will you do to them?" Johanna asked.

"The little riders will be my guests for as long as they want to be," Captain Braun said. "I owe that to them.

They are the first Dutchmen who looked at me in a friendly way and did not turn their faces away when I spoke to them."

Johanna felt her face grow hot and red as he spoke. She bent down and started to help him put the riders and the horses back into the sacks.

In a few minutes the riders were hidden and the radio, too. At a moment when Captain Braun had his back turned, Johanna pushed it deep into the closet. One day when he was out she would come back and get it. Grandfather couldn't be without his radio.

"Go down now," Captain Braun said. "It's better for all of us if no one sees us together."

Johanna went downstairs and alone she waited in the dark living room. Outside, the soldier was still standing guard. She pushed Grandfather's big chair near the window and sat down, her tired arms leaning on the windowsill. From there, she saw them come across the marketplace.

Grandfather had his arm around Grandmother's shoulders as if to protect her from the soldiers who were all around them. This time, there were more than nine. As soon as Grandfather opened the door with his key, the soldiers swarmed over the room. The big, red-faced soldier was again in charge. At his command the others pushed aside the furniture and looked behind it. They ripped open the upholstery, although Johanna couldn't understand why. The riders and the horses were much too big to be hidden in the upholstery of a chair. When they left to search the upstairs, the room looked as if a tornado had passed through.

Grandfather and Grandmother went upstairs, too, but they were always surrounded by soldiers, so that Johanna could not speak one word to them.

The soldiers began with the desk in the den, taking out the drawers and dumping the contents in a heap on the floor. Then they got down on their knees and looked under the bed and knocked on the wooden floor.

The soldiers finally gave up. They had realized that there was nothing hidden in these rooms. Only the attic room was left. They climbed the last stairs. Johanna felt weak and shaky again. Even when they found Captain Braun, they might still decide to search the room. She was glad now that Grandfather and Grandmother had no idea where the riders were hidden. They walked confidently up the stairs, Grandmother winking again at Johanna behind the soldiers' backs.

The soldiers must not have know that the room was occupied by one of their own officers, because they were taken aback when they found Captain Braun with his legs on the table, writing in his music book. He rose from his chair. The soldiers apologized profusely, and

the red-faced man especially seemed extremely upset at having intruded so unceremoniously on the room of a German officer. Captain Braun put all of them at ease with a few friendly words, and he must have made a joke, for they laughed. For one terrible moment, Johanna thought that, after all, Captain Braun's face looked no different from all the other soldiers. What he had done tonight could be a trap and he could betray them. But the soldiers now made ready to go, and they went without searching the room. Captain Braun took up his pencil and music book.

The attitude of the soldiers changed during their walk downstairs. When they came they had been sure they would find the riders. Now they seemed uncertain. The big red-faced soldier seemed to take it very much to heart that he had failed to find the riders. He and the other soldiers seemed suddenly to be in a terrible hurry and left the house without saying a word.

Grandfather picked up Johanna and swung her high in the air, as he had done when she had still been a little girl.

"Oh, Johanna, we are so proud of you, but where in this house did you hide the little riders?"

·Grandmother hugged Johanna, but she wouldn't let her tell the secret until they were all sitting quietly with a warm drink.

"Will they ever come back?" Johanna asked.

"I don't think so," Grandfather said. "They are convinced that the riders are not hidden here, and they can't prove that we ever had anything to do with their disappearance."

Johanna lay in bed that night, thinking about everything that had happened during the long day. She could hear the airplanes flying over the house. Every night it sounded as if there were more planes than the night before. This time, Johanna didn't think of her father; instead she thought of Captain Braun. She put on her slippers and walked upstairs. The door of the room stood ajar. Johanna pushed it open. Captain Braun was sitting at the table with his face buried in his hands. He looked up when he heard Johanna.

"I cannot sleep," Johanna said. "If I leave my door open, would you, please, play the flute for me?"

Understanding What You've Read

1. What real historical event prevented Johanna from returning to America?
2. What historical facts are used as details on pages 534–535 of the story?
3. Why did Johanna dislike Captain Braun when she first met him? Why did she change her mind at the end of the story?
4. Why do you think Johanna asked Captain Braun to play the flute?

Writing

1. Finish these sentences with fictional details. Each sentence is about an important historical person or event. You may want to look up some more facts in an encyclopedia.

   a. As President Washington shook my hand, I said, ". . ."
   b. The Declaration of Independence was being signed as the boy . . .
   c. The Wright brothers' plane might fly, but . . .
   d. Benjamin Franklin took off his bifocals, and . . .

2. One lesson you can learn from history is that ordinary people can display special courage during wartime. Explain in a sentence or two how Johanna showed her courage.

More Historical Fiction

Courage to Adventure: Stories of Boys and Girls Growing Up with America selected by Child Study Association of America/Wel-Met. T. Y. Crowell, 1976. Here are nineteen stories about American children from many different ethnic heritages at many different times in our nation's history.

The Princess and the Lion by Elizabeth Coatsworth. Pantheon, 1963. About 200 years ago, an African princess, followed by her pet lion, sets out to free her brother who is held prisoner on a distant mountain.

Bears on Hemlock Mountain by Alice Dalgliesh. Scribner, 1952. There aren't supposed to be any bears on Hemlock Mountain—but there are. And Jonathan must find a way to escape from them.

The Strange Voyage of Neptune's Car by Joe Lasker. Viking, 1977. This story is based on the true adventures of Mary Patten, the first woman to command a clipper ship around Cape Horn.

Sarah Bishop by Scott O'Dell. Houghton Mifflin, 1980. Sarah must build a new life after her farm is destroyed during the Revolutionary War.

Boris by Jaap ter Haar. Delacorte, 1970. Boris's story reflects the true hardships that World War II meant for many European children.

Dragonwings by Laurence Yep. Harper & Row, 1975. Moon Shadow leaves China to make a new home in San Francisco shortly before the earthquake of 1906.

Glossary

This glossary is a little dictionary. It contains the difficult words found in this book. The pronunciation, which tells you how to say the word, is given next to each word. That is followed by a word's meaning or meanings. Sometimes, a different form of the word follows the definition. It appears in boldfaced type.

The special symbols used to show the pronunciation are explained in the key that follows.

PRONUNCIATION KEY*

a	add, map	m	move, seem	u	up, done
ā	ace, rate	n	nice, tin	û(r)	urn, term
â(r)	care, air	ng	ring, song	yōo	use, few
ä	palm, father	o	odd, hot	v	vain, eve
b	bat, rub	ō	open, so	w	win, away
ch	check, catch	ô	order, jaw	y	yet, yearn
d	dog, rod	oi	oil, boy	z	zest, muse
e	end, pet	ou	out, now	zh	vision, pleasure
ē	even, tree	ōo	pool, food	ə	the schwa,
f	fit, half	ŏo	took, full		an unstressed
g	go, log	p	pit, stop		vowel representing
h	hope, hate	r	run, poor		the sound spelled
i	it, give	s	see, pass		a in above
ī	ice, write	sh	sure, rush		e in sicken
j	joy, ledge	t	talk, sit		i in possible
k	cook, take	th	thin, both		o in melon
l	look, rule	th	this, bathe		u in circus

Foreign: N is used following a nasal sound: French *Jean* [zhäN].
 ˜ indicates the [ny] sound: Spanish *señor* [sā·nyôr′].

In the pronunciations an accent mark (′) is used to show which syllable of a word receives the most stress. The word *bandage* [ban′dij], for example, is stressed on the first syllable. Sometimes there is also a lighter accent mark (′) that shows where there is a lighter stress, as in the word *combination* [kom′bə·nā′shən].

The following abbreviations are used throughout the glossary: *n.,* noun; *v.,* verb; *adj.,* adjective; *adv.,* adverb; *pl.,* plural; *sing.,* singular.

---

*The Pronunciation Key and the short form of the key that appears on the following right-hand pages are reprinted from *The HBJ School Dictionary,* copyright © 1977, 1972, 1968 by Harcourt Brace Jovanovich, Inc.

A

a·ban·don [ə·ban′dən] *v.* To leave; to fail to take care of. **—a·ban·doned,** *adj.:* an *abandoned* house.

a·bly [ā′blē] *adv.* With ability.

a·bun·dance [ə·bun′dəns] *n.* More than enough; an overflowing quantity.

ac·com·plish·ment [ə·kom′plish·mənt] *n.* Something done or completed; an achievement.

a·chieve·ment [ə·chēv′mənt] *n.* Something accomplished.

ac·tive [ak′tiv] *adj.* Busy or lively.

ac·tu·al [ak′chōō·əl] *adj.* Real.

ad·mit [ad·mit′] *v.* **ad·mit·ted** To accept as true.

ad·van·tage [ad·van′tij] *n.* Any circumstance that benefits someone or helps toward success.

af·fect [ə·fekt′] *v.* **af·fect·ed** To act on; have an effect on.

af·fec·tion [ə·fek′shən] *n.* A feeling of kindness, fondness, or love.

A·gi·ri·A·sa·sa [ä·gi′rē·ä·sä′sä] The wise man's name in "The Oba Asks for a Mountain."

air pock·et [âr′ pok′it] *n.* **1** A bubble of gas in the stomach. **2** A strong current of air that may cause an airplane to drop down sharply.

a·jar [ə·jär′] *adj., adv.* A little bit open, as a door.

al·ma·nac [ôl′mə·nak] *n.* A calendar in the form of a book or pamphlet that may state facts, predict the weather, or have wise little sayings or riddles.

Am·a·zon Riv·er [am′ə·zon riv′ər] *n.* A very large river which flows east across most of northern South America.

am·ne·sia [am·nē′zhə *or* am·nē′zhē·ə] *n.* Loss of memory. It can be caused by sickness, shock, or a hard hit on the head.

a·muse [ə·myōōz′] *v.* To entertain.

a·mus·ing [ə·myōō′zing] *adj.* Causing enjoyment, laughter, fun. **—a·muse,** *v.*

an·ces·tor [an′ses·tər] *n.* **1** A plant or animal of an earlier type from which later plants or animals have developed. **2** A person from whom one is descended, generally a person further back than a grandparent.

an·cient [ān′shənt] **1** *n.* A person who lived in early times. **2** *adj.* Very old.

an·tique [an·tēk′] *n.* Something very old, made a long time ago.

ap·pren·tice [ə·pren′tis] *n.* A person who works for another in order to learn that other person's trade or business.

arch [arch] *n.* A curve at the top of a gate, doorway, or window: A stone *arch* is often used as a doorway.

ar·chae·ol·o·gist [är′kē·ol′ə·jist] *n.* A scientist who studies how people lived in the past, often by digging up their camps, tombs, cities, etc.

ar·chi·tect [är′kə·tekt] *n.* A person who draws plans for buildings or other structures.

as·cend [ə·send′] *v.* **as·cend·ing, as·cend·ed 1** To succeed to; take over: *ascend* the throne (become king or queen). **2** To climb; rise.

as·sem·ble [ə·sem′bəl] *v.* **as·sem·bled** To bring together; collect.

at·om [at′əm] *n.* The smallest part of an element that can take part in a chemical reaction.

av·er·age [av′rij] *adj.* Usual, ordinary.

av·o·ca·do [av′ə·kä′dō] *n.* The green fruit of a tropical tree, eaten in salad and in other ways. It has one large pit.

awk·ward·ly [ôk′wərd·lē] *adv.* Being clumsy or embarrassing: walking *awkwardly* onto a stage.

B

bal·le·ri·na [bal′ə·rē′nə] *n.* A female ballet dancer.

bal·let [bal′ā *or* ba·lā′] *n.* A dance in which formal steps and movements are performed by costumed dancers. A ballet often tells a story.

bare·ly [bâr′lē] *adv.* 1 Only just; scarcely. 2 Plainly; openly.

bar·ter [bär′tər] *v.* To trade.

bate [bāt] **bat·ed** *v.* To eat or take nourishment—no longer used.

bea·gle [bē′gəl] *n.* A small dog with short legs and droopy ears.

Bell, Alexander Graham [bel, al′ig·zan′dər grā′əm] 1847–1922, the inventor of the telephone.

be·tray [bi·trā′] *v.* To give away a secret; to help an enemy.

bi·car·bon·ate of soda [bī·kär′bə·nit] *n.* A white powder that fizzes in water. Used in cooking or for an upset stomach. Also called *sodium bicarbonate.*

bind·er [bīn′dər] *n.* A notebook.

blow·hole [blō′hōl′] *n.* A nostril in the top of the head through which a dolphin, whale, etc. breathes.

bob [bob] 1 *v.* To move up and down or back and forth, with short, jerky motions. 2 *n.* A cork or float on a fishing line.

boom [boom] 1 *n.* A sudden increase in growth or riches: A *boom* usually does not last long. 2 *n.* The sound of an explosion. 3 *v.* To grow large and rich very quickly.

bore [bôr] *v.* **bored** 1 To make a hole in or through. 2 To make tired by being dull.

breath·tak·ing [breth′tā′king] *adj.* Taking one's breath away; very beautiful.

breed [brēd] 1 *v.* To produce young. 2 *n.* A particular kind of animal.

bur·den [bûr′dən] *n.* 1 A load. 2 Something difficult to carry or bear.

bur·lap [bûr′lap] *n.* A rough, loose cloth used for bags, sacks, etc.

bur·row [bûr′ō] 1 *n.* A hole or tunnel dug by an animal and used to live in, hide in, or escape through. 2 *v.* To make such a hole or tunnel.

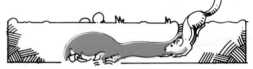

bus·y·bod·y [biz′ē·bod′ē] *n.* A person or animal that interferes in the business of others. — **bus·y·bod·ies,** *pl.*

C

ca·boose [kə·boos′] *n.* The last car of a freight train.

car·a·van [kar′ə·van] *n.* A group of traders, pilgrims, or others who travel together, as across a desert.

---

add, āce, câre, pälm;   end, ēqual;   it, īce;   odd, ōpen, ôrder;   tŏŏk, pōōl;   up, bûrn;
ə = a in *above*, e in *sicken*, i in *possible*, o in *melon*, u in *circus*;   yōō = u in *fuse*;   oil;   pout;
check;   ring;   thin;   this;   zh in *vision*.

ca·reer [kə·rir′] *n.* The main work of a person's life.

car·il·lon [kar′ə·lon] *n.* A set of bells on which a tune can be played.

car·ri·on [kar′ē·ən] *n.* Dead and rotting flesh.

cas·u·al·ly [kazh′ŏŏ·əl·ē] *adv.* In a cool manner, showing no emotion: He *casually* introduced himself to the famous writer.

cat·a·logue [kat′ə·lôg] *n.* **1** A list of things a store has for sale. **2** A card file showing the books in a library.

cell [sel] *n.* The basic unit of any living thing.

cen·sus [sen′səs] *n.* An official count of all the people in a country or city.

cen·ten·ni·al [sen·ten′ē·əl] *n.* The hundredth birthday of something: The Philadelphia *Centennial* Exposition was held one hundred years after the signing of the Declaration of Independence.

chal·lenge [chal′enj] **1** *n.* An invitation or dare to do something, usually dangerous or difficult. **2** *v.* To ask for a contest, duel, or fight.

char·ac·ter [kar′ik·tər] *n.* **1** A person, animal, etc., in a play, novel, story, etc. **2** All the qualities that make up the nature of a person. **3** Any letter, figure, or mark used in writing or printing.

charge [chärj] **1** *n.* An amount of stored electricity. **2** *v.* To fill with electricity. **3** *v.* To ask a price for. **—in charge** Having the care or control of.

Cher·o·kee [cher′ə·kē] *n.* A member of a tribe of American Indians. At first they lived in the southeastern U.S. Now many *Cherokees* live in Oklahoma.

cho·re·og·ra·pher [kôr′ē·og′rə·fər] *n.* A person who plans dancers' movements for performances.

cir·cu·la·to·ry [sûr′kyə·la·tôr′ē] *adj.* Having to do with movement around or through something, as of the blood.

cit·a·del [sit′ə·dəl] *n.* A building that overlooks a city in order to protect it.

ci·vil·i·za·tion [siv′ə·lə·zā′shən] *n.* The art, skill, science, knowledge, and culture of a particular group of people at a particular time.

claim [klām] **1** *v.* To demand as one's own. **2** *n.* A demand for something as one's own.

clasp [klasp] **1** *n.* A fastening or hook to hold two parts together. **2** *v.* To fasten with a clasp. **3** *v.* To grasp or embrace.

clog [klog] *v.* To plug or fill up so nothing can move. **—clog·ged,** *adj.*

clum·sy [klum′zē] *adj.* Not smooth or easy; awkward.

clus·ter [klus′tər] *n.* A group or bunch of similar things close together.

cob·ble·stone [kob′əl·stōn′] *n.* A rounded stone that was used for paving streets.

coin·age [koi′nij] *n.* **1** Money. **2** The right to make coins.

col·league [kol′ēg] *n.* A fellow worker in a profession or organization; associate.

co·lo·ni·al [kə·lō′nē·əl] **1** *n.* A person who lives in a land separate from the country that controls it. **2** *adj.* Having to do with a colony or colonies.

com·mis·sion·er [kə·mish′ən·ər] *n.* A person chosen or elected to be head of a government department or assignment.

com·mit·ment [kə·mit′mənt] *n.* The state of being bound to a promise.

com·mu·ni·ty [kə·myōō′nə·tē] *n.* **1** A group of people living together in one area. **2** A group of people living together who share the same interests.

com·mu·ni·ty re·la·tions [kə·myo͞o′nə·tē ri·lā′shənz] *n.* The dealings between a business or organization and the public in general.

com·pan·ion [kəm·pan′yən] *n.* A person who spends time with another, sharing what the other person is doing.

com·pa·ny [kum′pə·nē] *n.* **1** A group of dancers, actors, or singers gathered to perform together. **2** A group of people who have come together because of some common interest or purpose. — **com·pa·nies,** *pl.*

com·pel [kəm·pel′] *v.* **com·pelled** To force.

com·plex [kəm·pleks′ *or* kom′pleks] *adj.* Made up of many parts.

con·cern [kən·sûrn′] **1** *v.* To relate to; involve. **2** *n.* An interest or worry.

con·cer·ti·na [kon′sər·tē′nə] *n.* A small musical instrument like an accordion.

con·di·tion [kən·dish′ən] *n.* **1** Physical fitness; state of being healthy. **2** The state of being of a person or thing.

cone [kōn] *n.* The dry fruit of certain trees, mostly evergreens.

cone-bear·ing [kōn′bâr′ĭng] *adj.* Producing a dry fruit that holds seeds: Pines and many other trees are *cone-bearing.*

con·sid·er·a·ble [kən·sid′ər·ə·bəl] *adj.* Rather large; worth noticing.

con·stant [kon′stənt] *adj.* **1** Happening over and over, without end. **2** Faithful.

con·tact [kon′takt] **1** *n.* A coming together, meeting; the relation of touching or being in touch with. **2** *v.* To get in touch with.

con·tract [kən·trakt′] *v.* To become smaller; pull together into a smaller space.

con·trar·y *adj.* **1** [kən·trâr′ē] Determined to disagree: He was *contrary* in choosing a movie. **2** [kon′trer·ē] Totally different: *contrary* beliefs.

cor·al [kôr′əl] **1** *n.* A stony substance formed by many, many skeletons of tiny sea animals. **2** *n.* The animal whose skeleton forms coral. **3** *n., adj.* A pinkish or yellowish red color.

cor·ner·stone [kôr′nər·stōn′] *n.* A stone set into the corner of a building: The date the building was started is often carved in the *cornerstone.*

count·less [kount′lis] *adj.* Too many to be counted.

count·y seat [koun′tē sēt′] *n.* The place where the members of the county government meet and have their offices.

cove [kōv] *n.* A small, sheltered bay along a shoreline.

coy [koi] *adj.* **1** Shy. **2** Pretending to be shy in order to flirt.

craft [kraft] *n.* A skill, especially one done with the hands.

craft shop [kraft′ shop′] *n.* A place to buy supplies for practicing a craft.

cray·fish [krā′fish′] *n.* A small, freshwater shellfish like a lobster. Also called *crawfish.*

---

add, āce, câre, pälm;   end, ēqual;   it, īce;   odd, ōpen, ôrder;   to͝ok, pōol;   up, bûrn;
ə = a in *above*, e in *sicken*, i in *possible*, o in *melon*, u in *circus*;   yo͞o = u in *fuse*;   oil;   pout;
check;   ring;   thin;   this;   zh in *vision.*

cres·cent [kres′ənt] *adj.* Curved like a quarter moon.

crib [krib] *n.* **1** A cage for storing corn. **2** A baby's bed with railings on the sides.

crim·son [krim′zən] *n., adj.* Deep red.

crit·ic [krit′ik] *n.* A person who judges the value of music, books, plays, etc., and writes about his or her judgments.

crouch [krouch] **1** *n.* The position of crouching. **2** *v.* To stoop down with the knees bent, as an animal about to spring. — **crouch·es.**

cru·sade [kroo·sād′] **1** *v.* To fight for a cause or against an evil. **2** *n.* A vigorous struggle against evil or for a cause.

crush [krush] *v.* To press or squeeze as to break or injure. — **crush·ing** *adj.* Overwhelming, overpowering.

crys·tal [kris′təl] **1** *n.* A body formed when something turns to a solid: A *crystal* has flat surfaces and angles in a regular pattern: salt *crystals,* ice *crystals.* **2** *adj.* Colorless, transparent.

A salt crystal

cu·bic inch [kyoo′bik inch′] *n.* A unit for measuring volume, equaling one inch wide by one inch high by one inch deep.

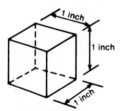

cue [kyoo] *n.* A word, action, etc., used in a play as a signal to another actor.

cul·ti·vate [kul′tə·vāt] *v.* **cul·ti·vat·ed** To prepare (land) for growing plants by loosening the soil.

cu·ri·os·i·ty [kyoor′ē·os′ə·tē] *n.* **1** A desire to find out. **2** Something strange or unusual. — **cu·ri·os·i·ties,** *pl.*

cu·ri·ous [kyoor′ē·əs] *adj.* Eager to know.

cur·rent [kûr′ənt] *n.* The part of a body of water or air that flows in a certain direction.

cur·ry [kûr′ē] *n.* A sauce or powder made of finely ground spices, used in cooking, especially in India and the Mideast.

curt·sy [kûrt′sē] **1** *n.* A bow made by bending the knees and leaning the upper body forward; used by females. **2** *v.* To make such a bow.

cy·cle [sī′kəl] *n.* **1** A series of stages in the growth of an animal or plant. **2** The time needed for these stages to take place. **3** A series of events that always happen in the same order and end back at the starting point.

D

---

darn [därn] **1** *v.* To mend cloth by stitching the hole with thread. **2** *n.* A place mended by darning. — **darn·ing** *adj.:* a *darning* needle.

da Vin·ci, Le·o·nar·do [də vin′chē, lā′ə·när′dō] 1452–1519, Italian painter, sculptor, engineer, and scientist.

dec·o·ra·tion [dek′ə·rā′shən] *n.* Something used to make something else more fancy or attractive; an ornament.

de·crease [di·krēs′] *v.* To get smaller.

ded·i·ca·tion [ded′ə·kā′shən] *n.* A giving over of one's life and/or time to a special purpose.

de·duc·tion [di·duk′shən] *n.* **1** A conclusion based on reasoning. **2** A subtraction: a thirty-dollar *deduction.*

de·fy [di·fī′] *v.* To refuse to follow (orders); resist openly.

de·mon [dē′mən] *n.* **1** A person having great energy or skill: a speed *demon.* **2** An evil spirit, devil.

de·part·ment [di·pärt′mənt] *n.* A separate part or division, as of a company, store, government, etc.

de·pend [di·pend′] *v.* **1** To be affected, influenced, or controlled by. **2** To trust; rely. — **de·pend·a·ble** [di·pen′də·bəl] *adj.* Worthy of trust; reliable.

de·scent [di·sent′] *n.* The act of going down to a lower point.

de·scrip·tive [di·skrip′tiv] *adj.* Telling what a person or thing is like.

de·sign [di·zīn′] *v.* **de·signed** To plan for a certain purpose.

de·sign·er [di·zī′nər] *n.* A person who plans the arrangement of the parts or features of something.

des·per·ate·ly [des′pər·it·lē] *adv.* Recklessly, carelessly — almost without hope.

de·vel·op·ment [di·vel′əp·mənt] *n.* **1** A growing larger or better. **2** The result of growing larger or better.

de·vice [di·vīs′] *n.* Something built for a specific purpose.

dig·ni·fied [dig′nə·fīd] *adj.* Having pride; calm and stately.

di·rec·tor [dī·rek′tər *or* di·rek′tər] *n.* A person who controls or manages, as in the production of a dance, movie, etc.

dis·ap·point [dis·ə·point′] *v.* **dis·ap·point·ed** To fail to meet the hopes of: Don't *disappoint* me.

dis·as·ter [di·zas′tər] *n.* An event causing great distress or ruin, as a fire, flood, etc.

dis·charge 1 [dis′chärj] *n.* The removal of an electrical charge. **2** [dis·chärj′ *or* dis′chärj] *v.* To set off or send forth an electrical charge.

dis·cour·age·ment [dis·kûr′ij·mənt] *n.* A feeling of being without hope or confidence.

Dis·ney, Walt [diz′nē, wôlt] 1901–1966, movie producer, especially known for animated cartoons *Mickey Mouse* and *Donald Duck.*

dis·tinct·ly [dis·tingkt′lē] *adv.* Very clearly.

dis·turb [dis·tûrb′] *v.* **dis·turbed** To break in upon with noise or change; upset.

dog·pad·dle [dog′pad′əl] *v.* **dog-pad·dling** To swim by paddling with each arm and kicking with each leg, as a dog does.

dol·ly [dol′ē] *n.* **1** A tool shaped like a small wooden stool on the end of a stick: The *dolly* was used to wash clothes by turning and pounding them in the water. **2** A flat frame set on wheels, used to move heavy objects. **3** A child's term for a doll.

do·na·tion [dō·nā′shən] *n.* Contribution, gift.

draw [drô] *v.* **1** To pull or drag. **2** To make a picture, cartoon, or likeness of with lines.

drib·ble [drib′əl] *v.* **drib·bling 1** To bounce or kick a ball very quickly. **2** Let fall in drops; drip or drool.

drift [drift] **1** *n.* Something piled up by wind or water: The snow piled in a *drift.* **2** *v.* To move or float in a current of water or air.

drift·wood [drift′wŏŏd′] *n.* Wood that is drifting in water or has washed up on shore.

---

add, āce, câre, pälm; end, ēqual; it, īce; odd, ōpen, ôrder; tŏŏk, pōŏl; up, bûrn;

ə = a in *above,* e in *sicken,* i in *possible,* o in *melon,* u in *circus;* yōŏ = u in *fuse;* oil; pout;

check; ring; thin; this; zh in *vision.*

drive [drīv] **1** *n.* The moving of cattle or sheep. **2** *n.* Ambition. **3** *v.* To direct and control the movements of.

drop·let [drop′lit] *n.* A little drop.

drought [drout] *n.* A long time without rainfall during which the ground becomes very dry.

dwin·dle [dwin′dəl] *v.* To grow steadily smaller.

E

East·ern Wood·land In·di·ans [ēs′tərn wood′land′ in′dē·ənz] *n., pl.* Those American Indians who lived mostly on land thickly covered with trees in eastern North America.

e·clipse [i·klips′] *n.* A complete or partial hiding of the sun or moon: An *eclipse* occurs when the moon passes between Earth and the sun or when the moon passes through Earth's shadow.

e·di·tion [i·dish′ən] *n.* All the copies of a book or paper printed at one time and without differences.

ef·fect [i·fekt′] **1** *n.* Influence; the ability to cause something to change. **2** *v.* To bring about or cause.

em·bel·lish·ment [im·bel′ish·mənt] *n.* Something added to make attractive; decoration.

en·a·ble [in·ā′bəl] *v.* **en·a·bled** To make able; give the ability to: Tennis lessons will *enable* me to play better.

en·chant·er [in·chan′tər] *n.* A magician; sorcerer.

en·tire·ly [in·tīr′lē] *adv.* Totally.

en·vi·ron·ment [in·vī′rən·mənt] *n.* The conditions and surroundings that have an effect on the development of a person, animal, or plant.

e·qua·tion [i·kwā′zhən] *n.* A statement that two or more quantities are equal, as $5 \times 5 = 25$.

e·qua·tor [i·kwā′tər] *n.* An imaginary line that circles the Earth halfway between the North and South Poles.

es·tab·lish [ə·stab′lish] *v.* **es·tab·lished** To set up on a firm or lasting basis.

e·val·u·a·tion [i·val′yoo·ā′shən] *n.* An examination, check-up, test.

e·ven·tu·al·ly [i·ven′choo·ə·lē] *adv.* In the end; finally.

ex·as·per·ate [ig·zas′pə·rāt] *v.* To annoy almost to the point of anger.

ex·cerpt [ek′sûrpt] *n.* A passage or section taken from a piece of writing.

ex·ec·u·tive [ig·zek′yə·tiv] *n.* One of the persons who is in charge of a business.

ex·pand [ik·spand′] *v.* To make or become larger.

ex·pose [ik·spōz′] *v.* **ex·pos·ing** To uncover; reveal.

ex·po·si·tion [eks′pə·zish′ən] *n.* A showing; a display of things.

F

---

face [fās] **1** *n.* An outer level or flat surface, as of a crystal or a cliff. **2** *n.* The front of the head extending from forehead to chin and ear to ear. **3** *v.* To meet with courage.

fac·tu·al [fak′choo·əl] *adj.* Made up of, or relying on, things known to be true.

faith [fāth] *n.* A religion or belief.

fa·mil·iar [fə·mil′yər] *adj.* Well known as through experience, study, or because often encountered.

far·sight·ed [fär′sī′tid] *adj.* **1** Showing good judgment in looking and planning ahead. **2** Able to see things at a distance more clearly than things that are near.

fas·cin·a·ting [fas′ə·nāt·ing] *adj.* Very interesting.

fas·cin·a·tion [fas′ə·nā′shən] *n.* Great interest or attraction.

fear·some [fir′səm] *adj.* Frightening.

fea·ture [fē′chər] *n.* **1** A special article, story, or column, as in a newspaper. **2** Part of the face, as eyes, nose, or mouth.

feed [fēd] **1** *n.* Food for animals. **2** *v.* To give food to.

feld·spar [feld′spär′] *n.* A hard mineral containing aluminum and other elements.

fid·dle·back chair [fid′(ə)l·bak′] *n.* A straight-back chair with no arms and a center piece down the back that is shaped like a fiddle (a violin).

field [fēld] **1** *n.* A large stretch of land. **2** *v.* To catch, as a ball. —**field·ed.**

fier·y [fīr′ē *or* fī′ər·ē] *adj.* Flaming; containing fire.

fife [fīf] **1** *n.* A small, shrill flute. **2** *v.* To play a fife. —**fifed.**

file [fīl] **1** *v.* To have something put on an official record. **2** *n.* A cabinet, drawer, or box in which papers are arranged according to a system. **3** *v.* To arrange and put in a file.

flash [flash] **1** *n.* A sudden blaze of light. **2** *v.* To shine brightly. **3** *v.* To move quickly. —**flashed.**

flus·tered [flus′tərd] *adj.* Confused; embarrassed; upset.

for·ty-nin·er [fôr′tē·nī′nər] *n.* Someone who went to California in 1849 to find gold.

Fo·rum [fôr′əm] *n.* The center for meetings, business, and courts in the ancient city of Rome.

fos·sil [fos′əl] *n.* The remains or impressions of an animal or plant of a past age, hardened and preserved in rock.

fossil

foul shot [foul′ shot′] *n.* In basketball, a free throw given to a player after an opponent makes physical contact, a foul, with that player.

frail [frāl] *adj.* Weak; easily damaged.

frame·work [frām′wûrk′] *n.* The inner structure around which something is built.

free·way [frē′wā′] *n.* A highway for fast traffic; expressway.

fre·quen·cy [frē′kwən·sē] *n.* Station or tuning on a radio receiver.

frus·tra·tion [frus·trā′shən] *n.* Defeat and disappointment.

fu·gi·tive [fyōō′jə·tiv] *n.* A person who is running from danger or arrest.

fu·ri·ous [fyŏŏr′ē·əs] *adj.* **1** Very great: at a *furious* speed. **2** Very angry.

fuss·budg·et [fus′buj·it] *n.* A fussy, hard-to-please person.

G

gai·ter [gā′tər] *n.* A covering, as of cloth or leather, for the lower leg or ankle.

gale [gāl] *n.* A very strong wind.

gasp [gasp] *v.* **gasped** To struggle for breath with the mouth open.

---

add, āce, câre, pälm;   end, ēqual;   it, īce;   odd, ōpen, ôrder;   tŏŏk, pōōl;   up, bûrn;
ə = a in *above*, e in *sicken*, i in *possible*, o in *melon*, u in *circus*;   yōō = u in *fuse*;   oil;   pout;
check;   ring;   thin;   this;   zh in *vision*.

gen·er·a·tion [jen′ə·rā′shən] *n.* One step or stage in the history of a family: My father is of a different *generation* than I.

ge·ol·o·gy [jē·ol′ə·jē] *n.* The study of the history and structure of the Earth's crust, especially as recorded in rocks.

gi·bral·tar [ji·brôl′tər] *n.* **1** A hard white candy, usually peppermint or lemon flavored. **2** With a capital letter, *Gibraltar* is the name of a place at the southern tip of Spain.

glare [glâr] *v.* To stare with a fierce and angry look.

gleam [glēm] **1** *n.* A ray or beam of light that is faint or shines for only a short time. **2** *v.* To shine with a gleam.— **gleam·ing.**

gloss·y [glôs′ē] *adj.* Smooth and shiny.

glow·worm [glō′wurm′] *n.* A firefly, or its larva, that glows in the dark.

Go·bi Des·ert [gō′bē dez′ərt] *n.* A rough, rocky desert about three times the size of California, in east central Asia.

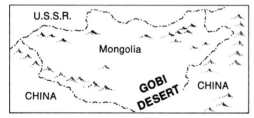

gog·gles [gog′əlz] *n., pl.* Large glasses that protect the eyes from wind, dust, and sparks.

gold rush [gōld′rush′] *n.* The hurrying of settlers to a place where they think they can find gold: In 1849 there was a *gold rush* to California.

gran·ite [gran′it] *n.* A hard igneous rock that will take a high polish. It is often used as a building material.

graze [grāz] *v.* To feed on growing grass.

Greek [grēk] **1** *adj.* Having to do with an ancient people of southern Europe, their lands, or their language. **2** *n.* A person from Greece.

grit [grit] *n.* Bits of stone; gravel: Chickens, which have no teeth, need *grit* in their stomachs to grind their food.

grot·to [grot′ō] *n.* A cave.— **grot·toes,** *pl.*

gruff [gruf] *adj.* Rough; rude.

guard [gärd] **1** *n.* A device, attachment, etc., that makes something safe to use or keeps it from being lost. **2** *v.* To watch with care.

H

haugh·ti·ly [hô′tə·lē] *adv.* Proudly and scornfully.

haz·y [hā′zē] *adj.* Unclear, misty.

he·li·um [hē′lē·əm] *n.* A gas that is lighter than air and does not burn.

hemp [hemp] *n.* A tall plant of Asia, grown for its tough fiber, which is made into cloth, rope, etc.

her·ald [her′əld] **1** *n.* A bearer of important news; messenger. **2** *v.* To announce or foretell.

hinge [hinj] *n.* A joint on which something turns.

hol·low [hol′ō] **1** *n.* Valley. **2** *adj.* Empty on the inside, not solid.

Ho·mer [hō′mər] A Greek poet who lived almost 3,000 years ago; the author of the *Odyssey.*

home·spun [hōm′spun′] **1** *adj.* Made at home. **2** *n.* Cloth made of yarn spun at home. **3** *adj.* Plain; simple.

home·stead [hōm′sted] *n.* **1** A piece of land given to a settler by the U.S. government to farm, improve, and eventually own. **2** A person's land and house.

Home·stead Act [hōm′sted akt′] *n.* One of several Homestead Acts—laws that allowed settlers to buy land in the West with their work plus a very small amount of money.

home·stead·er [hōm′sted′ər] *n.* A settler who farmed land in order to buy it.

ho·ri·zon [hə·rī′zən] *n.* The line where the Earth and sky seem to meet.

horn of am·mon [hôrn′ uv am′ən] *n.* A sea shell that curls like the horn of a male sheep. Statues of an Egyptian god, Ammon, showed him with a sheep's curling horns.

horse·car [hôrs′kär] *n.* A trolley or "bus" drawn by horses along a track.

house 1 [houz] *v.* To give shelter to or lodge. **2** [hous] *n.* A building that people live in.

hurl [hûrl] *v.* **hurled** To throw with a great force.

husk·y [hus′kē] *n.* A large, strong dog used to pull sleds through snow.

Hwei Ming [hwā′ ming′] *n.* A Chinese female's name which means "clever." The word *ming* can also mean "light."

hy·dro·gen [hī′drə·jən] *n.* The lightest of all gases; it burns easily and has no smell or color: *Hydrogen* combines with oxygen to make water.

I

i·den·ti·fi·ca·tion [ī·den′tə·fə·kā′shən] *n.* The action of identifying, describing, or recognizing.

ig·ne·ous rocks [ig′nē·əs] *n.* Rocks formed at very high temperatures, as by a volcano.

I·le·sha [ē·lā′shä] *n.* A city in southwest Nigeria.

im·ag·i·na·tive·ly [i·maj′ə·nə·tiv·lē] *adv.* In a creative way.

im·mense [i·mens′] *adj.* Very large; huge.

im·press [im·pres′] *v.* **im·pressed** To affect the mind or feelings of, usually favorably.

im·pres·sion [im·presh′ən] *n.* **1** The pressing of paper on type; printing. **2** An effect on the mind or feelings.

im·prove·ment [im·proōv′mənt] *n.* **1** The act of making better. **2** The result of becoming better.

in·au·di·ble [in·ô′də·bəl] *adj.* Incapable of being heard.

in·can·ta·tion [in′kan·tā′shən] *n.* The speaking of words or syllables that are supposed to have magical results: The wizard's *incantation* made a rabbit appear in the hat.

in·cor·por·ate [in·kôr′pə·rāt] *v.* To combine, bring together; to include as part of something else.

in·crease [in·krēs′] *v.* To get bigger.

in·de·pen·dence [in′di·pen′dens] *n.* Not having to depend or rely on someone or something; the condition of being independent.

in·de·pen·dent [in′di·pen′dənt] *adj.* Self-supporting; not subject to the authority or direction of others.

---

add, āce, câre, pälm;   end, ēqual;   it, īce;   odd, ōpen, ôrder;   toŏk, poōl;   up, bûrn;
ə = a in *above*, e in *sicken*, i in *possible*, o in *melon*, u in *circus*;   yoō = u in *fuse*;   oil;   pout;
check;   ring;   thin;   this;   zh in *vision*.

In·dies [in′dēz] *n., pl.* **1** Refers to southern and northern Asia and the islands nearby. **2** The East Indies. **3** The West Indies.

in·di·vid·u·al·ist [in′də·vij′ōō·əl·ist] *n.* A person who believes in or lives in his or her own way, no matter what other people think.

in·dus·try [in′dəs·trē] *n.* A business; branch of manufacturing or business. — **in·dus·tries**, *pl.*

in·flu·ence [in′flōō·əns] *n.* **1** A person with power to affect another person. **2** The power of a person or thing to have an effect on others.

inn·keep·er [in′kē′pər] *n.* A person who owns or operates an inn. An inn is a hotel or restaurant.

in·oc·u·late [in·ok′yə·lāt] *v.* To put a vaccine into a person's or animal's body to protect it against a certain disease.

in·sig·ni·fi·cant [in′sig·nif′ə·kənt] *adj.* Lacking importance, meaning, size, or worth: an *insignificant* difference.

in·stance [in′stəns] *n.* An example or illustration.

in·tel·lec·tu·al·ly [in′tə·lek′chōō·ə·lē] *adv.* Mentally; in a way having to do with intelligence.

in·tense [in·tens′] *adj.* Very strong, great, or deep: *intense* cold.

in·tent·ly [in·tent′lē] *adv.* With great attention.

in·trud·er [in·trōō′dər] *n.* One who enters without permission or welcome.

in·ves·ti·gate [in·ves′tə·gāt] *v.* **in·ves·ti·gat·ing** To look into, find out about.

in·vest·ment [in·vest′mənt] *n.* The use to which money or time is put in order to gain something.

i·o·ta [ī·ō′tə] *n.* **1** The ninth letter of the Greek alphabet. **2** A small amount.

ir·ri·gate [ir′ə·gāt] *v.* **ir·ri·gat·ed** To furnish (land) with water by using pipes, ditches, or canals.

ir·ri·ga·tion [ir′ə·gā′shən] *n.* The supplying of land with water by artificial means such as through pipes, ditches, or canals.

i·tem [ī′təm] *n.* Any one thing in a group of things.

J

---

jade [jād] *n.* A type of stone, usually green but sometimes white, used in jewelry or carving.

jet stream [jet′ strēm′] *n.* A current of strong winds, 9,000 to 13,500 meters above Earth, blowing from the west at speeds of often more than 400 kilometers per hour.

John·ny Ap·ple·seed [jon′ē ap′əl·sēd′] Nickname of *John Chapman*, 1775–1845, American pioneer who planted apple trees all over the Midwest.

K

---

kil·ler whale [kil′ər (h)wāl′] *n.* A fierce, mostly black whale which hunts in packs. Generally, the whale does not attack humans.

L

---

lack [lak] *n.* A state of being without.

la·crosse [lə·krôs′] *n.* A game first played by North American Indians, using rackets or sticks and a small ball.

land bridge [land′ brij′] *n.* A narrow strip of land serving as a passage, or bridge, between two bodies of land.

Lat·in [lat′ən] *n.* The language of ancient Rome.

launch [lônch] *v.* **1** To hurl or fling into the air. **2** To move or push into the water.

lead·ing [lē′ding] *adj.* **1** Most important. **2** At the front; first.

leaf [lēf] **1** *v.* To turn the pages. **2** *n.* One of the pieces of paper making up a book. A page is really one side of a *leaf.* **3** *n.* One of the flat, thin, usually green parts of a plant or tree.

leop·ard seal [lep′ərd sēl′] *n.* A spotted seal found near Antarctica.

lib·er·ate [lib′ə·rāt] *v.* **lib·er·at·ing** To set free.

lieu·ten·ant [loo·ten′ənt] *n.* A military rank below captain but above sergeant.

life·like [līf′līk′] *adj.* **1** Accurately representing real events: a *lifelike* movie. **2** Looking like a person or thing that is or was alive.

lime·stone [līm′stōn′] *n.* A common kind of rock made of the same substance as chalk.

lin·en [lin′ən] **1** *n.* Thread or cloth made from flax fibers. **2** *adj.* Made of linen.

link [lingk] **1** *n.* Connection. **2** *v.* To join, connect.

lla·ma [lä′mə] *n.* A South American animal related to the camel but smaller and with no hump.

lo·cal [lō′kəl] *adj.* In the nearby area.

lo·ca·tion [lō·kā′shən] *n.* The place where something is.

lock [lok] *n.* **1** An enclosed section of a canal in which ships can be raised or lowered by letting water in or out. **2** A device for fastening a door, safe, etc.

lo·cust [lō′kəst] *n.* An insect like a grasshopper that often moves in large groups and destroys crops.

loot [loot] **1** *v.* To rob by force. **2** *n.* Slang for money.

lu·na·tic [loo′nə·tik] *n.* A person who is mentally ill.

Lyme Re·gis [līm′ rē′jis] *n.* A seaside town in southwest England, on the English Channel.

M

mag·ni·fy [mag′nə·fī] *v.* **mag·ni·fied** To make something look bigger. — **mag·ni·fied,** *adj.*

mam·mal [mam′əl] *n.* Any of the animals that have backbones and whose young are fed with milk from their mothers' bodies.

man·sion [man′shən] *n.* A large, impressive house, as of a wealthy person.

man·tle [man′təl] *n.* **1** One of the layers inside the Earth. **2** A loose-fitting, usually sleeveless garment worn over other clothing; a cloak.

mark·ing [mär′king] *n.* (*often plural*) The color pattern of an animal's fur, a bird's feathers, etc.

mat·ter [mat′ər] *n.* **1** Anything that has weight and takes up space. **2** A particular kind or form of substance: volcanic *matter.* **3** The ideas, facts, or meaning of a book, speech, etc.

mel·o·dy [mel′ə·dē] *n.* A succession of single tones in music; tune.

mem·o·ra·ble [mem′ər·ə·bəl] *adj.* Worthy of being remembered; easily remembered as being important.

men·ace [men′əs] *n.* Threat, danger.

---

add, āce, câre, pälm; end, ēqual; it, īce; odd, ōpen, ôrder; took, pool; up, bûrn;
ə = a in *above,* e in *sicken,* i in *possible,* o in *melon,* u in *circus;* yoo = u in *fuse;* oil; pout;
check; ring; thin; this; zh in *vision.*

mer·chan·dise [mûr′chən·dīz *or* mûr′chən·dīs] *n.* Goods bought and sold for profit.

met·ro·pol·i·tan [met′rə·pol′ə·tən] *adj.* Having to do with a large city and its surrounding suburbs.

mi·cro·or·gan·ism [mī′krō·ôr′gən·iz′əm] *n.* A tiny living thing visible only through a microscope, as a bacterium.

mim·ic [mim′ik] *n.* A person who imitates others.

min·er·al [min′ər·əl] *n.* A natural substance, neither vegetable nor animal, that is important for nutrition in living things.

min·now [min′ō] *n.* A small fish commonly used for bait.

mis·chief [mis′chif] *n.* **1** A person or animal that teases or plays tricks. **2** Tricks or teasing.

mis·sion [mish′ən] *n.* **1** A calling; one's chief purpose. **2** The task or duty that a person or group is sent to do.

mis·un·der·stand·ing [mis′un·dər·stand′ing] **1** *v.* Not understanding or understanding wrongly. **2** *n.* A disagreement.

mo·bile 1 [mō′bēl] *n.* A sculpture made of movable parts and hung in balance so that any breeze moves or turns it. **2** [mō′bəl] *adj.* Easily moved.

mol·lusk [mol′əsk] *n.* A member of a group of animals with soft bodies that are not divided into segments; it is usually protected by a hard shell. Snails and clams are mollusks.

moor·ing [moŏr′ing] *n.* The line, cable, anchor, etc., that holds a ship in place.

more·o·ver [môr·ō′vər] *adv.* Besides.

mouth [mouth] *n.* **1** The place where a river meets the sea. **2** The opening through which food is taken into the body and sounds are uttered.

mu·ni·tions [myoō·nish′ənz] *n. (usually pl.)* Materials and supplies used in war; guns, cannons, bullets, and shells.

mus·ket [mus′kit] *n.* An old type of firearm, now replaced by the rifle.

mu·tin·y [myoō′tə·nē] **1** *n.* A rebellion against authority, as by a group of soldiers against their commander. **2** *v.* To take part in a mutiny.

N

name·less [nām′lis] *adj.* **1** Having no name. **2** Not known by name. **3** Not fit to be spoken of: *nameless* terror.

na·tion·al [nash′ən·əl] *adj.* Having to do with the nation as a whole.

na·tion·al·i·ty [nash′ən·al′ə·tē] *n.* A group of people who come from a certain country.

na·tive [nā′tiv] **1** *adj.* Born, grown, or living naturally in a particular area. **2** *n.* A plant or animal living in an area.

na·ture [nā′chər] *n.* **1** One's own combination of characteristics. **2** The world, except for things made by people.

nav·i·ga·tion [nav′ə·gā′shən] *n.* The art of charting the position and route of a ship, aircraft, etc.

nav·i·ga·tor [nav′ə·gā·tər] *n.* A person who charts the position and route of a ship, aircraft, etc.

net·ting [net′ing] *n.* Material made with strips woven together leaving holes between.

nev·er·the·less [nev′ər·thə·les′] *conj.* But, however.

New Am·ster·dam [n(y)oō′am′stər·dam] *n.* Early Dutch settlement on the site of what is now New York City. In 1664 the British renamed it New York.

New Zea·land [n(y)ōō′zē′lənd] *n.* An island nation in the southern Pacific, southeast of Australia. It is a member of the British Commonwealth.

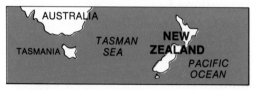

Norse [nôrs] *n., pl.* The early people who lived in northern Europe.

nudge [nuj] **1** *n.* A gentle push, as with the elbow. **2** *v.* To touch or push gently so as to attract attention.

O

O·ba [ō′bə] Powerful chief in the land of the Yoruba.

ob·ser·va·tion [ob′zər·vā′shən] *n.* The act of looking at something scientifically and making notes on it.

ob·serve [əb·zûrv′] *v.* To see or notice.

ob·ses·sion [əb·sesh′ən] *n.* An idea, thought, or feeling that fills the mind and cannot be driven out.

oc·ca·sion·al [ə·kā′zhən·əl] *adj.* **1** Happening now and then. **2** Made or suitable for a special occasion.

O·ke-U·mo [ō′kā·ōō′mō] *n.* A mountain in Nigeria.

o·me·ga [ō·mē′gə, ō·meg′ə, *or* ō·mā′gə] *n.* **1** The last letter in the Greek alphabet —symbol ω. **2** The end; the last.

or·di·nance [ôr′də·nəns] *n.* An order, or law, made by the government of a city or town.

or·gan·ism [ôr′gən·iz′əm] *n.* A plant or animal thought of as something built of parts and organs.

o·rig·i·nal [ə·rij′ə·nəl] **1** *n.* The first form of a piece of writing. **2** *adj.* Belonging to the beginning of something; first.

o·ver·pro·tect [ō′vər·prə·tekt′] *v.* **o·ver·pro·tect·ed** To protect (a child) too much and keep (the child) from normal experiences.

ox·y·gen [ok′sə·jin] *n.* A colorless, tasteless, odorless gas making up about a fifth of the Earth's atmosphere.

P

pains·tak·ing·ly [pānz′tā′king·lē] *adv.* Very, very carefully.

par·chee·si [pär·chē′zē] *n.* A game played on a cross-shaped board. *Parcheesi* is a trademark. The original game, called *pachisi,* is a very old game of India.

pat·ent [pat′(ə)nt] *n.* A government document giving an inventor the sole right to make and sell an invention or use a new process for a set number of years.

pa·trol [pə·trōl′] *n.* A person or group guarding an area.

pay dirt [pā′ dûrt] *n.* Earth in which something valuable, such as gold or silver, is found.

peer [pir] **1** *v.* To look closely in order to see clearly. **2** *n.* An equal, as in rank, talent, etc.: an artist without *peer.*

Pe·king [pē′king′] *n.* The capital of China.

Pe·nob·scot Bay [pə·nob′skot bā′] *n.* A bay in the state of Maine.

perch [pûrch] **1** *n.* A resting place for a bird. **2** *v.* To sit or place (something) on. —**perched.**

per·il [per′əl] *n.* Danger.

---

add, āce, câre, pälm;   end, ēqual;   it, īce;   odd, ōpen, ôrder;   tŏŏk, pōōl;   up, bûrn;

ə = a in *above,* e in *sicken,* i in *possible,* o in *melon,* u in *circus;*   yōō = u in *fuse;*   oil;   pout;

check;   ring;   thin;   this;   zh in *vision.*

per·ma·nent [pûr′mən·ənt] *adj.* Continuing without change, lasting.—**per·ma·nent·ly,** *adv.*

per·plexed [pər·plekst′] *adj.* Puzzled; bewildered.

phi·lan·thro·pist [fi·lan′thrə·pist] *n.* A person who gives a great deal of time or money to helping others.

Pied Piper of Hamelin [pīd′ pī′pər uv ham′lin] A musician in a German folk story who led the rats out of the city of Hamelin by playing his pipe—a small flute or whistle. In revenge for not being paid he led the children of the city away also. *Pied* means having or wearing two or more colors in patches.

pier [pir] *n.* A structure built on pillars and jutting over water, used as a landing place or walk.

pike [pīk] *n.* Road; turnpike.

pil·grim [pil′grim] *n.* A wanderer or traveler.

pix·ie or **pix·y** [pik′sē] **1** *n.* A fairy or elf. **2** *v.* To cast a magic spell over.—**pix·ied.**

plaque [plak] *n.* A flat metal plate with words or pictures pressed into it.

play out [plā′ out′] *v.* **played out** To use up, finish.

plun·der [plun′dər] *v.* **plun·dered** To rob of property or goods by force.

point [point] *n.* **1** A narrow piece of land extending out into water; cape. **2** The sharp end of something.

pol·i·cy [pol′ə·sē] *n.* A plan or method of action or conduct.

por·poise [pôr′pəs] *n.* A sea mammal similar to a small whale, mostly blackish with a blunt snout.

port·fo·li·o [pôrt·fō′lē·ō] *n.* A flat case for carrying papers or drawings.

pos·i·tion [pə·zish′ən] *n.* **1** The place where someone or something is, especially in relation to other things or people. **2** A job.

po·tion [pō′shən] *n.* A liquid that is supposed to have medicinal, poisonous, or magical qualities.

prac·ti·cal [prak′ti·kəl] *adj.* Useful.

prai·rie [prâr′ē] *n.* A large area of level grassy land having few or no trees.

praise [prāz] *v.* **praised** To give a high opinion of something; show approval.

pre·dict [pri·dikt′] *v.* To say what is going to happen before it happens.

pre·dic·tion [pri·dik′shən] *n.* The act of saying what is going to happen before it happens: The weather forecaster's *prediction* is rain for Friday.

pre·fer [pri·fûr′] *v.* To like better.

pres·ent-day [prez′ənt·dā′] *adj.* As of now; modern.

pres·to [pres′tō] **1** *interj.* Before you know it; quickly, suddenly: *"Presto!"* is what a magician says when pulling a rabbit out of a hat. **2** *adj.* In music, very quick.

pre·vail·ing wes·ter·lies [pri·vā′ling wes′tər·lēz] *n., pl.* The west winds that are common in middle latitudes both north and south of the equator.

prey [prā] *n.* Any animal seized by another for food.

prick·ly [prik′lē] *adj.* **1** Having small, sharp points, as a cactus. **2** Stinging: a *prickly* feeling.

prin·ci·pal [prin′sə·pəl] **1** *n.* The head of an elementary school or high school. **2** *adj.* First in rank or importance; chief.

prin·ci·ple [prin′sə·pəl] *n.* **1** Good moral standards; honesty; fairness: The judge is a woman of *principle.* **2** A general truth or rule on which other truths are based: the *principle* of democracy.

proc·ess [pros′es] *n.* A way of making or doing something.

pro·ces·sion [prə·sesh′ən] *n.* A formal and serious parade.

pro·claim [prō·klām′] *v.* To make known; announce to the public.

pro·fes·sion [prə·fesh′ən] *n.* An occupation requiring a good education and mental — rather than physical — labor.

pro·fes·sion·al [prə·fesh′ən·əl] *adj.* **1** Describing a sport with players who are paid to play and practice under a manager's control. **2** Of or working in a profession.

prof·it [prof′it] *n.* The amount of money gained in a business deal after deducting all expenses.

pro·fuse·ly [prə·fyoōs′lē] *adv.* In a generous way; abundantly.

proj·ect 1 [proj′ekt] *n.* A problem or task. **2** [prə·jekt′] *v.* To jut. **3** [prə·jekt′] *v.* To throw forward.

pro·nounce [prə·nouns′] *v.* To declare; to announce that something is so.

prop [prop] *n.* Any movable object needed on the stage for a play, except costumes and scenery.

pro·pose [prə·pōz′] *v.* **pro·posed** To put forward as a suggestion to be considered.

pros·per·i·ty [pros·per′ə·tē] *n.* The state of having more than enough on which to live.

pros·per·ous [pros′pər·əs] *adj.* Successful; thriving; wealthy and comfortable.

Pueb·lo [pweb′lō] **1** *adj.* Pertaining to a group of American Indian tribes in the Southwest. These tribes lived in towns with houses made of brick or stone. The Spanish word for "town" is *pueblo,* so the Spaniards called them the Pueblo people. **2** *n.* A member of a Pueblo tribe.

Puer·to Ri·co [pwer′tō rē′kō] *n.* An island in the West Indies that is a self-governing possession of the United States.

puf·fin [puf′in] *n.* A sea bird of the North Atlantic with a short neck and a triangular bill.

punc·ture [pungk′chər] *v.* To pierce with something sharp.

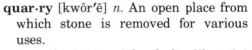

Q

quar·ry [kwôr′ē] *n.* An open place from which stone is removed for various uses.

quartz [kwôrtz] *n.* A hard glasslike mineral, sometimes found in colored forms.

ques·tion·naire [kwes′chən·âr′] *n.* A list of questions, usually printed, used to get information from a person.

R

raft [raft] *n.* A floating platform made of logs fastened together.

ram [ram] *n.* A male sheep.

rare [râr] *adj.* **1** Very unusual. **2** Hard to find. **3** Undercooked: *rare* meat.

---

add, āce, câre, pälm;   end, ēqual;   it, īce;   odd, ōpen, ôrder;   toŏk, poōl;   up, bûrn;
ə = a in *above*, e in *sicken*, i in *possible*, o in *melon*, u in *circus*;   yoō = u in *fuse*;   oil;   pout;
check;   ring;   thin;   this;   zh in *vision*.

ra·vine [rə·vēn′] *n.* A long, narrow gorge or depression in the earth, usually cut out by a flow of water.

raw [rô] *adj.* **1** Not cooked. **2** Not processed: *raw* sugar. **3** Damp and chilling: *raw* weather.

ray [rā] *n.* **1** In mathematics, a part of a line that begins at a given point on the line and extends in only one direction. **2** A beam of light.

re·ac·tion [rē·ak′shən] *n.* **1** The action of two or more chemicals on one another; chemical change. **2** An action in response to something.

read·y-made [red′ē·mād′] *adj.* Clothing that you buy in a store. *Ready-made* clothes fit people of various sizes.

re·al·i·ty [rē·al′ə·tē] *n.* An actual person, thing, or fact.

re·al·ize [rē′əl·īz] *v.* To understand fully.

rear ad·mi·ral [rir′ ad′mə·rəl] *n.* A rank in the U.S. Navy above captain.

re·cep·tion [ri·sep′shən] *n.* **1** A receiving or welcoming. **2** A party at which hosts greet their guests.

rec·og·ni·tion [rek′əg·nish′ən] *n.* Notice and approval.

rec·og·nize [rek′əg·nīz] *v.* To identify, know.

rec·re·a·tion [rek′rē·ā′shən] *n.* Play, amusement, or relaxation.

re·gion [rē′jən] *n.* An area of land, usually large; a district.

re·hears·al [ri·hûr′səl] *n.* A practice session or performance to prepare for a public performance.

re·jec·tion [ri·jek′shən] *n.* The act of refusing to accept something.

re·la·tion [ri·lā′shən] *n.* **1** A connection between people and groups brought about by business or other contacts. **2** A connection between people by family or marriage.

re·lease [ri·lēs′] *v.* **re·leased 1** To make available to the public; put on sale. **2** To set free.

re·mark·a·ble [ri·mär′kə·bəl] *adj.* Extraordinary, unusual, worthy of notice.

re·pro·duc·tion [rē′prə·duk′shən] *n.* The process by which animals or plants produce new life.

rep·tile [rep′til *or* rep′tīl] *n.* A cold-blooded animal that crawls on its belly or creeps on very short legs. Snakes, lizards, and crocodiles are reptiles.

req·ui·si·tion [rek′wə·zish′ən] *n.* A formal request or demand.

re·sist [ri·zist′] *v.* To refuse to give in to; to oppose.

re·solve [ri·zolv′] *v.* **re·solved** To decide firmly.

re·spect·ed [ri·spek′tid] *adj.* Honored; highly regarded. — **re·spect,** *v.*

re·spect·ful·ly [ri·spekt′fə·lē] *adv.* Politely.

res·pi·ra·to·ry [res′pə·rə·tôr′ē *or* ri·spīr′ə·tôr′ē] *adj.* Having to do with breathing.

re·spon·si·bil·i·ty [ri·spon′sə·bil′ə·tē] *n.* Duty or obligation.

re·stric·tion [ri·strik′shən] *n.* Something that limits something else.

re·view [ri·vyoo′] **1** *n.* An article that tells about and judges new books, plays, etc. **2** *v.* To go over again.

rib [rib] *n.* **1** One of the long, curving bones enclosing a person's or animal's chest. **2** A thing like a rib in use or shape, as the curved pieces in the framework of a boat.

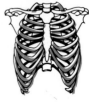

ridged [rijd] *adj.* Having a number of raised strips.

rif·fle [rif′əl] *v.* **rif·fling** To turn pages impatiently.

riled [rīld] *adj. informal* Angry.

Rip Van Win·kle [rip′ van′ wing′kəl] In Washington Irving's story, the hero who wakes after sleeping twenty years and finds the world changed.

ri·val [rī′vəl] *n.* Someone who wants the same thing that another person wants; a competitor: One team is a *rival* of another team.

rol·ling [rō′ling] *adj.* Hilly; swaying.

rough [ruf] *adj.* **1** Done quickly without worrying about small things. **2** Not smooth; bumpy.

S

sac [sak] *n.* A baglike part in an animal or plant. It usually contains a fluid.

Sac·a·ja·we·a [sä′kə·jə·wē′ə] 1787?–1884, an American Indian woman who helped the explorers Lewis and Clark.

sac·ri·fice [sak′rə·fīs] **1** *n.* The giving up of something. **2** *v.* To give up something.

sage·brush [sāj′brush′] *n.* A small shrub with white or yellow flowers found on the dry plains of the western U.S.

sand·bar [sand′bär′] *n.* A ridge of sand built by flowing water, as in a river.

scat·ter·ing [skat′ər·ing] *n.* **1** The breaking up and spreading of a beam of light by something that bends it in many directions. **2** A small number or amount of something spread all around.

schol·ar [skol′ər] *n.* A person who has learned a great deal through study.

schol·ar·ship [skol′ər·ship] *n.* Money that is awarded to a student to help pay for his or her education.

schoon·er [skōō′nər] *n.* A ship having two or more masts.

scoff [skof] *v.* **scoffed** To show disbelief; laugh at.

scull [skul] *n.* **1** A long oar worked from side to side over the rear of a boat. **2** A light, short oar, used in pairs by one person.

sec·tion [sek′shən] *n.* **1** A separate part or division. **2** A part of a city or community; district, area.

sen·si·tive [sen′sə·tiv] *adj.* Able to feel and recognize things easily and rapidly.

Se·quoi·a Na·tion·al Park [si·kwoi′ə nash′ən·əl pärk′] *n.* A national park in central California. It includes groves of giant sequoia trees and the highest mountain in the continental United States.

set [set] **1** *n.* All the scenery needed for one or more scenes of a play or movie. **2** *v.* To put in a certain position; place.

set·tee [se·tē′] *n.* A long bench or sofa with a back and arms, usually for two or three people.

---

add, āce, câre, pälm;   end, ēqual;   it, īce;   odd, ōpen, ôrder;   tŏŏk, pōōl;   up, bûrn;
ə = a in *above*, e in *sicken*, i in *possible*, o in *melon*, u in *circus;*   yōō = u in *fuse;*   oil;   pout;
          check;   ring;   thin;   this;   zh in *vision.*

set·ting [set′ing] *n.* **1** Surroundings; environment. **2** The time and place of a work of literature.

shal·low [shal′ō] **1** *adj.* Not deep. **2** *n.* (*usually plural*) A shallow place in a body of water.

shan·ty [shan′tē] *n.* A roughly made, hastily built shack or cabin.

Sho·sho·ne [shō·shō′nē] **1** *adj.* Coming from a group of American Indian tribes that spoke the Shoshone language. These tribes used to live in the land that is now California and the northwestern states. **2** *n.* A member of a Shoshone tribe.

shrill [shril] *v.* **shrilled** To say or ask in high, piercing tones.

shuf·fle [shuf′əl] *v.* **1** To drag (the feet) in walking or dancing. **2** To push about or mix together without order.

si·lo [sī′lō] *n.* A tower for storing grain.

Sin·bad the Sail·or [sin′bad] In the *Arabian Nights,* a merchant who has adventures when he goes on a voyage.

sin·is·ter [sin′is·tər] *adj.* Threatening evil, trouble, or bad luck.

skull [skul] *n.* The bony framework or skeleton of the head.

slash [slash] *v.* **slashed** To cut through quickly, as with a knife.

slosh [slosh] *v.* **slosh·ing** To move, wade, or plod through water or mud.

smoke·shed [smōk′shed′] *n.* A building or room filled with smoke for treating or curing meat, fish, or cheese.

smug·gle [smug′əl] *v.* To bring in or take out secretly.

snake [snāk] *v.* **snaked** To move, wind, or crawl like a snake.

sod [sod] *n.* The top layer of earth held together by twisted roots of grass.

so·lar [sō′lər] *adj.* Relating to the sun.

so·lo [sō′lō] *adj.* Done by one person.

soothe [sooth] *v.* **1** To calm. **2** To soften or relieve: to *soothe* someone's grief.

source [sôrs] *n.* The thing, place, or person from which something comes.

span [span] *v.* **spanned** To extend across.

spe·cies [spē′shēz] *n., pl.* A group of living things that are alike and able to breed with one another.

spec·u·late [spek′yə·lāt] *v.* To form theories; to imagine possible reasons or answers for something.

spell·bound [spel′bound′] *adj.* **1** Not able to move, as if tied down by magic. **2** Under a magic spell.

spiral [spī′rəl] **1** *adj.* Winding or curving like a cone-shaped coil. **2** *n.* A curve. **3** *v.* To move in a curving path.

sprang [sprang] *v.* Moved suddenly and rapidly; leaped. — past tense of **spring.**

spun [spun] *v.* Twisted into thread; made into (yarn) by spinning. — past tense and past participle of **spin.**

squawk [skwôk] **1** *n.* A harsh, shrill cry. **2** *v.* To make a harsh, shrill cry. — **squawked.**

squid [skwid] *n.* A sea animal with ten arms. It has a long thin body, tail fins, and two arms that are longer than the other eight.

stage name [stāj′ nām′] *n.* The name a professional performer uses instead of the name given at birth.

stan·dard [stan′dərd] *adj.* **1** Made just like the model. **2** Widely accepted; regularly used.

Stan·dard Time [stan′dərd tīm′] *n.* A system for having all the clocks in a large area set at the same time.

steed [stēd] *n.* A horse, especially a spirited war horse.

stee·ple [stē′pəl] *n.* A tall structure that narrows to a point at its top, rising above a church tower.

stock [stok] *n.* **1** Farm animals. **2** A supply of something kept for use or sale. **3** The wooden part of a rifle that serves as a handle or support.

strag·gle [strag′əl] *v.* **strag·gled** To lag behind those one is traveling with.

stretch [strech] **1** *n.* A large area. **2** *v.* To extend beyond normal size.

stride [strīd] *n.* A long, sweeping step.

strike [strīk] **1** *n.* Discovery. **2** *v.* To make contact with; hit.

strode [strōd] *v.* Walked with long, sweeping steps. — past tense of **stride.**

style [stīl] *n.* **1** An individual manner of singing, playing an instrument, writing, etc. **2** The way in which something is done, built, written, etc.: a Greek *style* of architecture.

su·per·sti·tion [sōō′pər·stish′ən] *n.* The fear or belief, without reason, that certain things or actions will cause good or bad luck.

surf [sûrf] *n.* The waves of the sea as they break on a beach or reef.

surge [sûrj] **1** *n.* A rush; a sudden swelling or flow. **2** *v.* To move with a strong rush or wave.

sur·vey [sər·vā′] *v.* To measure exactly.

sur·vey·or [sər·vā′ər] *n.* A person who measures land.

sur·vive [sər·vīv′] *v.* To live through; remain alive.

swell [swel] **1** *n.* The long, continuous body of a rolling wave. **2** To increase or cause to increase.

T

---

tack·le [tak′əl] **1** *n.* Equipment or gear for a certain use. **2** *v.* To grab or attack.

tap [tap] **1** *v.* To release liquid from (something) by drilling a hole. **2** *n.* A light blow. **3** *n.* A faucet that controls the flow of liquids: a water *tap.*

tar·pau·lin [tär·pô′lin *or* tär′pə·lin] *n.* A piece of canvas or other material that has been made waterproof, used to cover exposed objects.

tech·ni·cal [tek′ni·kəl] *adj.* Having to do with mechanical or industrial skills.

tech·ni·cian [tek·nish′ən] *n.* A person who can adjust and handle electrical or other equipment, such as that used in staging a play.

the·a·ter [thē′ə·tər] *n.* **1** The arts involved in putting on plays. **2** A place built for the presentation of plays, films, and other performances.

thick·et [thik′it] *n.* A thick, dense growth, as of trees and bushes.

Thor [thôr] The god of thunder, war, and strength worshipped in northern Europe in early times.

tire·some [tīr′səm] *adj.* Boring; time-consuming.

ti·tle [tīt′əl] **1** *n.* A descriptive name given to show rank or honor. **2** *n.* The name of a book, story, play, etc. **3** *v.* To give a name. — **ti·tled.**

tongue [tung] *n.* **1** A language or dialect: the Greek *tongue.* **2** The movable muscular organ in the mouth used in eating or speaking.

tor·rent [tôr′ənt] *n.* A rapid flow.

trace [trās] **1** *n.* A very small amount of something. **2** *n.* A mark or sign left by some person or thing. **3** *v.* To follow the course or development of.

tramp [tramp] *v.* **tramp·ing** To hike.

trans·fer [trans′fər *or* trans·fûr′] *v.* **trans·ferred** To move from one person or place to another.

trans·lu·cent [trans·lōō′sənt] *adj.* Allowing some light to pass through but blocking a view of objects.

---

add, āce, câre, pälm;   end, ēqual;   it, īce;   odd, ōpen, ôrder;   tŏŏk, pōōl;   up, bûrn;
ə = a in *above,* e in *sicken,* i in *possible,* o in *melon,* u in *circus;*   yōō = u in *fuse;*   oil;   pout;
         check;   ring;   thin;   this;   zh in *vision.*

trans·par·ent [trans·pâr′ənt] *adj.* So clear that objects on the far side can be easily seen.

tri·an·gu·lar [trī·ang′gyə·lər] *adj.* Having to do with, or shaped like, a triangle; having three sides.

trib·al [trī′bəl] *adj.* Having to do with a tribe or tribes.

trib·ute [trib′yōot] *n.* **1** Money or other payment given by one group of people to another on demand, often as the price of peace and protection. **2** A speech, compliment, gift, etc., given to show admiration, gratitude, or respect.

trig·ger [trig′ər] *n.* **1** Something that starts an action. **2** The small lever that fires a gun.

trill [tril] *n.* The rapid alternating of two tones that are nearly alike.

trol·ley [trol′ē] *n.* A kind of bus that runs on tracks through a city.

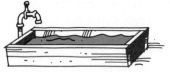

trough [trôf] *n.* A long, narrow, open box that holds food or water for animals.

tune [t(y)ōon] **1** *v.* To adjust the strings of, to make the tones correct. **2** *n.* A melody, usually simple and easy to remember. **3** *n.* The condition of being at the proper musical pitch.

tu·tor [t(y)ōo′tər] *n.* A person who teaches another, usually privately.

tweez·ers [twē′zerz] *n., pl.* A small instrument used for grasping and holding small objects.

Twin Cit·ies [twin′ sit′ēz] *n.* St. Paul, the capital of Minnesota, and nearby Minneapolis, the state's biggest city.

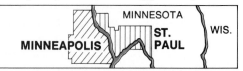

twine [twīn] *n.* A heavy string made up of two or more strands twisted together.

twit·ter [twit′ər] *v.* **twit·tered** To utter light, high, chirping sounds like a bird.

typ·i·cal [tip′i·kəl] *adj.* Having the qualities or features of a whole group.

U

U·lys·ses [yōo·lis′ēz] The Latin name for *Odysseus,* the Greek hero of Homer's *Odyssey.*

un·cer·e·mo·ni·ous·ly [un′ser·ə·mō′nē·əs·lē] *adv.* In an informal, sometimes rude, way.

un·furl [un·fûrl′] *v.* **un·furl·ing** To spread out or open; uncurl or unroll.

un·paved [un·pāvd′] *adj.* Not paved; said of a surface that is not covered with concrete or other material.

ur·ban [ûr′bən] *adj.* Of, in, or having to do with a city.

V

valve [valv] *n.* **1** Half of the shell of a clam, oyster, etc. **2** A device in a musical instrument that opens and closes an air passage and so changes the pitch of a tone. **3** Any device that controls the flow of liquid, as through a pipe. *Valve* comes from the Latin word *valva,* meaning "the leaf of a door."

vane [vān] *n.* A device that shows the wind's direction. A fin at the rear end turns a pointer toward the wind.

vast [vast] *adj.* Huge; of very large size.

ven·i·son [ven'ə·sən] *n.* The flesh of deer, used as food.

vice·roy [vīs'roi] *n.* A person appointed to rule a country, colony, etc., as the personal agent of the king or emperor.

vic·to·ry [vik'tər·ē] *n.* Success; the overcoming of an enemy or of difficulty.

vir·tue [vûr'chōo] *n.* Good quality; moral excellence.

vis·i·ble [viz'ə·bəl] *adj.* Capable of being seen.

vo·cal cords [vō'kəl kôrdz'] *n., pl.* Either of two pairs of folds of membrane that stick out into the throat. The lower pair can be made to move back and forth and produce voice sounds when air from the lungs passes between them.

W

wake [wāk] **1** *n.* The track of disturbed water left behind by a moving ship. **2** *v.* To stop sleeping.

wal·lop [wol'əp] **1** *n. informal* A hard hit. **2** *v.* To strike with a wallop; beat soundly. — **wal·lop·ing**, *adj.* Large, impressive.

wal·low [wol'ō] **1** *v.* To roll or tumble about; to flounder, as in mud or water. **2** *n.* A muddy area used by animals for wallowing.

war·ble [wôr'bəl] *v.* **war·bling** To whistle or sing with trills, as some birds do.

ward·robe [wôrd'rōb'] *n.* **1** A collection of costumes, as in the theater. **2** A collection of clothing.

wash·board [wäsh'bôrd' *or* wôsh'bôrd'] *n.* A board with a rippled metal surface: Sudsy clothes are rubbed on a *washboard* to squeeze the dirt out.

wea·ry [wir'ē] *adj.* Tired.

weath·er [weth'ər] *v.* **weath·ered** To change in looks and color by rain, wind, cold, etc.: The white house had *weathered* and was now gray.

weath·er·ing [weth'ər·ing] *n.* The process of breaking down rock by the weather's action.

well [wel] *v.* **welled** To rise up or flow, as water from a spring.

West [west] *n.* **1** North America, South America, and Europe. **2** The western part of the United States, especially west of the Mississippi River.

West In·dies [west' in'dēz] *n.* A chain of islands extending eastward from southern Mexico past Puerto Rico, then bending south to South America.

wet·land [wet'land'] *n.* Swamps and marshes.

whol·ly [hō'lē] *adv.* Fully, completely.

win·dow box [win'dō boks'] *n.* A long box in which flowers can be planted. The *window box* may be either hung outside a window or set on a porch.

wink [wingk] *v.* **wink·ing 1** To give off light in short flashes; twinkle. **2** To close and open the eye rapidly, often as a sign or hint.

World's Fair [wûrldz' fâr'] A large fair in which a number of nations exhibit their goods, inventions, art, etc.

wring [ring] *v.* **1** To squeeze or twist, usually to get water out of. **2** To get by force, violence, or threats: to *wring* an answer out of someone.

---

add, āce, câre, pälm;   end, ēqual;   it, īce;   odd, ōpen, ôrder;   tŏŏk, pōōl;   up, bûrn;
ə = a in *above*, e in *sicken*, i in *possible*, o in *melon*, u in *circus*;   yōō = u in *fuse*;   oil;   pout;
check;   ring;   thin;   this;   zh in *vision*.

Y

yam [yam] *n.* A kind of sweet potato.

yelp [yelp] *v.* **yelped** To cry or bark sharply.

Yo·ru·ba [yō·rōō′bə] *n.* West African tribe from what is now Nigeria.

Z

Zeus [zōōs] The chief and most powerful of the ancient Greek gods.

zo·ol·o·gy [zō·ol′ə·gē] *n.* The science that has to do with animals, their classification, structure, development, etc.

---

add, āce, câre, pälm;   end, ēqual;   it, īce;   odd, ōpen, ôrder;   tŏŏk, pōŏl;   up, bûrn;
ə = a in *above*, e in *sicken*, i in *possible*, o in *melon*, u in *circus*;   yōō = u in *fuse*;   oil;   pout;
check;   ring;   thin;   this;   zh in *vision*.

Index of Titles and Authors

C 3
D 4
E 5
F 6
G 7
H 8
I 9
J 0